LITERARY PORTRAITS

LITERARY PORTRAITS

BY

CHARLES WHIBLEY

Essay Index Reprint Series

 BOOKS FOR LIBRARIES PRESS
FREEPORT, NEW YORK

First Published 1920
Reprinted 1968

LIBRARY OF CONGRESS CATALOG CARD NUMBER:

68-55864

MANUFACTURED
BY
HALLMARK LITHOGRAPHERS, INC.
IN THE U.S.A.

CONTENTS

RABELAIS

FOR so many centuries has the name of Rabelais stood for a book that the world sometimes forgets that it was ever borne by a man, who in his busy life played the many and diverse parts of scholar, priest, doctor, courtier, humourist. John Milton calls up other images than *Paradise Lost* : we do not straightway confuse him with Lucifer ; we remember also Cromwell's accomplished secretary, and the author who proved in his *Areopagitica* that prose, no less than verse, might echo with noble music. Even Shakespeare, though he eludes the biographer, is seldom mistaken for his works : we do not ascribe to him the joviality of Falstaff, the misanthropy of Hamlet, the madness of Lear ; we still recognise the poet who came from Warwickshire to conquer London, and who held his own against the wits and rufflers of Elizabeth's glorious age. But Rabelais is merged in the ' Lives, Heroick Deeds, and Sayings of Gargantua and his Sonne Pantagruel,' until the amiable doctor and learned gentleman are both forgotten. And the injustice done to François Rabelais is the more profound, because of all men that ever thought and wrote he is the most clearly detached from his own

creations. Moreover, since his speech is ever open
and courageous, he is involved by the witless in the
flagrant charge of indecent buffoonery. The illustrious
extravagances in word and deed of Gargantua,
Panurge, and Friar John are too readily ascribed to
their creator, who is insulted by modern censors as
he was injured by the monks and Calvinists of his
own day. But François Rabelais was a very real man,
who worked, laughed, and fought with the best of his
contemporaries ; and, happily for his memory, the
materials for a portrait are not lacking.

I

    François Rabelais, Extractor of the Quintessence
and High Priest of the Sacred Isles, was born as the
fifteenth century was tottering to its close. The
year of his birth is uncertain, and while tradition
sets it down as 1483, some commentators would
advance it as far as 1495. On either side the arguments are sound and irrelevant. Says one : he could
not have begun the masterpiece of his life at forty-
nine ; says another : his friends and he must surely
have been of the same age. Experience warrants
the truth of neither assertion, and no enterprise is so
hazardous as to fit a date to imagined circumstances.
Rabelais' birthplace, on the other hand, is not doubtful. Touraine is the province wherein he first saw the
light, the garden of France, as Pantagruel calls it :
Touraine, splendid with castles and the golden Loire ;

rich in vineyards, carpeted with flowers; richer still in beautiful women and great men. For Touraine is the mother-country, not only of Rabelais, but of Descartes, the apostle of method and pure style, of Balzac, the truest historian of modern France. So that her pride ends not with her palaces : her builders have builded with something better than dead stones. ' It is all with Live Stones,' to turn the phrase of Panurge, ' that she sets up and erects the Fabricks of her Architecture, to wit, Man.'

And in Touraine it is Chinon [1] that Rabelais calls his own, ' the famous City, noble City, ancient City, yea, the first City in the World, according to the judgment and assertion of the most learned Massorets.' The debt he owed to his birthplace he repaid with an eloquent generosity. The praise of Touraine, of Chinon, of la Devinière (his father's vineyard), is constantly in his mouth, and this is the one certain spark of autobiography which illuminates his works. His father, 'tis said, dwelt at the sign of the Lamprey, and is variously described by rumour as an apothecary and as an innkeeper. That he should have been called an innkeeper accords with the legend, and the same confusion, no doubt, persuaded De Thou to declare that in his day the house of Rabelais was a tavern. François, the youngest of several sons, was early dedicated to the Church. After a brief sojourn at the abbey of Seuilly, he passed to the monastery

[1] *Rabelesus Chinonensis* he describes himself in his matriculation at Montpellier.

of La Baumette; he did not tarry there long, and presently we find him a Grey Friar in the monastery of Fontenay-le-Comte.

His reception into this order was, in a sense, the good fortune of Rabelais' life. The time and the place were alike favourable : the New Learning, which was coming over the Alps, descending from Rotterdam, or traversing the Channel, had nowhere more fervent zealots than in this corner of Poitou. During the many years that Rabelais passed at Fontenay he might devote himself, so long as the secret was kept, to every branch of knowledge. Nothing eluded his curiosity : an expert in law and theology, he acquired so deep an insight into medical science as set him above all his contemporaries. He became as ready as Pantagruel himself to discuss the insoluble problems of magic, alchemy, geomancy, and philosophy. He plumbed ' the true Well and Abyss of Encyclopedic learning.' Above all, he devoted himself to the study of Greek. He mastered the many authors whose works he was destined to quote with so fantastic an erudition; nor was his task so simple as it might seem. He had to fight, not only with the scarcity of books and manuscripts, but with the bitterly declared prejudice of the age. Greek, in fact, was the forbidden tongue, the plain mark of heresy, and the controversy raged most bitterly during the years spent by Rabelais among the Grey Friars.

' Time was,' said Erasmus, ' when he was a heretic,

who dissented from the Gospels or the Articles of
Faith. Now whatever is displeasing or unintelligible
to the abbots is heresy. To know Greek is a heresy,
to speak with polish is a heresy, in brief all is heresy
which they do not do themselves.' So the principles
of right and wrong were reshuffled. Sobriety, truth,
and chastity were virtues insignificant beside the
great virtue of all : ignorance of Greek. Jean de Boyssone narrowly escaped the heretic's death of burning
at Toulouse, because with other sins he ventured to
read the New Testament. Yet, for all the strength
of the Church, Greek had its champions all the world
over. When Erasmus dared to publish the New
Testament in the original tongue, he threw down a
gauntlet which the priests were not slow to pick up.
For, in truth, this memorable work was a challenge as
well as a masterpiece, a monument both of satire and
theology, which castigated the Church, while for the
first time it revealed the hidden foundations of belief.

Erasmus, then, declared war in the spirit of one
who said that he would pawn his coat rather than
lack a newly found example of Greek literature ; and
nowhere was the war waged with more acerbity than
in England. Oxford became, for a while, the last
stronghold of the Old Learning : the Greeks were
opposed by a compact body of reactionaries, who in
an ill-omened moment styled themselves Trojans, and
gave their leaders the august names of Priam, Paris,
and the rest. The result of the combat was foreseen
and not long delayed. Thomas More, at the instiga-

tion of Henry VIII., the constant friend of true learning, addressed a letter of remonstrance to the University, wherein he freely mingled threat with
objurgation.   Even when the battle was won in
England, it was still fought in France with increasing
bitterness ; and though Rabelais never wavered in his
allegiance, he did not come off scatheless from the
encounter.   However, a prudent courage always
supported him : the persecution of the Church was
no check upon the learning whose cause he was to
advocate with so noble an eloquence in Gargantua's
famous letter to Pantagruel. 'Now it is that the
minds of men'—so writes the King—'are qualified
with all manner of discipline, and the old sciences re-
vived, which for many ages were extinct : now it is
that the learned languages are to their pristine purity
restored, viz. Greek, without which a man may be
ashamed to account himself a scholar, Hebrew,
Arabick, Chaldæan, and Latine.' In these words
Rabelais expresses with admirable lucidity his own
point of view.   Without Greek a man may not account
himself a scholar !   And it is not without significance
that the man of genius, who was destined to rival
Aristophanes and Lucian, to weld the folklore of his
country and the satire of Greece into a masterpiece
of humour, should have begun his literary career with
a translation of Herodotus.[1]

[1] Tiraqueau states in a second edition of his *De Legibus
Connubialibus* that Rabelais had translated into Latin the First
Book of Herodotus.   Of this work we have no other trace.

II

Thus was the Revival of Learning achieved in such secluded corners as the monastery of Fontenay-le-Comte. Within these quiet walls Rabelais laid the foundation of his vast learning; and his reputation was not obscured by the taunts of his colleagues. In Pierre Amy, at any rate, he found a generous and sympathetic friend, and it is pleasant to think of the two scholars pursuing in unity of mind and contempt of disaster the studies which were presently to disgrace them. They purchased books, and they read them; they did their utmost to make Fontenay a centre of learning; and with a freedom which doubtless affrighted the monks, they held a lettered intercourse with the outside world.

One document remains,[1] which gives us an intimate view of their ambition and enthusiasm : this is nothing less than a receipt for seven crowns, which Henri Estienne, the publisher, declares was paid him by Pierre Amy for books sold to the Bishop of Maillezais. Now, this bishop—Geoffrey d'Estissac by name—was the lifelong friend of Rabelais; to him are addressed Rabelais' letters from Rome; and no doubt the books purchased of Estienne were eagerly read by the two

[1] The document is printed in M. Fillon's *Lettres écrites de la Vendée.* By a curious irony the receipt was discovered pasted on one of the wooden boards used to bind the works of Dun Scotus (printed by Jean Granjon, 1517), whom of all the schoolmen Rabelais and his friends most cordially despised.

monks of Fontenay. They were, moreover, precisely
the books which eager apostles of the New Learning
would desire—Aristotle, Cicero, Homer, the Chronicle
of Nuremberg, *la Voye Celeste*, and the *Querela Pacis*
of Erasmus.

So it was not only within the walls of Fontenay that
Rabelais found sympathy and encouragement. While
Geoffroy d'Estissac sat upon the throne of the neighbouring bishopric, André Tiraqueau, the Bailiff of
Fontenay, and the once famous jurisconsult, Aymery
Bouchard, were among Rabelais' devoted friends. And
Rabelais, who never loosened an attachment, remembered them both in dedications, and always refers to
Tiraqueau with affection and respect. The 'learned,
wise, courteous and just civilian, André Tiraqueau,'
he calls him in the Prologue to the Fourth Book;
and when the youthful Pantagruel goes abroad,
does he not visit that erudite scholar and sound
lawyer ?

The friendship with Tiraqueau was the more important, since to it we owe one of the few references
to the young friar; and the slight sketch drawn by
the lawyer has at least a hint of the gaiety which
always distinguished Rabelais. Now Tiraqueau, too,
was beset by the prevailing ambition of literature; he
too could write Latin in a style of easy familiarity;
moreover, he was engaged with Bouchard in a controversy on that question of women, which has
agitated the world since Aristophanes, and has not
yet received a final answer. The Bailiff, in his *De*

Legibus Connubialibus, made what Aymery Bouchard considered an insolent attack upon the sex; whereon Bouchard replied in a pamphlet περὶ τῆς γυναικείας φύτλης; and Tiraqueau in his second edition not only attempts to demolish Bouchard, but invokes the approving aid of Rabelais himself. That Rabelais should be on the side of the misogynists we, who know his book, can readily understand; and Tiraqueau could not quote a sounder authority. Bouchard, said his enemy, believed himself an orator, and all the world knows that one of the tricks recommended in Lucian's Ῥητόρων Διδάσκαλος is to show one-self amiable to women. 'That, at any rate,' says Tiraqueau, 'is the opinion of our friend François Rabelais, a friar, well skilled both in Latin and Greek.'

Such controversies tightened the bonds of acquaintanceship, and Rabelais, despite the persecution of the friars, enjoyed an intellectual freedom rare in the sixteenth century. What, indeed, would he have done at Toulouse, ' where they did cause burne their regents alive ' ? But Poitou seems to have been endowed with a liberal intelligence, and the profound learning of Rabelais was speedily noised abroad. Above all, the friendship of Pierre Amy contrived an introduction to the celebrated Guillaume Budé, and a correspondence followed, partly in Latin, partly in Greek. Now Budé, or Budæus, was the first scholar of France, the one rival in Europe to Erasmus. Unhappily, the oblivion that waits upon scholars long since overtook him, and his letters to Rabelais, clumsy as they are, have been longer remembered than his once admired treatise, *De Asse*.

Rabelais was young and a friar; wherefore he approached the great man cap in hand. And for a while the great man kept a silence which Rabelais' vanity did not easily brook. A second letter [1] is proof enough of wounded pride and hurt humility. He confesses that he would rate the intimate friendship of Budæus more highly than dominion over the whole of Asia. And he asks: 'What can a young man look forward to who is unlettered and obscure, an utter stranger to fair courtly phrases, at the hands of one who is of the highest repute in literature, and who has excelled all men in merit and genius?' He throws the blame, in a mock-heroic strain, upon his friend Amy: 'If I were disposed to proceed to the extremity of justice against him, I see no skulking-place, no harbours of refuge in which he could hide himself.'

The pleasantry is heavy-shotted, and not of the kind that we should expect from Rabelais' hand; yet if this Græco-Latin letter does not prove his wit, at least it proves his erudition. On the other hand, the reply of Budæus might have been written by Mr. Barlow himself: it is lofty, grave, pretentious; it attacks Rabelais in a vein of portentous irony for suspecting Pierre Amy of bad faith. 'Where now is

[1] I have quoted this letter from Mr. W. F. Smith's valuable edition of *Rabelais*, to which students are profoundly indebted.

your brotherly love,' writes the learned doctor, ' the chain of monasteries, the pillar of religion, the glue of unanimity, which you keep on declaiming almost in every other word must be revered as a Deity ? If a friend, who is not the first-comer, but chosen, reverenced, and faithful, makes a statement neither at hazard nor in the way of a joke, a statement in fine which demands credit, should you not believe him ? '

So the correspondence is continued, now in Greek, now in Latin, and, dull as it is, it casts a very clear light upon Rabelais' character and erudition. Budæus was not the man to write to any scholar that could address him in the decent prose of either language. But Rabelais was already known to his contemporaries as *doctissimus*, and he was fighting the same battle as Budæus himself. ' Furthermore we know,' says Budæus, ' that those theologians, haters of the Greeks, have spent their utmost zeal and diligence that they might blot out the Greek tongue, as nothing else to be sure than the trial and test of their own ignorance.' Nor were they anywhere more active than among the Franciscans of Fontenay-le-Comte, when at last the tardy suspicion was aroused. The cells of Rabelais and Amy were searched by the enemies of Greek (so much we gather from the letters of Budæus), and incriminating literature was discovered, supplied, may be, by the Bishop of Maillezais himself. For this sin there was no palliation. What could be said in defence of a ruffian who had trans-

lated Herodotus, upon the tip of whose pen were
constant tags from Lucian and Homer, who not only
read the abhorred tongue, but wrote it like a scholar ?
Budæus intervened in vain ; at last the life of erudition, passed in the walks and gardens of Fontenay, was
over : Rabelais left the brotherhood with a hatred of
friars in his heart ; a vast material was stored up for
the satire that was to come ; and in spite of persecution he could declare with truth that to the seclusion
and leisure of Fontenay-le-Comte he owed the ency-
clopædic learning which has made him for ever
famous.

The blow was weakened by the championship of
powerful friends. Rabelais was always a man of care-
fulness and foresight : the fate of the red herring had
no charm for him, and no sooner was he expelled from
Fontenay than he took refuge with the old companion
of his studies, Geoffroy d'Estissac, Bishop of Maillezais. And he did not then, nor at any other time,
quarrel with the faith. A hatred of the friars and
their morals was no interruption to his orthodoxy ; he
was as little tainted by Lutheranism as Budæus himself ; and unto the end he found room in the same
church which sheltered Erasmus. Indeed, a promotion instantly followed his expulsion from the Fran-
ciscan monastery. A special indulgence from the
Pope permitted him to enter the order of St. Benoît,
'with the title and habit of regular canon, and to
receive and hold, despite his vows of poverty, such
secular benefices as were afterwards his.' Meantime

he was free, under d'Estissac's protection, to pursue
his studies as he would : he dwelt at Liguge in
honour, and cultivated the Muses perhaps with more
elegance and less labour than heretofore.

An epistle, in verse, which he addressed to Jean
Bouchet, and which recalls the easy familiarity of
Martial, still remains to us, and certainly suggests a
life of lettered ease. Therein he compliments his
friend upon his 'escritz, tant doulx et meliflues';
begs him, 'differer ceste solicitude de litiger et de
patrociner'; and advises him, having procured 'les
tallonniers de ton patron Mercure,' to visit him at
once. Of course, there is a classical allusion to every
ten lines, and the whole letter might have been
written by any exquisite of the sixteenth century.
Thereto, as in duty bound, Bouchet, an advocate of
Poitou, replies with a like array of policy and compliment. 'Va, lettre, va de ce fascheux Palais,' he
explains with proper coxcombry, 'te presenter aux
yeux de Rabelays.' Alas! though he can compliment Rabelais and the whole house of d'Estissac,
he cannot leave Poitou and visit 'le tien hermitage,'
because there he is detained by 'le petit tripotage
de plaictz, proces et causes.' Not an important
correspondence, but memorable, because it is marked
rather by benignity than by talent, and because
benignity is the last quality wherewith posterity has
credited the man whom the great Budæus called
χρηστὴ κεφαλή.

III

Rabelais stayed not long at Ligugé : in 1528 began his life in the world. Hitherto, no doubt, books had said more to him than men. Neither Latin nor Greek withheld its secrets from him, and, monk as he was, he had made himself master of pagan antiquity. At whatever date his birth be fixed, he was no longer young, and for all the profundity of his studies he was neither pedant nor dry-as-dust. The blood of Touraine was warm in his veins ; his courage, as may be seen in his encounter with the Franciscans, was always high ; and now began the years of wandering *per saeculum*, which were to supplement the erudition of his youth. It was towards Lyons that he first turned his steps, *presbyteri saecularis habitu assumpto*, as he said in a supplication to the Pope. Nor could he with his enterprise in view have chosen a more favourable city. The Lyons of 1528 was devoted to polite letters and active enterprise. It was as though Venice had crossed the Alps, bringing bankers and printing-presses in her train. Learned men sought the gracious capital of the South, for there they found a freedom and a welcome denied them by the Sorbonnists of Paris. Clement Marot sojourned there for a time, and Etienne Dolet, who at Lyons practised the art embellished by the Aldi ; while neither Budæus nor Erasmus was a complete stranger.

At Lyons, then, Rabelais met many of the famous

men whose works had been an inspiration to the friars of Fontenay, and in erudition he was a match for the best of them. Meanwhile he had interrupted the practice of religion. It was bodies that he healed at Lyons, not souls; and though the fame of his medical skill was growing, he threw himself heart and soul into the proper business of Lyons—the editing and printing of books. He became, in brief, a bookseller's hack, expert and energetic. He read proofs, may be, if proofs were read in those days; he wrote prefaces, he compiled almanacks. Of the Lyonnese printers the greatest, of course, was Sebastian Gryphius, a profound scholar and elegant writer of Latin, who dreamed of rivalling the press of Venice with his editions of the classics. And while Gryphius appealed to the learned few, Claude Nourry and François Juste devised such trivial little books as amuse the people; and it is a clear symbol of Rabelais' career that he worked for all three. Some day he was to prove to the world that the chap-book transformed by humour and learning might take its place among the great literature of the world: that Aristophanes need not disdain, if he read beyond the grave, a set of little volumes which were thrust into a pedlar's pack and carried up and down the countryside of France.

Meantime he played the part of the professed scholar, and his first work was an epistle dedicatory to his old friend André Tiraqueau, which served as preface for the *Medical Letters* of Manardus. There is perhaps in a single borrowed phrase—'Boys have now a Rhinoceros nose all the world over'—a trick of the real Rabelais. For the rest, the epistle is commonplace enough. Compliments are paid to Tiraqueau himself, and to the Bishop of Maillezais, 'my kindest Mæcenas'; a regret is uttered that in his own practice of medicine very few adapt themselves to better methods. 'So it is,' writes Rabelais, 'that as we know is the common fate of them that perish by shipwreck, whatever they snatch at when the ship is wrecked and founders, be it beam, or coat, or straw, they cling to it with clenched hands, forgetful meanwhile of swimming and without care, so long as that which is in their hands fall not away, until they are sucked down in the vast whirlpool: in the same way our doctors hold on to their loves in the books, to which they have been accustomed from their boyhood with all their might and careless of wrong, even if they see their bark of false knowledge battered and leaking in every corner. And, if they are pushed off, they think that their very soul is driven from its seat.' Here, of course, is sketched the sound doctrine of Rabelais, the hatred of false authority, the contempt of stale-grown custom. That spirit of raillery, which reshaped the world, was not yet awake within him.

His next enterprise was the *Aphorisms* of Hippocrates, collated in accord with an ancient Greek manuscript in his own possession. He undertook the work with peculiar care, because, said he, inaccuracy in a physician's book is not merely a fault, but a sin which demands expiation. 'A single little word added, or erased, nay, even an accent inverted, or set in a wrong place, often involves the death of many thousands.' Sebastian Gryphius, 'that most consummate and highly finished printer,' printed the little book with his accustomed care, and it was dedicated with all the eloquence of gratitude to Geoffroy d'Estissac. Rabelais, in truth, forgot neither his friends nor his enemies, and we readily condone his extraordinary flattery for its eloquent expression. 'Whatever my labour can achieve properly belongs to you'—thus he writes to the Bishop of Maillezais—'who have until now cherished me so warmly with your kindness, that wherever I cast my eyes, nothing confronts my senses save the sea and sky of your munificence.' [1] The compliments are turned prettily enough; the allusions to the literature of Greece and Rome are constant and appropriate; but many another scholar of this generation might have indited these flimsy prefaces, and we are still many leagues from the admirable Pantagruel.

Rabelais' third performance brings us no nearer to his genius : rather it involves him in the ridicule which his scorn would joyfully have hurled at a rival. With a heedlessness foreign to his character, he assumed a wanton responsibility for two scraps 'saved by a happier fate from fire, shipwreck, and the

---

[1] Rabelais leaves the quotation from Homer, οὐδέν ἦ οὐρανὸς ἠδὲ θάλασσα, in its original Greek.

ruin of age.' The one was the will of Lucius Cus-
pidius, the other an ancient contract of sale. Rabelais,
confessing in a dedication to Aymery Bouchard that
he has never seen the original manuscript, is content
to evoke the authority of the renowned Gryphius.
The fragments were the work of one Pontanus,
who had mystified the learned more darkly than he
had dared to hope. And Rabelais treated the matter
with characteristic nonchalance : he waited for his
Gargantua, and therein held up Pontanus, Secular
Poet, to inapposite contempt.

Did Rabelais ever meet Erasmus in the flesh—
Erasmus, whom above all men he might call his
master ? The question has been asked many times,
and never found a satisfactory answer. Yet one
would like to think that he who wrote the *Moria* once
encountered his greatest disciple. Of all the heroes
who fought the fight of freedom in the sixteenth
century, Rabelais and Erasmus present the strongest
resemblance. Each had suffered the terrors of
monkish discipline ; each had come forth into the
world armed with vengeance and resentment. Erasmus,
no doubt, was the finer scholar ; and while Rabelais
had no reason to fear his rival, they were both brilliant in satire, as they were pitiless in contempt.
Obvious as is the resemblance, the contrast also is
notable. Wit was the weapon of Erasmus, humour
the weapon of Rabelais : the one pressed home the
rapier's point, the other laid about him with a solid
bludgeon. No man has the right to call the dainty,

the elegant, the polished Erasmus a coward; none
the less it is true that had his intellect allowed
him he would have lived at peace with all men. His
pleasures were the children rather of refinement than
of joyousness. He must drink good wine, and ride a
good horse, because these gifts of life were due to a
gentleman and a scholar. The storm which he let
loose in Europe appalled him, and, rather than be
shipwrecked himself, he would have run into the
nearest harbour of safety. When he was reproached
with laying the egg whence came forth the Reforma-
tion, ' Yes,' he said ; ' but I laid a hen's egg ; Luther
has hatched a fighting cock.'

Rabelais, on the other hand, preferred joyousness
before refinement. He, too, loved wine, but he held
an over-nice taste in liquor for a sign of age. Again,
laughter was as urgent a necessity for him as the
combat ; and, if his blows were less deft, they were
always heavier than the blows of Erasmus. Yet for
scholarship and grandeur of intelligence Erasmus and
Rabelais are the twin forces of the intellectual renaissance; and, but for the ill-fortune that persuaded
Erasmus to hide his thoughts in the obscurity of a dead
tongue, who knows how exalted a position he would
have held in the world of letters ? Did the two, then,
ever meet ? An interview between them would have
been far more remarkable than the encounter between
Pope and Dryden ; nor is there any hindrance in the
path of those who would imagine it. Erasmus surely
visited Lyons, and Rabelais, who had read his works

in Fontenay, surely sought him out. One thing, at least, is certain : a letter, reprinted in the *Clarorum Virorum Epistolae centum* (1702), bears internal evidence that it was addressed by Rabelais to Erasmus. Though it gives greeting to Bernard Salignac, a name unknown in history, a copy has been found in the Library at Zürich addressed to Erasmus himself. Nor could it well have been addressed to any other. The scholars mentioned were all intimate (for friendship or enmity) with the author of the *Moria*. Hilary Bertholf had been his private secretary ; Aleander had enjoyed his interrupted acquaintance.

Above all, the tone which Rabelais adopts towards his correspondent could have befitted none other than the scholar of Rotterdam. The excuse for the letter was the restoration to its owner of a *Jewish History*, once borrowed by the Bishop of Rhodez. ' I gladly seized this handle and occasion,' says Rabelais, ' of making known to you, my humane father, by some pleasing office, with what feeling and affection I regard you. I called you my father, I would also say mother, if in your indulgence you would allow it. For that which we find daily happens to those who bear offspring in their womb, that they nourish children which they have never seen, protecting them from the dangers of the ambient air, you too have suffered the very same, you, who have educated me, unknown to you in face, unworthy to be known by name.' Thus Rabelais confesses an obligation which he might reasonably have felt, and at the same time

declares that hitherto he had never looked upon his
' humane father.' Such a gracious letter must needs
have met with a response, and it is likely that Erasmus
hereafter discovered his ardent disciple at Lyons.

IV

Meanwhile Rabelais was quietly deserting the wide
fields of scholarship for the meadows of eternal gaiety.
If he did a pedant's work for the illustrious Sebastian
Gryphius, he was already, under the auspices of
Nourry and Juste, appealing to the larger world of
courtiers, wits, and people. Almanacks were the
fashion of the hour, and who so well skilled to provide
the mob with a safe prediction of the future as
François Rabelais, doctor of medicine and ironic
searcher into the secrets of astrology ? So we find
him contriving the trivial chap-books, which the
people loved, and with no better motive for the work
than to supplement a modest income. Many are the
almanacks which we owe to his pen, and though mere
fragments of them remain, there is enough to prove
their worthlessness. In vain we look for any hint of
the real Rabelais : we find nothing more characteristic than a casual quotation from the classics.
The first (of 1533) is marked by a mild piety. He
hints—as who would not, at that time ?—that the
conjunction of Saturn with Mercury indicates a
change of kingdoms and religions. Having given
the hint, he refrains from further speech. ' These,'

says he, ' are the secrets of the close council of the
Eternal King ' ; and so he implores his readers to let
the veil fall on what is written in the eternal registers.
' It is not for you to know the times or the seasons,
which the Father hath put in His own power. . . .
Whoso searcheth out His Majesty, shall be crushed by
it.' The almanack of 1535 is even more discreet. ' If
the kings, princes, and christian communities have
in reverence the divine word of God . . . we have
never seen in our times a year more healthy for the
body, more peaceful for the soul, more fertile in
blessings than this shall be.' To such a prediction
as that none could be found to object, and if Rabelais'
experiments in divination are dull and trivial, he
must at least be pronounced a safe prophet. Far
more important is the fact that he has now appeared
as a writer of French : henceforth, save in letter or
preface, he deserts the Latin tongue, and thus it was
that through the bookseller's shop he reached the
gates of immortality. Had he remained as loyal as
Budæus to scholarship and Latinity, he never would
have taken his place by the side of the masters of
living literature.

While there is neither amusement nor promise
in the little almanacks, with the *Pantagrueline Prognostication* Rabelais' true career begins. This chap-
book, published in 1533, scintillates with a spark,
at least, of Rabelaisian humour. The author declares
himself for the first time, ' Alcofribas Nasier, Archi-
triclin to the afore-mention'd Pantagruel,' and dedi-

cates the work in a style that seems natural enough,
' for the Benefit and Noddification of the giddy-
brained and weather-wise *Would be's.*' The *Prognostication* is, indeed, a frank and free parody of the
popular almanacks. Rabelais laughs with contempt
at the Astrologers of Lyons, among whom he was
lately enrolled, and writes with something of his
own dash and vigour. The satire is coarse, even
brutal, and the prophesies are sure for any year in
the world's history. As for the golden number, *non
est inventus*, but the true spirit of Pantagruelism is
already there; the renowned vocabulary is busily
forming itself; and while Rabelais' previous works
throw no ray of light upon his talent, here at last we
suspect the real Alcofribas.

So far we are on certain ground : the *Prognostication* is pure Rabelais, and acknowledged as such. Only
Rabelais could have written it : Pantagruel, King of
Utopia and Dipsody, is already introduced, and the
praise of wine is sung as lustily as in the masterpiece
itself. But a year before was published, possibly
by the same bookseller, a little chap-book of proper
style and fitting type, which bears another familiar
name. The woodcut which adorns the first page is
characteristic of the pedlar's wares, and the title
arouses a just curiosity. ' Les grandes et inestimables
Croniques,' thus it runs : ' du grant et enorme geant
Gargantua : contenant sa genealogie, La grandeur et
force de son corps. Aussi les merveilleux faicts
darmes qu'il fist pour le Roy Artus comme verrez

cy après. Imprimé nouvellement, 1532.' Was it from another's work that the real author of *Gargantua* borrowed his hero's name and descent ? Or is this the work of Rabelais ?

If another writer than Rabelais were in question, one would instantly say no. It is contrary to the general experience that the author of Pantagruel, or even of the *Pantagrueline Prognostication*, should a brief year before have composed so tiresome and bombastic a work as *les Grandes Croniques*. On the other hand, there is no reason why the author of the dedicatory epistles to Tiraqueau and the rest should not have described the foolish creation of Grant-Gosier and Galemelle by Merlin the Wizard. The epistles and the *Croniques* are alike the work of a literary hack, and in 1532 Rabelais was the hack not only of Gryphius, but of Claude Nourry. Above all he was a man who kept his head, so to say, in water-tight compartments. The right half of his brain, it seems, knew not what the left was doing. And we have no right to declare on internal evidence alone that the *Grandes Croniques* are or are not the work of his hand.

Thus we are thrown back upon uncertainty and the division of the critics. M. Brunet holds that Rabelais is the true author of the *Croniques*, and his argument is not unsound. Apart from the similarity of name, which is wholly unimportant, the *Croniques* suggest the real Gargantua in more than one incident. The destruction of the trees by a whisking of the

mare's tail, the theft of the church bells, the con-
cealment of his prisoners in a hollow tooth, King
Artus's banquet of four hundred salted hams, and
Gargantua's gorgeous and giant wardrobe—all these
are familiar episodes. Moreover, in a second edition,
as M. Brunet points out, there is a definite allusion
to Pantagruel, in which Rabelais' own hand might
be traced. ' Gargantua vesquit cinq cens et ung an,'
thus ends the text, ' et eut de grosses gueres, desquelles
je me tays pour le present. Et eut ung filz de
Badebec son epouse, lequel a faict autant de vaillances
que Gargantua. Et le pourrez veoir par la vraye
Chronicque laquelle est une petite partie imprimée.
Et quelque jour que messieurs de Sainct Victor voul-
dront, on prendra la coppie de la reste des faictz de
Gargantua, et de son filz Pantagruel.'
At first sight this quotation seems conclusive, but
there is no reason why the publisher, with a full knowledge of Rabelais' design, should not have concluded
his chap-book with a useful advertisement. There
is still less reason why Rabelais should not have
borrowed from the *Croniques* such incidents as were
fit for his ampler scheme. No writer ever plagiarised
with a stouter heart and more manifest justice. His
masterpiece is haunted by memories not only of the
world, but of books, and if we relied on resemblances
alone, we might as easily prove him author of the
Iliad as of the *Grandes Croniques*. I prefer to believe
him innocent ; I see no trace of his hand in the guilt
of the chap-book ; yet a conclusive verdict is obviously

impossible, and no jury of critics will be persuaded to agree.

The question gains a certain importance because its answer affects our judgment of the real *Gargantua* and the real *Pantagruel*. Which was written first ? *Pantagruel* bears on its second edition the date 1533. We know no copy of *Gargantua* earlier than 1535. And *Gargantua* is obviously the first book, obviously intended as such by Rabelais himself. Nor is the knot loosened by the author's own confusion. In *Gargantua* he refers to *Pantagruel*, in *Pantagruel* to *Gargantua*, with provoking impartiality. What, then, does it all mean ? The easiest solution is to suppose that the first edition of *Gargantua* has perished down to its last copy ; and the fate of books favours the solution, especially as *Gargantua* might easily receive the supreme compliment of being read to rags. M. Brunet, however, sternly regards *les Croniques* as the work of Rabelais, which he presently discarded that the real *Gargantua* might accord in humour and spirit with *Pantagruel*. Where documentary evidence fails, it is idle to dogmatise, especially when the author is Rabelais, whose brain eludes the laws of probability.

Meanwhile, Rabelais had not sojourned all these years in one city. Though he had practised at Lyons the two arts of letters and medicine, the lust of wandering had already overtaken this child of the cloister, and henceforth the composition of his romance was but an interlude in a life of travel. In 1530 he was at

Montpellier, where, as we know by the register of
the University, he matriculated and proceeded to
his bachelor's degree.[1] No sooner was he made
bachelor than he delivered a famous course of lectures
upon the *Aphorisms* of Hippocrates. And in the
fifth chapter of *Pantagruel*, which is as nearly auto-
biographic as may be expected in romance, he records
his own impression : ' He went then to Montpellier '
—to Pantagruel the adventure is ascribed—' where
he met with the good wines of Mirevaux, and good
jovial company withal, and thought to have set himself to the study of Physick ; but he considered that
the calling was too troublesome and melancholick,
and that Physicians did smell of glisters like old
devils.' For Pantagruel the study was perhaps too
' melancholick ' ; not so for Rabelais, who speedily
gained the highest renown for his skill and learning.
It was at Montpellier, too, that he acted in ' the moral
comedy of him who had espoused and married a
Dumb Wife.' Here, at least, we have an anecdote,
established not upon idle gossip, but upon his own
word,[2] and it is a pleasant picture that he paints, a
staid professor and his colleagues playing the part of

---

[1] Here is his bachelor's declaration preserved at Montpellier,
and printed in Mr. W. F. Smith's edition :—'Ego franciscus
'Rabelesus diocesis Turonensis promotus fui ad gradum bacca-
'laureatus die prima mensis Novembris Anno domini millesimo
'quingentesimo trigesimo sub Reverendo artium et medicinae
'professore magistro Joanne Scurronio. Rabelesus.'

[2] Book III. chap. xxxiv. The story is by this familiar all
the world over, if it be best known in Molière's adaptation.

drolls in presence of the students. 'I never in my Lifetime,' quoth Panurge, 'laughed so much as at the acting of that Buffoonery.'

It was in 1534 that Rabelais made his first distant journey: he went to Rome, for the visiting of which shrine his whole life had been a preparation. In his days Athens lay beyond the known world; Rome was the goal of the pilgrim's ambition; and Rabelais, when he left Lyons in the train of Jean du Bellay, was as well equipped for the study of antiquity as was Winckelmann two centuries later. Little, indeed, had he to learn of the past: he could no more than confirm by the sight of his eyes the erudition of his mind. He made the journey, moreover, under the highest auspices. Jean du Bellay, then Bishop of Paris, travelled as ambassador to the Holy See, that by pleading the cause of Henry VIII.'s divorce he might buckle more closely the alliance between France and England.

Though politics did not engross the scholar, he was doubtless on the side of Henry, since Ortuinus and the monkish rabble had espoused the cause of Catherine. Literature and archæology were his true interests, and in a preface to Marliani's *Topography of Rome* he has left us a record of his discovery. He intended, so he said, first to visit the great men of the city; second, to collect such drugs and herbs as were foreign to France; and then to portray the city with his pen. For this last enterprise he was fortified with a farrago of notes collected from both literatures; and though we cannot regret that, for the rest of his life, he was faithful to his masterpiece, a treatise on Rome by François Rabelais would have been a veritable curiosity. He found no plants unknown to him. ' I saw one plane-tree,' says he, ' at the Mirror of the Arician Diana ' ; and there was no need for him to describe the aspect of the city when Marliani had his *Topography* ready for the press.

He was content, therefore, to introduce this work to his patron and to France. Nevertheless, he did not abate his studies ; for not only did he devise a plan for the partition of Rome, using the quadrant of Thales the Milesian, but he examined Rome with so great diligence that, says he, ' I believe no man knows his own house better than I know Rome and all its alleys.' And the preface gave him an opportunity of paying a lofty compliment to his friend Du Bellay. ' Ever since I had a sense of polite letters,' he wrote, ' the end of my desire has been to cross Italy and to visit Rome, the capital of the world. But for me to have seen you at Rome is a higher privilege than to have seen Rome itself. To have been at Rome lies within the fortune of all who are not maimed and crippled in all their limbs ; to have seen you at Rome, distinguished by the incredible congratulation of man, was a pleasure ; to have played any part in policy, when you undertook that noble embassy, upon which you were sent by Francis, our unconquerable king, was glory indeed.' The compliment was not undeserved, and a lifelong friendship is sound proof of its sincerity. But to Rabelais what mattered most was that he had been to Rome in the train of an ambassador, and so had shaken off one other shackle that bound him to the service of the Church.

His return from this triumphant embassy was inauspicious. *Pantagruel* had already brought him into conflict with the authorities : the Sorbonne was furious at his insolence, and he fared no better at the hands of Calvin and his school. Moreover, the Grand Hospital at Lyons, indignant that a doctor, to whom it paid an income of forty *livres*, should vanish without leave, had appointed a successor ; and there is small wonder that another year saw Rabelais back again at Rome with Du Bellay, who had attained the dignity of a cardinal's hat. At this moment all Europe trembled at the name of Charles v., and Rome was in terror at his threatened approach. But Rabelais, in his correspondence with Geoffroy d'Estissac, does not prove himself a profound politician. He speaks of wars and their rumours ; he speaks also of seeds for the Bishop's salads, and gives directions for their planting ; he relates the scandals of the papal courts ; above all, he speaks of the *supplicatio pro apostasia*, which he had presented in due form to the Pope. For many years, Rabelais confesses, he has wandered up and down the rough places of the world ; he has worn the habit of the secular priest, and now he approaches the Holy Father in an attitude of penitence for the recklessness of the past, and asks that he may be received again into the order of St. Benoît, and that he be allowed to practise medicine ' without the use of fire and the knife.' His petition was granted, and Rabelais having done penance, and been duly cleansed from the stain of ill-repute, could regulate his estate without too large a sacrifice of freedom.

Despite the Pope's forgiveness, he continued his wanderings. Now we find him at Montpellier, a new-made doctor, whose lectures are busily frequented, and who, despite the prohibition of fire and knife, gives a lesson in anatomy upon the body of a gallows-bird. So much we know from Etienne Dolet, the profound scholar, ingenious printer, and violent controversialist, with whom Rabelais was many years intimate.[1] Now, Dolet celebrated Rabelais' innovation by writing a sham epitaph to the victim, who is supposed to speak in his own person through Dolet's verses. ' *Spectaculo lato expositus*,' murmurs the corpse :—

> *Secor ; medicus doctissimus planum facit*
> *Quam pulchre, et affabre, ordineque*
> *Fabricata corpus et hominis rerum Parens.*
> *Sectum frequens circumspicit*
> *Corona miraturque molem corporis*
> *Tanto artificio conditi.*

While their friendship lasted Dolet and Rabelais peppered one another with Latin verse of no peculiar

---

[1] See Mr. Copley Christie's erudite *Life of Etienne Dolet*, to which I am much beholden.

merit.   From Rome Rabelais sent the printer a receipt
for the *garum* of the ancients, and one cannot admire
too highly the pedantry of the two scholars.   Dolet
replied in appropriate terms, and presently celebrated
his friend in the best known and most often quoted of
his verses.   When Dolet was acquitted of murder in
1537, a banquet was given in his honour, a banquet
attended by the great Budæus himself, by Marot, ' the
Gallic Virgil,' by François Rabelais, ' that honour and
glory of the Paeonian art, who is able to recall the
dead even from the threshold of Pluto, and to restore
them to the light.'   Nor was grave converse wanting
at this feast.   The humanists of France sang the
praises of such foreign scholars as Erasmus, Melan-
chthon, and Sannazar, and demonstrated that when
Latin was the universal language, learning knew not
the common boundaries of geography.

But presently a quarrel separated Rabelais and
Dolet, as quarrels were wont to separate Dolet from
his friends ; and there can be no doubt that the
printer's conduct was indefensible.   In 1542 Rabelais
published a new edition of his First and Second
Books, whence with characteristic caution he removed
certain stumbling-blocks of offence.   Dolet, less cunning than his friend, and not averse from involving
another in his own ruin, printed an edition of his
own, described as ' revised and augmented by the
author,' from which no guilty words had been
removed.   Dolet's edition appeared first, and Rabelais
or his printer prefaced their own by a sharp and

justified attack upon the pirate. After this interchange of insult no intimacy was possible, and thus,
through no fault of Rabelais, a famous friendship
came to an end.

So Rabelais, ever restless, resumed his travels.
After a sojourn in Montpellier, he is in Piedmont with
Guillaume du Bellay, the cardinal's brother. Now he
is discussing seven-months' children, with the grave
circumstance which he despised in others; now (at
a later date) he is buying Greek books and Syriac
manuscripts for the King's library; and whoever it
is that speaks of him treats him with the respect due
to a scholar. At another time he is keenly interested
in the Aldine Press, and introduces the famous Aldus
Manutius to his patron. Again, in 1542, as we gather
from the verses of Claude Chappuis,[1] he is a master
of requests to the King :—

> *Et Rabelais a nul que soy semblable*
> *Par son scavoir partout recommendable.*

And he was soon to need all the support he could
get. His champion Guillaume du Bellay died in
1542, and Rabelais was present to solace his last
hours. As his friends grew less, his enemies increased in strength : if the scholars of France fought
upon his side, the Sorbonne was yet more bitter than
before. But François i., under whose auspices the
Third Book was printed in 1546, proved a loyal as

---

[1] For this quotation I am indebted to M. Heulhard's *Rabelais
en Voyage*, a mine of curious information.

well as a powerful protector. 'King Francis of
eternal memory,' says Rabelais in the dedication of
the Fourth Book, 'had been made sensible of the
false accusations : And having caused my books (mine,
I say, because several false and infamous have been
wickedly layd to me) to be carefully and distinctly
read to him by the most learned and faithful Anag-
nost in this kingdom, he had not found any passage
suspitious ; and he abhorred a certain envious,
ignorant, hypocritical Informer, who grounded a
mortal heresy on an N put instead of an M by the
carelessness of the Printers.'

No sooner, however, did the King fall sick, than Rabelais thought it wise to take refuge at Metz, where he
was appointed doctor at a salary of 120 *livres*. 'Tem-
pora etiam Rabelaesum ejecerunt e Gallia,' wrote Jean
Sturm, ' φεῦ τῶν χρόνων,' and during the next few
years Rabelais was again in exile, now at Metz, now
at Rome. None the less, he managed (in 1547) to
publish a fragment of the Fourth Book, which
appeared complete five years later under the august
patronage of Monseigneur Odet, Cardinal of Châtillon.
Two years later he was at Rome when Louis d'Orléans,
the second son of Henri ii., was born, and there he
was witness that ' the very day there ran through the
banks of Rome a common rumour, without certain
authority, of this happy birth, not only of the place
and day aforesaid, but also of the hour, *i.e.* about
nine o'clock by the computation of the Romans.'
That news should travel instantaneously from St.

Germain-en-Laye to Rome might have seemed
supernatural to any save a profound scholar; but
Rabelais had many an instance ready culled from
antiquity, and, like the wise astrologer he was,
he set about casting the horoscope for the young
prince.

The occasion fired Rome and Rabelais with an
ardent flame. A mighty festival, such as was never
before seen, was designed in honour of the King's son
—a Sciomachia it was called, that is, a mimic repre-
sentation of battle both by sea and by land. Leroy,
the loyal and patient panegyrist of Rabelais, declares
that it was his hero and none other that designed
the festival. Whether that be so or not, we owe
to Rabelais its eloquent description, conveyed in a
letter to the Most Reverend the Cardinal de Guise.
It is as pleasant a picture of a pageant as exists, and
happily Rabelais reserved the Latin tongue for the
Sapphics, which conclude what may be described
as a model of ' special correspondence.' Unluckily
the sea-fight, which had for its main incident the
destruction of a vast galleon, was brought to nought
by the sudden rising of the Tiber. The bull-fight
and encounter which followed in the Piazza of
Saint Apostollo, the Gargantuan banquet, and the
display of fireworks, were such as no eyes had ever
looked upon, and no pen described. If we may
believe Leroy, the people of Rome were so enchanted
with the spectacle that they said to Jean du Bellay:
' Leave us Rabelais, your magician.' And Du Bellay

answered : ' No, he is mine, and I keep him—an old Frenchman whom I shall restore to France.'

We may not believe Leroy; and with the Scio-machia ends the official career of François Rabelais. Returned to France, he was appointed curate of Meudon, and held the curacy rather less than two years, for on the 9th of January 1552 he signed a document of resignation. Why he resigned is still a mystery; it is probable that he deemed the publication of the Fourth Book of *Pantagruel* a bar to the duties of a priest. Like Heliodorus, he was asked to choose between his book and the Church, and, like Heliodorus, he chose his book. That he acted rightly is certain. *Pantagruel* was the work of his lifetime; the curacy of Meudon, though it is closely linked to his name, was but an interlude of repose. And Rabelais was not destined for peace : the Fourth Book aroused a louder clamour even than the others. Fezandat, the printer, was forbidden to sell the book for fifteen days, on pain of corporal punishment. Yet again Rabelais won a king's pro-tection, and the book was free : his last achievement, for in a few months he was dead, honoured by his friends, hated by the Sorbonnists, and revered in his parish of Meudon, says tradition, as ' a watchful, honest, and charitable pastor.'

V

Such was Rabelais the man, who is too often obscured by a very different personage—the Rabelais of legend. Now, the Rabelais of legend is a monster of hideous mien and low morals, clumsily put together by declared enemies. It was but natural that the monks, whom he scarified in his book, should have employed their ingenuity in detraction; and since they were troubled by no scruples of truth or conscience, they found little difficulty in creating a bogey. 'Who drives fat oxen must himself be fat'—such was their argument, and therefore they boldly declared that the author was no more than the living image of his work. It was not for them to understand a masterpiece which offended the dignity of their order; they did not trouble to search out the honourable life and employments of their victim; they were content to sow their slanders broadcast over the world, in the vain hope that the tares of their foul fancy might grow up and choke the harvest of intelligence.

The miscreant who scattered the first seeds was a monk of Fontevrault, Puy-Herbault by name, whom Rabelais, in a single passage of retaliation, classes with 'Your mad Herb-stinking Hermits, gulligutted dunces of the cowl.' The attack of Puy-Herbault [1] was at once clever and cleverly delivered. He in-

---

[1] *Theotimus, sive de tollendis et expurgandis malis libris . . . libri tres.* Parisiis, 1549.

volved Rabelais in the welter of wrath which he hoped would overtake his writings. 'Nihil aliud,' says he, 'quam perpotat, heluatur, graecatur, nidores culinarum persequitur, ac cercopissat.' Nor is this all. 'I have heard,' says Puy-Herbault, 'from those who live on terms of familiarity with him, that he is of a bad character, and that his life is far more disgraceful than his speech. And more than once I have deplored the fate of a man, who, despite the brilliance of his attainments, shrouds himself in so dense a cloud of vices. . . . He is never mentioned by pious men without loathing ; he is never praised, even at table, except perhaps for having a gullet always dry. . . . This only remember, that vices are heaped up in Rabelais without limit, and that the piety which he has abandoned is every day properly avenged.'

Never was an indictment more hypocritical and more false. A long and honourable career is the best answer to such slanders as this. Rabelais is never mentioned without loathing, says Puy-Herbault ; he is never praised but for drunkenness. The evidence of a hundred friends clears the scholar's character, and it is plain that the 'Herb-stinking Hermit' was lying insidiously when he appealed to the authority of his intimates. However, the harm was done. The followers of Puy-Herbault merely echoed his falsehood. Rabelais, the drunken buffoon, the bawdy trickster, the impious impostor, the truculent enemy of God and man, was already invented, and gossip was free to do the rest. The adventures of his life were perverted to his disgrace; wherever he went he was tracked and convicted of an imbecility. So that the man, whom we know to have been a grave scholar and wise healer, is tricked out in the rags of a mischievous, intoxicated schoolboy. The wonder is that the rascals who maligned him in truth's despite did not make him vast as Gargantua, while they pictured him cunning and unscrupulous as Panurge. For their case rests wholly upon the freedom of his book : they reck nothing of his honest career and the worthy affections he inspired. And had they been consistent, they must have turned him into a harlequin, ingeniously composed of Panurge and Friar John, of Pantagruel and Epistemon, of Gargantua and the Limosin.

At this hour it is superfluous to suggest that Petronius is not the same as Trimalchio, that Shakespeare is not Shylock, that Fielding is not Jonathan Wild. We are all too wise to put faith in so blatant a heresy. But Rabelais, once confused with his book, could hardly disentangle himself. Since his own life was honourable, anecdotes were invented to besmirch his fame, and his career was punctuated (so to say) with drunken and licentious orgies. He was expelled from the monastery, we are told, for frequent acts of indecent blasphemy ; wherever he went he played the silliest jests upon his companions. Once when he was penniless at Lyons and wished to reach Paris, he put up a handful of dust into packets, which he labelled *Poison for the King, Poison for the Queen,*

Poison for the Dauphin; the plot being known, he was of course arrested and carried to Paris, where he explained his trick, and so got his journey for nothing. The story, characteristic enough, anticipates the artifice of the scoundrel Latude; and to involve a distinguished man in so silly an enterprise is to lose hold of history and common-sense. Even when he died, his enemies must compose for him a burlesque will: ' I am worth nothing; I owe much; I leave the rest to the poor.' This jest, as M. Moland points out, was made by Erasmus in a letter addressed to Beda five-and-twenty years before the death of Rabelais. But facts are as little to the man who would prove his slander, as is truth to the writer whose pen is inked with malice. Ronsard, moreover, had little love for Rabelais, and he did his best to thicken the prevailing misunderstanding by a foolish epitaph, wherein he displayed him ' barbouillant dans le vin Comme une grenouille dans la fange.'

Here, then, are the opposing sides, nor is it difficult to discover the inclination of the truth. Shall we believe Puy-Herbault, Ronsard, and the forked tongue of gossip ? Or shall we put faith in the wise Budæus, in Tiraqueau, in the Bishop of Maillezais, in Du Bellay, in all the scholars and courtiers of the age ? Surely the character of Rabelais is never in doubt : from the moment that he entered the convent of Fontenay, he won the respect and admiration of his fellows; though the fame of the humourist was captured late, the fame of the scholar and physician was early conceded; and Rabelais would have been famous in the history of learning had he never created Pantagruel or Panurge. Moreover, though he fought the same fight as Erasmus, Dolet, and a hundred others, he never failed to obtain the help of powerful friends. When he needed a king's protection, it was not denied him; nor in the many documents that throw a light upon his career is a single word spoken in his dispraise.

And strangely enough, we know more of Rabelais than of many another great man: we can trace his shifting action, and follow his august vagabondage. The energy of French scholars has collected a vast array of indisputable facts which concern his life; yet only one circumstance may be set down to his discredit even by an enemy. Rabelais was father of a bastard son, born at Lyons about 1536. We should not have known of the one love-episode in his career, had not his friend Boyssone celebrated the death of the unhappy infant in a dozen sets of verses. The mother remains unknown, though it is clear that the father acknowledged the son; and it is significant that it was Boyssone who deplored the death of Theodulus. For Boyssone was irreproachable at once in scholarship and in character. Once, indeed, he had come near to incur the martyr's doom, and it was only by a recantation that he saved himself from following Jean de Caturce to the stake.

Indeed he was not a man to countenance buffoonery or to excuse a life of sin; and he makes the death of

Theodulus an opportunity for eulogising his father.
' You ask,' he writes in a copy [1] of hendecasyllabics,
' who lies under this little tomb ?   It is the little
Theodulus, little in all things, save in his accomplished father.'   Not a word in Boyssone's verses is
spoken to Rabelais' disgrace ; on the contrary, the
hendecasyllabics are a direct, unconscious refutation
of Puy-Herbault.   No pious man, declared the monk
of Fontevrault, could think of Rabelais without loathing, and Boyssone comes forth to vaunt his learning,
piety, and honour.   Nor have we a right to judge
Rabelais by a modern standard.   He was vowed to
celibacy ; and, as every student of the sixteenth
century knows full well, that vow did not prevent,
nor even discourage, bastardy.   Rabelais was permitted a licence that was readily given to the Popes.
In one of his letters, addressed to the Bishop of Maillezais, he answers a question put by that prelate,

[1] The verses are not the best in the world, but as an undesigned eulogy of Rabelais they have a unique interest:—

> De Theodulo Rabellaeso puero pusillo defuncto.
>> *Quaeris quis jaceat sub hoc sepulchro*
>> *Tam parvo ?   Theodulus ipse parvus.*
>> *Parva aetate quidem, simulque forma,*
>> *Et parvis oculis et ore parvo :*
>> *Toto denique corpore ipse parvus,*
>> *Sed magnus patre docto, et erudito,*
>> *Instructo artibus omnibus, virum quas*
>> *Aequum est scire bonum, pium atque honestum.*
>> *Has omnes Theodulus iste parvus,*
>> *Vitam si modo fata non negassent,*
>> *Erepturus erat patri, exque parvo*
>> *Magnus tandem aliquando erat futurus.*

whether the Lord Peter Farnese is a legitimate son
of Pope Paul III. or a bastard. 'Rest assured,'
answers Rabelais, with no comment, 'that the Pope
was never married : that is to say, the aforesaid
gentleman is assuredly a bastard.' And it is also
noteworthy that none of Rabelais' bitterest detractors
—and they were both many and vicious—ever reproached him with the little Theodulus.

Indeed, wherever we look, we find confirmation of
Rabelais' honest life. When Thevet was in Rome, as
you may read in his *Cosmographie*, he wished to
examine some monuments in the garden of an Italian
nobleman ; and assuredly he would have been arrested
as a spy, had not Rabelais declared upon his own
authority, which could not be denied, that Thevet
was a harmless archæologist. So, too, Joachim du
Bellay sang the praise of him whom his family had
supported. '*L'utile-doux Rabelais*,' he calls him,
with a reminiscence of Horace ; and surely none has
better deserved the double epithet. Moreover, in
his *Defense et illustration de la langue françoyse*, a work
of capital importance, wherein is exemplified the
theory turned by Rabelais into practice, he puts his
hero in the forefront of modern literature. 'The
learned men of France,' says he, 'have not always
despised their vernacular. He who calls Aristophanes
to life again, and feigns so well the nose of Lucian, is
good evidence of that.' Where, indeed, will you
find a wiser criticism, a worthier appreciation ?
Several centuries of study have not bettered it, and

the fame of Rabelais can despise detraction, when even in his own lifetime he found a champion so wise and valiant.

And there is one other plea for the defence, potent and unanswerable. It is easy for priests and pedants from the depths of their arm-chairs to charge with the grosser vices of debauchery and drunkenness a writer whom they cannot understand. There is one thing they forget. A man who, like Rabelais, led a full life, who packed every hour with work or travel, is not called upon to vindicate his character. Vice is for the idle, not for the life of invincible energy ; and though Rabelais, in his eulogy of frolic, may praise the wine-cup, he praises it as the poets of the Greek Anthology praised it, as Horace praised it, or as a hundred of our own. It is the story of Harry Fielding over again— of Harry Fielding, whom the critics have seen stained with claret, and tumbling upstairs drunk to bed. As though the reveller could rise in the morning to the easy composition of a masterpiece ! No, Rabelais may laugh at his enemies : when they prated, he did his work, he wrote his masterpieces, he went on his embassies, he studied the great writers of Greece and Rome ; and while Puy-Herbault and his fellows are nailed upon the barn-door of history, as a warning to other vermin, he goes gaily down the fields of time, laughing his honest laugh, and awaking in each generation the laughter of honest men.

VI

For all the noble energy of his life, it is Rabelais'
great work which gives him immortality, and which
classes him, as Coleridge said long ago, 'with the
creative minds of the world, Shakespeare, Dante,
Cervantes.' He was already old when he began to
write it, between forty and fifty, whatever date we
give to his birth; the last book did not appear in
print until he had been in the grave ten years; and
it held the accumulated learning and experience of a
busy, well-spent life. So far, indeed, it may be called
autobiographical, as it was the result of forty years'
study and observation. Though, as I have said, it is
criminally foolish to ascribe the sins of his personages
to their creator, who speaks now behind one mask,
now behind another, and cannot be at once Pantagruel and Panurge, the masterpiece is none the less
a reflection of a vast brain and vivid temperament.
Nor did Rabelais begin to write a day before he knew
that his material was wholesomely digested. 'Mace-
rate your subject,' said Mr. Stevenson in a passage of
rare wisdom, 'let it boil slowly, then take the lid off,
and look at it—and there is your stuff, good or bad.'
So Rabelais took off the lid after forty years of slow
boiling, and behold the stuff was very good indeed.

It is a superstition, hoary with age and mould,
that he wrote *Gargantua* and *Pantagruel* to help a
bankrupt printer. There never was a more foolish
libel uttered. In composition, in thought, in humour,

Rabelais' work is deliberately intentioned. He had
no more thought of the publisher, when he sat him
down to write, than he had of his own skin. His
multicoloured life had taught him to see all things
in a right relation; he knew that his command
over both form and substance was absolute; and he
needed no spur of friendship or expediency to sing
the pæan of freedom and joy that was humming in
his head.

The very texture of the romance is original and
sincere. In the warp of folklore he entangled the
woof of high intellect. The warp was nothing rarer
than the chap-books and almanacks of the time, which
he knew (none better) how to compile; the woof was
the threads which he had curiously gathered from the
literature of all countries and ages. It is as though
Guy Earl of Warwick or *Jack the Giant-Killer* were
intricated with *Hamlet* or the *Novum Organum*. And
that Rabelais was wholly conscious of his plan is
evident from the mere form and impression of his
books. To the eye as to the touch the early editions
are veritable chap-books: the *Gargantua* of 1537, for
instance, is a *livre de colportage*, even to the woodcut
which stands at the head of the first page. And by
form and substance alike Rabelais appealed to the
wider world which lay beyond the high wall of
scholarship. His anxious choice of French is proof
enough of his purpose. Budæus and the rest, who
wrote in respectable Latin, narrowed their audience,
as they narrowed the scope of their expression. The

Ciceronian, fit subject for Erasmus's scorn, was driven
to blasphemy because his blind-eyed respect for a dead
master compelled him to speak of the Virgin in terms
of Paganism. Rabelais knew enough of monasteries,
enough of Villon, to recognise that the common
truths of life might best be expressed in the common
tongue. So he chose French, as he chose the chap-
book, for the medium of his work.

Where did he find Gargantua ? That is a question
which has deeply troubled the historians; yet it is
not of vital import. Rabelais, like Molière, who rifled
Pantagruel, picked up his pearls where he found them ;
and whether or not he wrote *les Grandes Croniques,* he
did not invent his giant's name. For Gargantua was
already famous before Rabelais put pen to paper;
and though his romance quickened a popular interest,
the many rocks known as Gargantua's Chair were
probably thus entitled long before Rabelais came to
Lyons. While that is matter of dispute, one fact
admits of no argument. Gargantua stood in type as
early as 1526,[1] in which year Charles Bourdigné wrote
his *Ballade aux Lysans,* and put upon paper 'Gargantua qui a chepveulx de plaistre.' The plaster-
haired one, therefore, is not nominally Rabelais' invention. In essence he is; and we need not follow
M. Gaidoz, who, with an ingenuity misguided as

[1] It is suggested in the *Revue des Études Rabelaisiennes* (1er
fascicule) that, as the date is found only on the border, which
frames the title of Bourdigné's book, it is earlier than the book
itself, and that the *Ballade aux Lysans* may be later than the
work of Rabelais. The argument is not conclusive.

Professor Max Müller's, would prove that Gargantua is nothing better than a solar myth.

Folklore and intellect, then, are the twin elements of the Rabelaisian romance, and it is interesting to note that the two elements changed their proportions as the work progressed. In the First Book folklore predominates; in the Second the reader loses hold of the gigantesque idea; and in the Third a lofty, humorous intellect is dominant. Afterwards, the work declines in vigour as in wit: the inspiration seems rather literary than sensitive. But the chapbook is soon forgotten; and, indeed, it may be said that no sooner does the admirable Panurge appear on the scene, than the personages are higher than men only in the activity of their intelligence. Truly, if we would unlock the secret of Rabelais, we shall find the key in his own writings. His prologues are a manifest explanation of his style and purpose. Mirth, he declares, was his first object: 'When I did dictate these jovial new Chronicles of mine, I thought no more upon them than you, who possibly are drinking (the whil'st) as I was; for in the composing of this lordly book, I never lost nor bestowed any more, nor any other time than was appointed to serve me for taking of bodily refection, that is, whilst I was eating and drinking.' So also in the Prologue to the Third Book he sings a song to 'a draught of this bottle.' Says he: 'It is my true and only Helicon; it is my Caballine Fountain. . . . Drinking thus, I meditate, discourse, resolve, and conclude.' Whereon he appeals to the example of the ancients, declaring that 'Ennius drinking, wrote; and writing, drank. Æschylus (if Plutarch in his Symposiacs merit any Faith) drank composing; and drinking, composed. Homer never wrote fasting, and Cato never wrote until after he had drunk.' Thus he praises wine more highly than oil, and would rather have his writings smell of the bottle than of the lamp. In truth, they smell of both.

In another place he declares that he wrote with no other object than to solace his patients. 'I aimed not at glory and applause,' said he, 'when I diverted myself with writing; but only designed to give by my Pen to the absent that labour under affliction, that little help which at all times I willingly strive to give to the Present that stand in need of my Art and service.' This, no doubt, is a half-truth. Though no book was ever a better solace to weariness than Rabelais', his modest claim is partly satire and mystification. Nor does he attempt to preserve an urgent consistency with himself. The first page of his first Prologue is evidence of a lofty purpose. He compares his work to the Silenes of old, which, says he, 'were little boxes, like those we may now see in the shops of Apothecaries, painted on the outside with wanton toyish figures, as Harpyes, Satyrs, bridled Geese, horned Hares, saddled Ducks, flying Goats, Thiller Harts, and other suchlike counterfeited pictures at discretion, to excite people unto laughter, as Silenus himself, who was the foster-father of good Bacchus, was wont to do ; but within those capricious caskets were carefully preserved and kept many rich jewels, and fine drugs, such as Balme, Ambergreece, Amamon, Musk, Civet, with several kindes of precious stones, and other things of great price.' And the moral is no less vivid than the image : ' You must open the book, and seriously consider of the matter treated in it, then shall you finde that it containeth things of farre higher value than the boxe did promise ; that is to say, that the subject thereof is not so foolish, as by the Title at the first sight it would appear to be.'

The bone of the book, then, to use another Rabelaisian image, is humour, pure humour ; the marrow of the book is wisdom, pure wisdom ; and the safer the marrow is concealed in the bone, the greater the difficulty which stayed its discovery. For the rest laughter is the keynote of the book—laughter loud and wholesome. No man in the world's history was so palpably shaken by hilarity as Rabelais ; no man ever had the like genius of evoking merriment from others. Above all, he meant men to laugh ; and though beneath his text there runs a stream of seriousness, he did not demand that the stream should be plumbed from source to sea. In other words, he scorned a minute and literal interpretation, and his good sense enabled him to anticipate the folly of objection. He found men sad and serious, and once more he wreathed human lips in smiles. This result could not be achieved by simple means :

argument had failed; contempt passed unregarded; there was nothing could regenerate the torpid world save boisterous ridicule.

So it is that destruction must always precede reform; and Rabelais, with an intellectual courage which he shares with Lucian and Swift, killed with laughter the vain ignorance of his generation. The result to him has been misunderstanding and obloquy : even his staunchest admirers are constrained to apologise for him, though indeed the rough, rugged humour of old Gaul should stand in need of no defence. But where attack is constant, defence becomes imperative, and we cannot speak of Rabelais without remembering that he is still in the general imagination ' a filthy priest.' For his enemies' sake, this much may be conceded : he uncovered the secret places of life ; he wrote openly of those things which are commonly discussed in the privacy of speech ; he knew as little of reticence as of cowardice, and his book may be (and is) too strong a posset for the weak and faltering. The weak and faltering are free to leave it alone : assuredly the *esprit gaulois,* with its untrammelled licence, is not for them. Every man, I take it, is either born a Rabelaisian or he is not. If he have the good fortune to be a wise Pantagruelist, let him appreciate his master with a stout heart, and never thrust a like appreciation upon his fellows. Let the Scotist and the monk, as Rabelais would say, keep an ox upon their tongue, and not bring charges which are founded merely on their own lack of understanding.

In the first place, then, Rabelais' foulness has always seemed the greater because it has been taken out of its environment. The Frenchmen of the sixteenth century knew not the restrictions imposed by the squeamishness of a new refinement. They spoke boldly, as they acted freely; and so long as they escaped the censure of the Church, they might interpret their life as joyously as they chose. Moreover, the literature of the time was not confined within the limits that we mark to-day. The work of Rabelais is rather a symptom of the prevailing licence than an isolated phenomenon. There is many an earlier book that is almost as gross and outspoken as his. When Ulrich von Hutten wrote his *Epistolae Obscurorum Virorum* he convulsed Europe with laughter; he horrified even Erasmus; and he has never suffered the insults that have been cast upon Rabelais. Yet his book is as fearless a lashing of the monks as *Pantagruel* itself, and it is from all points of view that masterpiece's closest parallel. It professes to be a collection of letters addressed to Magister Ortuinus, who is remembered to-day by the satire of Rabelais; and, both by the style of its Latin and the ribaldry of its scorn, it deserves the admiration of all those who hate cant and appreciate humour. Set this curious little work by the side of Rabelais, and it will not excuse him (he needs no excuse); it will prove that Rabelais did not surprise his generation, as he surprises ours, by his singularity. Or study the incomparable *Praise of Folly*, and note the licence which a far more closely restrained wit than Rabelais allowed himself. Or read that other little masterpiece of satire, *les Quinze joyes de mariage*, which doubtless helped to suggest Panurge's immortal difficulty, and does not the recklessness of Gargantua find a match ? Truly, in his own day Rabelais had many competitors, and he used or he quoted them all. The Macaronic verses of Merlin Coccai are not miracles of delicacy; and doubtless they would have been forgotten to-day, had not the French satirist laid a careful hand upon them, and found therein more than a hint for the sophistries of Panurge. Nor to those who are familiar with the classics, another source of inspiration to our author, will his frivolity appear astonishing. We do not gird at Aristophanes to-day : rather we read him in our schools, though the difference between him and his most illustrious pupil is a difference not of kind, but of degree.

It is not merely on the ground of authority that we would defend Rabelais. Foul as his book is in certain passages, it is never indecent. There are ten outbursts of laughter to every page; there is not a single smirk from beginning to end. Rabelais always drags away the veil with a strong hand : he does not leave his impropriety half covered, and so prompt his reader to a filthy curiosity. Indecent writers exist, without doubt, but Rabelais is not of the number; and we do not envy the mind of those ' squint-minded ' fellows, who could suffer harm from the study of this wholesome literature. Never once does Rabelais incite to vice, which is joy's antithesis ; never once does he tickle a prurient fancy, which he never means to satisfy. In all things he is a man, and he easily shakes off the censure that is properly thrown at emasculated impropriety. More often than not his very bawdry is a burlesque of what is called ' sexuality ' ; and it is one of his faults that he has no interest, sentimental or intellectual, in womankind.

Save in the splendid interlude of the Abbey of Thélème, he gives no proof of a chivalrous temper. That, I say, is a fault—a fault whose corresponding virtue is a perfect absence of eroticism. Moreover, his foulness is rather an affair of words than of thoughts. He does not tempt the reader to imagine the situations which he sketches. In truth, the situations exist merely in word, and a list of synonyms is rather an occasion for hearty laughter than for zealous censure. To use a cant phrase, *Gargantua* and *Pantagruel* are never realistic. Their atmosphere is not the atmosphere of life. The mere size of the giants puts them above and without a narrow process of reasoning, and it is idle to saddle with vice a set of characters who were never meant to resemble our frail humanity. No, the work of Rabelais is a vision of pure intellect with a setting of romance, and romance and intellect alike carry us away from the squalor of actual life. And when in his style he takes on the robes of romance, he instantly puts off the broken boots of ribaldry. Then, the crown of intellect

always adorns his brow. We do not care what his
personages do ; in fact, they do very little : we care
infinitely how they think, and in what marvellous
words they express their daring thoughts. In brief,
no book is indecent which does not purposely evoke
indecent images ; and Rabelais does not stoop from
the high domain of intellect to achieve so paltry
a result.

But he, good soul, knew that his laughter would be
misunderstood by the timid, and in the Epilogue to
his Second Book he fashioned the barb which should
pierce his detractors. ' If you say to me, (Master)'—
it is the Master who speaks—' it would seem that you
were not very wise in writing to us these flimflam
stories, and pleasant fooleries : I answer you, that you
are not much wiser to spend your time in reading them:
neverthelesse, if you read them to make your selves
merry, as in manner of pastime I wrote them, you
and I both are farre more worthy of pardon, than a
great rabble of squint-minded fellowes, dissembling
and counterfeit Saints, demure lookers, hypocrites,
pretended zealots, tough Fryars, buskin-Monks, and
other such sects of men, who disguise themselves
like Maskers to deceive the world. . . . As for their
study, it is wholly taken up in reading of Pantagruelin
books, not so much to passe the time merrily, as to
hurt some one or other mischievously.' We all know
these monsters too well ; they abounded in the time
of Rabelais ; they are more frequent and mischievous
in our own. And we must e'en take Rabelais' advice,

and be tranquil : ' Fly from these men, and abhorre and hate them as much as I do, and upon my faith you will feel your selves the better for it. . . . Never trust those men that always peep out at one hole.' That is sound counsel soundly administered, and all good Pantagruelists will follow it with good heart.

There is another reason why Rabelais should not mask his meaning. Monstrous ills require heroic remedies, and the world which Rabelais essayed to heal was dying of a foul disease. He battled for the real against the unreal, for honest joy against itching asceticism, for the outspoken word against the unclean thought. The literature of his time discloses the enemies against whom he fought, and it is his triumph to have uncovered the ambuscade which threatened the people. The world was sick, he cured it ; the world was beset by secret foes, he repulsed them ; the world was asleep, he awoke it with the trumpet-call of good sense. The awakening was rude, no doubt. It was no fairy-princess rising from her beauty-sleep ; rather it was a bound and passionate giant bursting the chains at once of slumber and of captivity. How, then, should he awake but with a snort and a hiccup ? All knowledge was expressed in meaningless formulæ ; the old tradition of learning had been infamously broken ; the classics, once the scholar's inspiration, had been condemned as the mother of heresy ; and for the bread of learning men had received the stone of monkish indiscipline.

Rabelais, therefore, was a type of the full, brutal
Renaissance : he preferred to the barren maxims of
the schoolmen the amenity of paganism and the lust
of nature. And nature did not mean for him what
it meant for Rousseau, a half-hearted change of
culture, the substitution of a barbered garden for a
powdered court. In effect, he suppressed a thousand
years, and pictured man as he was before the artifice
of law and church got hold of him. So he preached
in a louder voice the same doctrine as Erasmus. And
while Erasmus may be compared to a crystal-clear
well, whose unruffled surface is broken only by the few,
Rabelais is like a turbid, tumultuous torrent, clanking
over half-covered rocks, and reverberating in the ears
of all men.

Loudly as he declaimed, bitterly as he fought, he
never shared the fanaticism of his enemies. His
opinions are generous even to liberality : he had cause
enough to hate the Church, yet he never assailed it
without reason, and Calvin was no more acceptable
to his intellect than the Sorbonne. And from his
absence of fanaticism there sprang the second quality
of caution. It was not for him to run his head into
a brick wall, that he might destroy at once the life that
he loved and the opinions which he championed. In
fact, Erasmus and Rabelais followed the line of least
resistance. They did not, and would not, abate one
jot of their principles. They put a wise diplomacy
before martyrdom, and who should say that they chose
the worse course ? Even if it were the worse for them,

it was the better for us. The irony of Erasmus, the humour of Rabelais, have had far more effect than the reckless deaths of such heroes as Caturce, who were sacrificed to the trickery of nameless persecutors. Not that Rabelais and Erasmus escaped the attacks of madmen. They opposed fanaticism by intelligence, and took care to cover themselves with the shield of kingly support. Maybe the martyr is a more comely figure than the man of calm and cunning sense. Yet they also are worthy soldiers who, instead of attacking their foe in front, find him unaware and turn his flank.

The enemies of Rabelais, then, were the false 'Theologues, who for the greater part are Hereticks,' 'the false Lawyers, who never go to law with one another,' the false 'Physicians, who never take any Physic.' And he belaboured them with a violence trebled by oppression. There is scarce a chapter of his book that does not wing a shaft at the Church and the monasteries. For the monks, indeed, his fiercest scorn is reserved. He likens them to apes, who neither keep the house nor drive the plough, but instead spoil and defile all things. So says he : ' A Monk (I mean those bitter, idle, lazie Monks) doth not labour and work as doth the Peasant and Artificer ; doth not ward and defend the country, as doth the man of warre ; cureth not the sick and diseased as doth the Physician.' No, they merely pray to God, and ' with a tingle-tangle jangling of bells trouble and disquiet all their neighbours.' And, says Friar John,

with the note of seriousness which is never long silent
in Rabelais : ' They say many patenotres, interlarded
with ave-maries, without thinking upon or appre-
hending the meaning of what they say, which truly I
call mocking of God and not prayers.'

So in the chapter on powdered beef he declares that
the monks live to eat rather than eat to live, and he
insults the gulligut, gulching friars in the same terms
and with the same epithets which Lucian applies to
the philosophers of his time. What can be better,
again, than the ridicule cast upon Janotus de Brag-
mardo, and through him upon all the sophisters of the
Sorbonne ? The good man, packed with insignificant
pretence, marks the place in his discourse where a
cough is appropriate, after the fashion of Olivier
Maillard.

For all this, let it not be thought that Rabelais
was a heretic. He hated Calvin more bitterly than
he contemned his ancient colleagues, and he repudiated
the charge with acerbity. ' The least of their detrac-
tions,' writes he of the cannibals, misanthropes, and
perpetual eavesdroppers, ' were that my books were
all stuffed with various Heresies, of which nevertheless they could not show one single instance ; much
indeed of comical and facetious fooleries, neither
offending God nor King : but of heresy not a word,
unless they interpreted wrong and against all use of
reason, what I had rather suffer a thousand deaths
than have thought.' This, indeed, we may take to be
no more than the truth, remembering only that the

heresy of to-day is the orthodoxy of to-morrow, and
that at a brief distance of time revolt and reaction are
insensibly merged the one in the other. Sir Thomas
More, a true reformer, lost his head rather than
follow his king to a logical conclusion.

Against the law Rabelais inveighed with equal
bitterness. 'The cosenages of Cepola,' who taught
litigants how they might prolong a legal process, were
shocking to his sense of honour and justice; and it
was not in mere satire that in the famous suit between
the Lords of Kissebreech and Suckfist—surely as fine
a piece of foolery as ever cast discredit on a foolish
system—all the papers stored up by the ingenuity of
attorneys were mercilessly burned. And what should
he say of scholars who worshipped Master John of
Scotland, and reverenced the college of Montaigu, who
saw no shame in comparing Ovid and Naso, or in
repeating parrot-like the maxims of the logicians?
'Then it was,' says he, 'that men began to tie their
breeches to their doublets, and not their doublets to
their breeches: for it is against nature, as hath been
most amply shewed by Ockam upon the exponibles
of Master Hautechaussade.' The question at issue
is as gravely intelligent as those which engrossed the
schools, and might properly be resolved by a prolonged study of the books that were treasured in the
stately library of St. Victor.

Wherever folly was, Rabelais attacked it, with a
courage and insight which give his satire an eternal
truth. When Pantagruel met a Limosin, he encoun-

tered a creature who is even more familiar to our own
century than to the sixteenth. The scholar, who
' came from the alme, enclyte and celebrate Academie,
which is vocitated Lutetia,' still frequents the Latin
Quarter, where he is known as decadent or deliques-
cent. Still he flays the Latin, imagining that by so
doing he doth highly Pindarise in most eloquent
terms; and not seldom does he die the death of
Roland, like the Limosin himself, the death in plain
English called thirst. Thus Rabelais runs atilt at all
the pedantries : the pedantry of faith, the pedantry
of medicine, the pedantry of style. And it is not
surprising that, compelled to fight his foemen with
their own weapons, he outdoes them all in an affectation of shallow thought and pretentious diction.

VII

Bitterly destructive as was the criticism of Rabelais, he was no apostle of mere negation. He
denied the false that he might affirm the true ; he
destroyed that he might build up a fairer monument.
The positive teaching of his book, in fact, is clearer
and more forcible than the negative ; and this is
proved by nothing so clearly as by his half-resolve
to teach nothing else than the duty of laughter.
In spite of himself and his own declaration, he could
never forget that he was a Silene, and that, however grotesquely his outside might be painted with
' wanton, toyish figures,' he held within many fine

drugs and rich spices. Above all, he was the champion of a sane and active life : he would always be doing something, or learning something. The spectator was contemptible. 'In my opinion,' said he, ' little honour is due to such as are mere lookers-on, liberal of their eyes, but of their purse parsimonious.' His bringing-up had disgusted him with the anæmic inactivity of the monasteries, and he never gave to ' good ' that falsest of all meanings—the absence of evil.

His scheme of education was more wholesome and practical than the vaunted system of our public schools. Read how Gargantua was instructed by Ponocrates, and note that nothing was neglected that might strengthen his body or set a fine edge upon his wit. Good order was always observed, and the young giant was even ' combed, curled, trimmed and perfumed.' Then after three good hours of lecture, he went into the meadows, where they played at the ball, ' most gallantly exercising their bodies, as formerly they had done their mindes.' And sport was as little an infliction as study : ' All their play was but in liberty, for they left off when they pleased, and that was commonly when they did sweat over all their body, or were otherwayes weary. Then were they very well wiped and rubbed, shifted their shirts, and, walking soberly, went to see if dinner was ready. . . . In the mean time Master Appetite came, and then very orderly sate they down at table ; at the beginning of the meale, there was read some pleasant history of the warlike actions of former times, until he had taken a glasse of wine.' Thereafter were discussed ' the nature and efficacy of all that was served at table,' and such appropriate authors as Athenæus, Pliny, and Aristotle were quoted. At last, after some ' fine Canticks made in praise of the divine bounty and munificence,' cards were brought, not for play, but to learn a thousand pretty tricks founded on arithmetic, and so the science of numbers was encouraged. Then came music and sports of all kinds, until at ' last they prayed unto God the Creator, in falling down before him, and strengthening their faith towards him, and glorifying him for his boundlesse bounty for the time that was past, they recommended themselves to his divine clemency for the future, which being done, they went to bed, and betook themselves to their repose and rest.' Thus he sketched an education which might have befitted a great king, without a word of ribaldry or scorn, and in such a spirit as proves that he gravely condemned the lazy, lither system of the monasteries.

Being a true man of letters, he loved best of all the ' celestial manna of honest literature,' and he has composed in Gargantua's letter to Pantagruel the simple gospel of humanism. This eloquent plea for the liberal arts, for the dignity of the classics, above all for the supremacy of Greek, is as good an argument against the superstition of the Church as may be found in the books of the century. Moreover, the famous letter is inspired with a lofty intelligence

and a wise fervour which the enemies of Rabelais do
not suspect. ' But because, as the wise man Solomon
saith '—thus he writes—' Wisdome entereth not into
a malicious minde; that knowledge without conscience is but the ruine of the soule, it behooveth
thee to serve, to love, to feare God, and on him to
cast all thy thoughts and all thy hope, and by faith
formed in charity to cleave unto him, so that thou
mayest never be separated from him by thy sins.'
Knowledge, without conscience, is but the ruin of
the soul! The man who echoed that profound sentence was no buffoon, and it is only a perverse criticism which has obscured the real character of his
book. The world has lived nearly four centuries
since Rabelais, and we are not within a league of
realising his noble, humane ideal of education.

A French critic has pointed out, with perfect ineptitude, that Rabelais lacked a sense of beauty; and
in his famous Abbey of Thélème he drew a living
sketch of a noble, pleasant life. Whatever amenity
or scholarship was possible in the seclusion of a religious house was marred by the constant restraint of
monkish prohibition. ' Thou shalt not ' were the
words with which every ordinance began, and for this
commandment Rabelais would substitute the ampler,
more generous ' Thou shalt.' ' Do what thou wilt,'
so said Gargantua, in the full certainty that those
who entered his Abbey could do nothing wrong.
In all respects the Abbey of Thélème was designed
as the monastery's antithesis. First, said Gargantua

to Friar John, you must not build a wall about your
convent because all other abbeys are mured around;
and as, if chaste and honest women enter certain
convents, the ground upon which they trod is newly
swept, so at Thélème the rooms, through which any
man or woman entered into orders chance to pass,
should be thoroughly cleansed. No bell should call
the inmates to dinner or rouse them from their sleep;
since there can be no ' greater dotage in the world than
for one to guide and direct his courses by the sound
of a Bell, and not by his own judgment and discretion.'
Nor did Thélème put a foolish restriction upon sex.
Women that were fair and well dispositioned were
no less free of the Abbey than men; and, as an open
defiance of the final vow, they might come and go
as they pleased.

So they lived a sweet, untrammelled life, disporting
themselves in full and honest gaiety of heart, as did
the courtiers in the golden garden of Boccaccio. In
all things elegance and beauty were enjoined. Rich
robes were the proper adornment of fair ladies and
valiant knights; pure goldsmiths' work and sparkling
jewels lent a brilliance to the amiable scene; if they
had a mind to ride, ' the ladies mounted upon dainty,
well-paced nags'; if an interchange of wit suited
them, they sent the time along with pleasant converse, or with the composition of verse and prose.
They hunted, they played, they sang, and in all things
they followed their inclination. And they never
transgressed the laws of amenity, ' because men that

are free, well-borne, well-bred, and conversant in
honest companies, have naturally an instinct and
spurre that prompteth them into vertuous actions,
and withdraws them from vice, which is called honour.'
Thus Rabelais for once sang the praise of the outworn
chivalry, and showed to the modern world that an
ideal of beauty and of conduct might still be shaped.

And the abbey which should enclose them—if the
word be not too harsh for the freedom of Thélème—
was a casket worthy of the precious jewel. As the
ladies and the gallants, who obeyed their mistresses
in all things, were the declared enemies of monkery,
so the unwalled castle wherein they dwelt was an
abbey in nothing but its name. Rabelais, in truth,
contrasted with the dark, immuring convent the
splendid liberty of the châteaux, which were and still
are the glory of Touraine. It matters not whether
his Thélème was designed in imitation of Chambord,
or of Amboise, which it recalls by its wonderful
' scalier or winding-stair, the entry whereof was
without the house, in a vault or arch six fathom
broad,' and which was made ' in such symmetrie and
largenesse, that six men at armes with their lances in
their rests might together in a breast ride up to the
very top of all the Palace.' This, I say, matters not
a jot, for there is little doubt that Rabelais pieced
together his abbey from many a desirable reminiscence. The free, frank life of his Touraine shines
forth in every page. The fountains, the tiltyard, the
tennis-court are the appanage of magnificence, and

orchards full of fruit-trees, ranged in quincunxes, may yet be seen as Rabelais designed them. 'Do what thou wilt' is a wise motto, if opportunity be added; and nought was lacking at Thélème for the proper enjoyment of life. Yet, says the critic, Rabelais had no sense of beauty.

Thus freedom and beauty are two chapters in Rabelais' gospel of life; and, while Gargantua sketched the perfect happiness, Pantagruel lent his name to the ideal of joyful sanity. Nothing better illustrates the growth of Rabelais' mind than the shifting definition of Pantagruelism. In the First Book, this quality denotes no more than 'drinking stiffly to your heart's desire, and reading the dreadful and horrifick acts of Pantagruel.' Gradually it took an ampler meaning; it transferred its virtue from the body to the soul. In the Second Book, to be a good Pantagruelist means 'to live in peace, joy, health, making yourselves always merry,' until at last it is stripped of selfishness, and enables man 'to bear with anything that floweth from a good, free, and loyal heart.' Such, then, was Rabelais' doctrine: from freedom and loyalty nothing can proceed that is not excellent; and we are content to take him at his word, with the full knowledge that a dissembling mind and squint eye are the worst obstacles to the understanding of his book.

His style is accurately fitted to his substance. As, for the matter of his work, he welded together the folklore of France and the wisdom of the ancients, so his language is the popular language of France,

haunted by memories of the classics. He disdains
neither proverbs nor slang ; if he cannot find a word
ready to his use, he scruples not to invent one ;
on the other hand, he fashions Greek as easily as he
fashions French, and there is scarce a line in his work
that does not carry the reader back across the centuries.
The master of an admirably lucid style, he chooses at
times to be dark and obscure ; and you may be sure
that, when his meaning is not instantly clear, he
deliberately intends to befog you. The real difficulty
of his book lies less in its construction than in its
vocabulary. Curious words may elude any one who
has not Cotgrave at his elbow— and even Cotgrave is
now and then at fault—but the syntax is never
tenebrous. Indeed, Rabelais wrote a French far
nearer to Latin than the language of to-day. The
words, which depend one upon another, are knit
together (so to say) with a stouter string than is
employed in modern French. To vary the metaphor,
the stones of his building are joined by a stiffer mortar
than we find (for example) in the building of Voltaire,
who sets his blocks, nicely squared and chiselled, one
upon another, and hopes that their own weight will
keep them in their place. Above all, the influence
of Greek is detected in the turn of his sentence, in
the facture of his phrase. What he owed to Lucian
and Aristophanes has already been pointed out, and
this debt is a debt of thought rather than of language.
As the Greek satirists turned the lantern of their
scorn upon the waste places of Paganism, so Rabelais

flashed his lamp upon the putrefactions of Catholicism. But his debt to Homer, for instance, is a debt of style. Again and again he gives an epic twist to his romance, until you hear the Homeric hexameter thundering through his quick and moving prose. The monk fighting his enemies might well be Achilles assailing the Trojan host : ' Then did the Monk with his staffe of the Crosse give Captain Drawforth such a sturdie thump and whirret betwixt his neck and shoulders upon the Acromion bone, that he made him lose both sense and motion, and fall down stone dead at his horses feet.' Whenever the narrative quickens, then Rabelais is mindful of Homer, whom he studied long since at Fontenay-le-Comte ; and it was not without a valid reason that the ingenious Dufresnoy composed his treatise on Homer and Rabelais.

And Rabelais has yet another claim upon our regard : he may be said to have invented the literature of digression. In other words, his thoughts move more quickly than his personages. Whatever purpose he have on hand, he is always ready to cut round the nearest corner, and discover a fresh point of interest. The nativity of Pantagruel prompts him to a long and curious disquisition on why the sea is salt, and there are few adventures which he does not interrupt with a like discussion. From the moment that Panurge asks if he shall marry, the romance is conducted by the method of digression. The artifice has been employed by Sterne and many another imitator, but never with the full humour which Rabelais brought to his task. And for this enterprise his erudition precisely fitted him. With a quotation always on his tongue, with his thumb always between the pages of a well-worn classic, he was never at a loss for an illustration ; and thus it is that his work is in one aspect the greatest commonplace book the world has ever seen—far greater than Burton's *Anatomy*, to which he was an inspiration, because whatever he quoted he vitalised and made his own. Truly in his brain the seeds of erudition found fertile soil, for it is only the shallow-pate whose invention is impoverished by the contemplation of another's learning.

VIII

And there is one quality which Rabelais owed to his native genius alone. A century of study could not have taught him to draw such characters as will live in the eternal memory of mankind. Pantagruel, Panurge, and Friar John are something more than bundles of qualities : they are men who may still have a part in our memory and experience. Pantagruel, the wise monarch and intelligent counsellor, is always true to the doctrine of his name. 'He was,' says Rabelais, ' the best, little, good man that ever girded a sword to his side ; he took all things in good part, and interpreted every action in the best sense.' That truly did he, or he could not have loved Panurge better than any man he ever saw. He delighted in wine as he delighted in wisdom and truth. Did he not, as set forth in the *Pantagrueline Prognostication,* appoint agents to sift the false news from the true before it came into his kingdom, an excellence to which no civilised nation has ever since attained ? In fact, he hath always been 'the idea, pattern, prototype, and exemplary of all jovial perfection and accomplishment.' His judgment between the two Lords was worthy of Solomon, and under Gargantua's auspices he was so admirably educated that he might symbolise all the learning of his age. Yet was he never morose with scholarship : he loved good cheer as heartily as his creator loved it ; and he found his friends not among the pedants, but among the ingenious spirits of his court. Was he not worthy, then, to give his name to a gospel of life, as well as to the all-important, priceless herb, Pantagruelion ? [1]

And while Pantagruel was the wisest of monarchs, Friar John of the Gobbets is the bravest, stoutest monk who ever donned a cowl. True, he was better at a fight than at a sermon ; true, also, he handled his crucifix like a cudgel. He is pictured as the escaped monk, who knows the folly of a wicked system, and esteems the world more highly than a vile seclusion. Worthy is he, in honour as in knowledge, of the

[1] Rabelais is rumoured to have been Pantagruel's rival in that he brought the lettuce into France. It is proved by his letter to Geoffroy d'Estissac that he was learned about salads. Should he not then have received the same compliment as Pantagruel, and heard the lettuce called 'Rabelaesia' ?

incomparable Abbey, given him by Gargantua. When
the King would have granted him Bourgueil or
St. Florent, he returned a very peremptory answer
that he would never take upon him the charge nor
government of monks. 'For how shall I be able,'
said he, ' to rule over others, that have not full power
and command of myself ? ' Thus he, too, was a good
Pantagruelist, and at Thélème put into practice the
gospel of his lord and master.

The greatest of them all is Panurge, the true
πολύτροπος, the man of shifts and wiles, the rascal
ready for any blackguardism, the prophet with a word
of wisdom ever on his tongue. No sooner does he
enter upon the scene than the romance assumes a
larger style ; and most properly does he show himself
in the rags which befit his life of dodges and escapes.
That the rest of the work should be devoted to his
whimsies is but just and wise, for he inspires Rabelais
to his boldest flights, his wittiest phantasies. 'Poor
Panurge bibbed and bowsed of it most villainously,
for he was as dry as a red-herring, as lean as a rake, and
like a poor, lank, slender cat, walked gingerly as if he
had trod upon egges' : such did he appear to his
patron, when he had escaped out of the hands of the
Turks, and it was upon eggs that he walked, intellec-
tually, unto the end. His qualities and conditions
are industriously set forth : a cheater and cony-
catcher, he was none the less a very gallant and proper
man, while his aquiline nose, like the handle of a
razor, was a clear advertisement of his character. To

his vices and deceits there was no end : he was a very
' dissolute and debauched person if there was any in
Paris ; otherwise, and in all matters else, the best and
most virtuous man in the world.' On the other hand,
his ingenuity was boundless. The argument whereby
he put the Englishman to a non-plus is a masterpiece
of silent oratory ; and his love-affairs, though unscrupulous, were conducted with a cleverness which
might have astounded the ladies of Paris. Despite
his gallantry, it must be confessed that he was a ' little
lecherous, and naturally subject to a kinde of disease,
which at that time they called lack of money.' Indeed,
he was seldom out of countenance, save when he
had a ' flux in his disease ' ; and it is not strange that
this flux was constant, since, while he had threescore
and ten ways of getting money, he had two hundred
and fourteen of spending it, besides his drinking.
Being a true gutter-brat, he was as quick as he was
mischievous : in less than two days he knew all the
streets, lanes, and turnings in Paris as well as his *Deus
det* ; and his cowardice was equal to his knowledge,
for no sooner had he played his prank, than he ran
away as fast as he could, for he was naturally fearful
of blows. So careless a spendthrift was he, that not
even the lordship of Salmagondy could fill his pocket :
in fourteen days he spent all the certain and uncertain
revenues for three whole years. He gave banquets,
he kept open house, he burnt great logs for the ashes,
he borrowed money beforehand, he bought dear, he
sold cheap, he ate his corn, whilst it was but grass.

And for all his excesses he had a ready excuse. Why should he cut his wheat in the blade when from it you might make ' a good green sauce ' ? At any rate there is no thrift in that, and it is thrift which aroused his bitterest scorn. ' Everybody cries up thrift, thrift, and good husbandry,' says he ; ' but many speak of Robin Hood that never shot in his bow.' Above all, he worshipped his creditors : ' The Lord forbid that I should be out of debt, as if, indeed, I could not be trusted.' So to debt he sings a song of triumph : to debt, whence spring kindliness and good fortune ; to debt, whereby man fulfils the end of his creation, which was ' but to owe, borrow, and lend ' ; to debt, on which depends the harmony of nature, the well-ordered policy of life. All the pæans of debt which have been chanted ever since, even down to Disraeli's immortal Fakredeen, owe their inspiration to Panurge, yet not one rivals the original either in eloquence or ingenuity.

Truly Panurge is always at his best when Pantagruel serves him for a foil ; and the discourse whether Panurge shall or shall not marry is Rabelais' final triumph of wit. The argument is tossed to and fro with the lightness of a puff-ball. ' Then marry, in the name of God, quoth Pantagruel. But if, quoth Panurge, my Wife should make me a Cuckold ? ' Panurge has made up his mind at the very outset : marry he will, but he will not be a cuckold, nor will he be beaten. Pantagruel can no more than argue ' yea ' or ' nay ' ; and feeling neither passion nor preference, he keeps always within the bounds of logic. In Coleridge's phrase : ' He stands for the reason as contradistinguished from the understanding or choice; that is, from Panurge.' But Coleridge's phrase is only half luminous. Panurge is at once more and less than ' understanding ' ; rather he opposes his temperament to his companion's intelligence, his *inconscience* to the other's *conscience*. Pantagruel gives the counsel best suited to Panurge's facts ; Panurge rejects such advice as does not chime with his instinct. He cares as little for divination as for oracles ; and, like a wrestler smeared with oil, he always extricates him from an embarrassing interpretation. The humour is perfect, because the contrast is at once ludicrous and subtle ; and had Rabelais written no more than two or three chapters of his Third Book, he would be secure of immortality.

One other quality Panurge shares with no other character in the romance : he has a physical as well as an intellectual existence. He is projected visibly from the ground-plan of the romance : if you met him in the street, you would surely know the man of guile and cunning. And this projection is the more remarkable, because Rabelais is usually careless of appearances : you are seldom conscious of his backgrounds or his trappings. His personages drink, but the shape of their flagons is never suggested : they walk or they sit, but they reveal neither the shape of the avenues wherein they wander, nor the form of the couches which gives them repose. When Pantagruel

was young, he was hairy : so much we know, yet the
aspect of his later years is never revealed ; nor should
we easily recognise Epistemon and Carpalin. The
accent of their speech is familiar ; themselves remain
strangers unto the end. Not so Panurge, whose
sharp features, thin nose, and hatchet face are as
intimate as the gaiety of François I., or the stout
rotundity of our eighth Henry.

So it has come about that Panurge has been iden-
tified with the author himself, with the Bishop of
Valence, with we know not what other prelate. But
the process of identification is barren and senseless.
One assertion may be confidently made ; *Gargantua*
and *Pantagruel* are not *romans à clef*, and the keys
which misplaced ingenuity has devised are but an
expression of human folly. Gargantua was a king,
so were Henry of Navarre and Francis of France ;
with the kingship begins and ends the imagined
resemblance. Moreover, the ignorance of the commentators is confessed by their divergence. How can
Friar John be at once Cardinal Châtillon, whom
Rabelais loved, and Martin Luther, whom he assuredly
despised ? The true Pantagruelist will sweep away
all these theories, being content to enjoy the flimflam
stories for their own humour, and to admire what
Coleridge truthfully styles ' the moral elevation of
Rabelais' work.'

IX

The success of *Gargantua* and *Pantagruel* was vast and immediate. 'The printers have sold more of them,' said their author, 'in two months' time, than there will be bought of Bibles in nine years' : which, considering that the Church forbade the study of Holy Writ, is not remarkable. Yet they had not the direct influence in France which we might have expected. They became part of the popular thought and of the popular speech : they did not challenge the men of letters into an open rivalry. The *Moyen de parvenir* is a flagrant imitation ; the *Compère Mathieu* touches Rabelais through the medium of Sterne. And what other works shall you set side by side with *Pantagruel* ? Molière cultivated the *esprit gaulois* after his own fashion ; the *Contes Drolatiques* descend in a straight, if parallel, line from the *Cent Nouvelles Nouvelles*. On the other hand, the books did not stay long within the boundaries of France : they early crossed the Channel, and *Gargantua* was known perhaps to Shakespeare and certainly to Ben Jonson.[1] Moreover, Nash and Harvey use such terms as Gargantuan and

[1] See *Every Man in His Humour*, ii. 1 : 'I 'll go near to fill that huge tumbrel-slop of yours with somewhat, an I have good luck : your Gargantua breech cannot carry it away.' And *As You Like It*, iii. 2 : 'You must borrow me Gargantua's mouth first.' See also *Othello*, i. 1, ll. 116, 117. But it is not easy to detect in the Elizabethans a certain debt to Rabelais. In the first place, Shakespeare and his contemporaries oftentimes arrived at the same goal as Rabelais by a different route. In the second place, Gargantua is not only the name of Pantagruel's father,

Gargantuist when they will ; and of Nash it is scarce too much to say that he owed not a little of style and vocabulary to the curate of Meudon. *Have with You to Saffron Walden*, for example, would not have been written as it was, had not its author deeply studied the romance of Rabelais. And criticism followed close on the heels of imitation. 'That merry man Rablays' is celebrated as early as *An Almond for a Parrot*; while Guilpin,[1] attacking in his *Skialetheia* the *Lydian Airs*, then popular, makes Rabelais a staff to beat his enemies. 'Let Rabelais,' he writes,

'Let Rabelais with his durtie mouth discourse,
   No longer blush, for they 'll write ten times worse.'

The wise Sir Thomas Browne, one regrets, fought some fifty years later on the same side with Guilpin ; and it is but natural that he, for whom Lucian was but of a giant familiar to the reader of chap-books. For instance, when Francis Meres, in his *Palladis Tamia*, condemns *Gargantua* with the *Four Sons of Aymon* and the *Seven Champions*, he is assuredly not thinking of Rabelais ; and it is likely that Shakespeare had nothing more than a chap-book in his mind when he wrote the passage quoted from *As You Like It*. So, too, in Beaumont and Fletcher's *Knight of the Burning Pestle*, the barber, in answer to the apprentice's cry, 'St. George for me !' shouts 'Gargantua for me !' And it is clear that the reference is to the book sold by the hawkers in the street with *Boris of Hampton* and *Guy, Earl of Warwick*. With Jonson and Nash the case is different. The author of *Bartholomew Fair* was obviously a reader of Master Alcofribas, while he who wrote *Pierce Penniless* was not merely a reader, but a conscious imitator.

[1] See M. Jusserand's *Shakespeare in France*, p. 18.

the Rhetorick of Satan, should depreciate Rabelais.
'There are a bundle of curiosities,' says he in *Religio
Medici*, 'not only in Philosophy, but in Divinity,
proposed and discussed by men of much supposed
abilities, which indeed are not worthy our vacant
hours, much less our serious studies. Pieces only
fit to be placed in Pantagruel's library, or bound up
with *Tartaretus de modo cacandi.*' Bacon, on the
other hand, praises him, as he should, and therewith
repeats an anecdote which befits only the Rabelais
of legend. 'When Rabelais, the great jester of
France, lay on his death-bed'—it is *Apothegm* 46—
'and they gave him the extreme unction, a familiar
friend came to him afterwards, and asked him how
he did. Rabelais answered, " Even going my journey,
they have greased my boots already." ' The value
of such anecdotes has already been demonstrated;
but it is significant that as early as Bacon the legendary
Rabelais was familiar on our side the Channel. And
the influence of Rabelais steadily increased in the
seventeenth century. Milton's son-in-law, John
Phillips, imitated him with an intelligent fidelity, and
so stout a Puritan as Sir William Waller did not
disdain to profit by his wisdom. These writers, however, were but accidental Pantagruelians, and after
Nash the inheritors in England of the Rabelaisian
spirit were Burton, Swift (*anima Rabelaesii habitans
in sicco*, according to the luminous phrase of Coleridge), and the author of *Tristram Shandy*, who owed
more to the master than he chose to acknowledge.

x

A century after Rabelais' death, Sir Thomas Urquhart published the first two books of his peerless Translation. The work was prefaced by a set of verses 'to the translatour,' signed J. de la Salle, and by some pages of doggerel, for whose false quantities and ineptitude Sir Thomas afterwards apologised. The doggerel, says he, was designed to be prefixed to a dozen books, and no more; the printer, mistaking his order, sent forth the learned author to the world as one capable of closing an hexameter with the words, '*pars est praeterita nostri*.' De la Salle, on the other hand, who is a Scot, and may be Sir Thomas himself, is well qualified for the task of adulation. It was thus, if we may believe the panegyrist, that Sir Thomas achieved the Translation :—

> 'Leaving your brave Heroick cares, which must
>   Make better mankinde and embalme your dust,
>   So undeceiving us that now we see
>   All wit in Gascone and in Cromartie,
>   Besides that Rabelais is conveighed to us,
>   And that our Scotland is not barbarous.'

Assuredly Scotland is not barbarous, and among many rich gifts we owe to the country over-Tweed is a translation, which has no rival in profane letters. Indeed, it can scarcely be called a translation at all; rather it is the English Rabelais. That Urquhart made mistakes is obvious : now he did not under-

stand his author's meaning; now an obstinate love
of elaboration caused him to annotate his author
rather than to translate him. ' 'Tis good to have
translations,' says Selden, ' because they serve as a
comment, so far as the judgment of man goes.' And,
in sooth, Urquhart's version serves as a comment, not
only on Rabelais, but upon himself. By knowledge,
as by temperament, he was perfectly fitted for his task.
French and English were both foreign tongues to him,
and he knew them equally well. In the remote
recesses of Cromarty he doubtless spoke the vernacular,
which the people understood. When he put pen to
paper he used the strange language of the south—
a language which he had acquired with pain, and
wrote with circumstance.

Thus it is that you will search his book wellnigh in
vain for Scotticisms. A few only have rewarded a
diligent reading : doup, dounby, bannock, and laird
are unmistakable. South of the Tweed ' the doup
of an egg ' has a very strange look. But it is noteworthy (and natural) that in the famous list of games
Urquhart should revert most easily to the speech of
his childhood. ' Nivinivinack ' is still familiar in
Scotland, while ' shear and threave,' ' soilie smutchie,'
and ' Joanne Thomson,' among others, can have but
one origin. And his foreign speech helps to explain
the excellence of his version : his style, assumed with
deliberate care, might have been bent to any purpose ;
the tongue which he wrote, being half strange, might,
perchance, have taken on a spurious simplicity. Yet

here his temper chimed with this study : he knew
Rabelais to the bone, as is proved by his original
works ; and being unbiassed in the use of English,
he was free to embroider it until it matched the speech
of Rabelais.

Nor could the French prose of the sixteenth century,
new-formed and unweakened as it was, have found
a better match than Elizabethan English run to seed.
And if his style was absolutely appropriate, so also
the translator's temperament suited the peculiar
characteristics of his author. For he was, in a sense,
Rabelais reincarnate : Rabelais with his humour
obscured by pedantry and his trick of ridicule turned
to seriousness. Sir Thomas would not have laughed
at the Limosin : he would have taken him to his heart
as a brother, and it seems as though Shakespeare were
a prophet when he drew Holofernes, who, bearing
no resemblance to honest John Florio, throws his own
shadow in front of Urquhart. Rabelais, in fact, had
he known Urquhart, would have turned him to scorn,
adding another masterpiece to his portrait gallery.
Though Urquhart might not have detected the
justice of the satire, his talent would have shown him
how to express it in English ; and it is a curiosity
of literature that an ingrained pedant should have
represented without flaw the bitterest scourge the
pedant has ever known. As I have said, you read
Urquhart with no thought of translation. Surely it
is an original that you hold in your hand, with its
perfect sense of narrative, and its accurate echo of a

complicated phrase. Moreover, the translator is always strongest where Rabelais himself is strong. If his slang bears no relation to the slang of Rabelais, in wealth and character it is unsurpassed. Now and again the English chafes against the restraint of the French, and, breaking all bounds, the synonyms of Urquhart rush and riot at their will. Each of Rabelais' lists seems to exhaust a branch of human knowledge ; and Urquhart pounces upon them with gusto, proving that his vocabulary is even richer than the Frenchman's.

In the composition of his work he enjoyed the valuable aid of Randle Cotgrave, whose *Dictionary*, the first of its kind, is still unsurpassed. Of Cotgrave [1] himself we know too little ; we do know that in 1611 he published *A Dictionarie of the French and English Tongues*, which alone made possible the proper understanding of Rabelais. How Urquhart would have accomplished his task without the aid of Cotgrave it is idle to speculate : it is certain that he never wrote except with Cotgrave on his table. Nor could there

[1] The dates of Cotgrave's birth and death are alike uncertain. He was educated at St. John's College, Cambridge, and, as he tells us in the dedication of his Dictionary, he was in the service of Sir William Cecil. Contemporary references to him are scanty and infrequent. It therefore gives him an unexpected touch of reality, when we read in *the manuscripts preserved at Belvoir Castle* (*Historical Manuscripts Commission, Twelfth Report, Appendix, Part V.*) under the date 31st August 1611-12 : ' Geven to Mr. Cotgrave that presented his French Dictionary ' to my Lady, 3l.' Here at any rate he is alive and in the flesh.

be a better connecting-link between Rabelais and Urquhart than this treasure-house of words. Florio's masterpiece is its only rival, and Cotgrave holds his own even against Florio. In those days the making of dictionaries was not a science, but an art; the lexicographer had not yet become a 'harmless drudge.' While he instructed his generation, he left behind him a finished portrait of himself. By his preferences you shall know a man, and by his preferences is Randle Cotgrave revealed to us. Not only was he a profound scholar; not only had he a wide and accurate knowledge of French and French literature: he was, to boot, a man of rare and curious lore. Scholar though he proves himself to be, he shared with Urquhart a love of the street-corner and the tavern. It was not in the houses of the great that he gathered the outcasts and footpads of speech, for which his dictionary is (so to say) a literary doss-house. Many an hour must he have spent wandering up and down among the thieves and rascals of London, or in the narrow streets which filled the Latin Quarter of ancient Paris. And he was no mere loafer in the cities of Europe: he knew the countryside as well as the tavern, and you can picture him as he tramps between the hedgerows, or sleeps at necessity under the stars. To the raffish knowledge of the city he added a deep acquaintance with nature. He collected flowers; he noted the flight and the plumage of strange birds; he made such a store of proverbs as has seldom been gathered within the compass of a book; no doubt he knew the travelling tinker as well as Burns, or as Borrow knew him in a later age; and upon whomsoever he saw, were he tinker, or poet, or assassin, he levied his toll of words.

Deepest of all he had studied Rabelais, whose true interpreter he remains to-day. Scattered up and down his book you will find a string of words marked by the following sign, Rab., and then you may be certain that Urquhart has been there before you. For this is the strange character of the translator: that he depended from first to last upon Cotgrave. His book has all the sound and rhythm of an original work. And not only is it a studied version: it is a version which owes many of its happiest effects to a dictionary. In one respect Urquhart's debt is open and confessed. Though he was born in the wilds of Cromarty, he was essentially a haunter of towns. For sport he cared nothing at all, and he was profoundly ignorant of natural history, so that one corner of Rabelais' omniscience was to him a sealed book. Here it was that Cotgrave was a sure guide, whom Urquhart never scrupled to follow. Only Urquhart forgot that, while it was his business to interpret, it was Cotgrave's to explain, and he does not always distinguish between an equivalent and a commentary.

For instance, when the simple word *flamans* perplexes him, he turns to his *Dictionary*, whence he adapts the following marvel: ' The reddish-long-billed - stork - likt - scrank - legged - sea - fowles.' It is wonderful, but it is not Rabelais; nor would it be clear why Urquhart should render *leuce* by ' the colour of the savage elk,' if we did not turn to our Cotgrave and find ourselves referred from *leuce* to *elland*. Thus he trusted Cotgrave even in his errors, and it is to the *Dictionary* that we owe the misleading name, ' Friar John of the Funnels '—by this wellnigh as famous as Frère Jean des Entommeures. For the translator, in doubt, sought counsel with his friend, and from *Entommeure* was sent to *Entonnoir*, which, being interpreted, is ' a funnell, or tunning-dish.' ' *Humanum est errare*, say the Latinists, to whom verie many '—so writes Cotgrave—' have been exceedingly beholden for an excuse upon just accusations. I (who am no God, nor Angell) either to prevent, or to profit others, am willing ynough to accuse myself.' The accusation, however, is light indeed. The errors of the book are few, its merits incalculable ; and when we praise the masterpiece of Urquhart, let us remember the credit due to this ' bundle of words,' which is no dictionary but a living thing.

XI

The life of Thomas Urquhart, Knight, was wellnigh as adventurous and many-sided as his style. He was born to an ancient family of Cromarty in the first decade of the seventeenth century. Aberdeen gave him his education : Aberdeen, which, said he, ' for honesty, good fashions, and learning, surpasseth as far all other towns and cities in Scotland as London doth for greatness, wealth, and magnificence, the smallest hamlet or village in England.' And, having learned all that Aberdeen and Scotland could teach him, he set forth on his travels after the habit of his class. Now, in those days the grand tour was not an affair of curiosity and amusement. The wandering Scot was forced to support himself by his scholarship, and to defend his honour with the sword; nor when Urquhart started upon his journey were examples lacking him. There was Francis Sinclair, for instance, who to ' accresce his reputation ' fought a duel with a gallant nobleman in High Germany, and who once in Spain slew seven adversaries ' epassyterotically, that is, one after another.' And Sinclair was no mere sharking fencer : at Paris he professed the mathematics, and if the sword was his pastime, it was the pen that fed him. Then, again, there was Master Alexander Ross, ' that minion of the Muses '; with Cameron, known in France as a ' walking liberary '; and before and above them all the Admirable Crichton, who was prepared not only to dispute, after Mirandola, *de omni re scibili et quibusdam aliis,* but to tilt against the whole world in the courtyard of the Louvre. With these examples in his mind, Sir Thomas made a ' peragration ' of France, Italy, and Spain. He fought, he argued, may be he lectured : at any rate he spoke all languages with ' the liveliness of the country accent '; and since a repartee leaped as easily from his tongue as the sword from his scabbard, it is not surprising that he was constantly embroiled.

The one purpose of his life, as of his works, was, indeed, to vindicate the honour of Scotland; and when a Frenchman or a Spaniard suggested, with an exquisite flattery to what he might have called his linguistical proficiency, that Spain or France was his true fatherland, he repelled the compliment with fury: 'He plainly told them, without any bones, that truly he had as much honour by his own country.' Thrice he fought for Scotland, and thrice he disarmed his antagonist, whose life he sold for an apology. So, says he, 'in lieu of three enemies that formerly were, I acquired three constant friends both to myself and my compatriots.' Not even patriotism turned him from the love of learning. Wherever he went he collected books, and he carried back to Cromarty a library, which he valued especially because it did not contain three books 'which were not of his own purchase, and all of them together, in the order wherein he had ranked them, compiled like to a compleat nosegay of flowers, which in his travels he had gathered out of the gardens of above sixteen several kingdoms.' It is a pretty conceit, and the library, though it came not from sixteen kingdoms, would seem to-day an inestimable treasure. Alas! The greed of creditors, and the harsh politics of the age, dispersed it, until at Worcester fight he had nought left to lose but his precious manuscripts.

His return to Cromarty was of evil omen. He found his father ruined by the importunity of creditors, and his own leisure imperilled by grinding poverty.

Nor was poverty his only foe: the Civil Wars drove him to the unpopular side, and the success of the Parliament sent him into exile. He was not utterly cast down: he continued a brave fight for literary ambition against disaster until the day of his death. Being a staunch Royalist, he hated the new Church and the new Democracy. The Presbyterians engrossed, in his view, the vices of the age. 'The minister,' said he, 'is the greediest man in the parish'; and he pursued the clergy of his own Cromarty with implacable hatred. Moreover, in 1641, he had been knighted by the King, so that gratitude as well as principle persuaded him to espouse the Royalist cause. He foresaw with horror the uniformity which threatened to level all men, and to destroy what was for him the dignity of life. He insists, as well he might, upon 'the sin of dismantling the honour of a house'; he points out, with a touch of characteristic recklessness, that the lands from which he is debarred were acquired by his ancestors two-and-twenty hundred years ago; and he deplores, with fantastic sincerity, 'the rigid levellers who would inchaos the structure of ancient greatness into the very rubbish of a neophytick parity.'

Attacked, at home by debt, abroad by a policy which he could not tolerate, he complains that 'our intestine troubles and distempers . . . were as an oxymel julep wherewith to indormiat them in a bitter-sweet security.' His worst invective is reserved for Robert Lesly of Findrassie, the greatest and most ruthless of his father's creditors. Now, his father's death—in 1637—had left poor Sir Thomas in narrower straits than ever: he inherited but a meagre six hundred a year, along with thirteen thousand pounds of debt, and ' five brethren, all men, and two sisters almost marriageable.' Had it not been for Findrassie, he might have borne up against even this load of debt and responsibility; but Findrassie did his utmost to thrust his debtor deeper into the mire. A scoundrel, fit for any baseness, the dishonest creditor kept ' his daughters the longer unhusbanded that they might serve him for so many stalking horses, whereby to intangle some neighbouring woodcocks.' And he not only demanded instant payment of the bankrupt Sir Thomas: he attacked his castle with whatever forces he could command; he quartered a troop of horse upon his poverty; and, finally, he seized upon his library, and wantonly destroyed a priceless treasure of manuscripts.

These blows were sufficient to destroy a less valiant knight, but Sir Thomas endured them all with dignity, and his greatest sorrow was that he might never realise his cherished dream of grandeur. He would have made Cromarty a valiant city: the fleets of all nations should have proudly ridden at anchor between the Suters, where was harbourage for a fleet of ten thousand; merchant adventurers would have sent their richest argosies to the Highland village; Sir Philbert Vernati, who ' had a great ascendant in counsel over all the adventurous merchants of what nations soever,' would

have given his loyal aid ; while, under the auspices of
the heritable Sheriff, ' men of literature and exquisite
spirits of invention ' would have deserted Paris, Cambridge, Aberdeen itself, for the culture of Cromarty.
In fact, says he : ' I would have been a Mæcenas to
the scholar, a pattern to the soldier, a favourer of
the merchant, a protector of the tradesman, and
upholder of the yeomen, had not the impetuosity of
the usurer overthrown my resolution, and blasted
my aims in the bud.' The dreams of Urquhart
vanished with the tangled skein of sleep. He awoke
to find his enemies ready, ' cannibal-like, to swallow
him up at a breakfast ' ; and Cromarty is still unseen
save by the eye of a curious tourist.

His ill-fortune found its climax at Worcester fight—
the only battle whereat, as he proudly says, he ever
gave ground. For there he lost not only his freedom,
but those precious manuscripts whose production was
the serious employ of his life : ' Master Spilsbury's
house, which sheltered Sir Thomas, was broken by
the Parliament's soldiery, and though the host was a
very honest man and hath an exceeding good woman
to his wife,' it was impossible to save more than a
few shreds. Thus it was that the works, which were
to reform the world and to restore Cromarty to affluence, were sacrificed to wrap up ' figs, dates, almonds,
caroway seeds, and other suchlike dry confections.'
Urquhart was in nowise cast down by the final
disaster. A prisoner of Cromwell, who treated him
with the utmost consideration, he devoted himself

valiantly to repair a loss, which other men would have thought irreparable, and, within two or three years, he had published the few tracts, which, with the Translation, made up his literary baggage.

XII

Already, in 1641, he had printed a volume of foolish epigrams, which reveal his character as little as his style. He now hurried through the press the fantastic pamphlets which gave him a niche in the temple of literature. The object of them all is to attain the unattainable : no problem, that was not insoluble, tempted him to a solution. He would square the circle, invent a universal language, and deduce his pedigree from Adam. These projects, indeed, had always engrossed him : even in the few solvent years which he had passed at Cromarty he never cared for such sports as amuse the country gentleman. When others went a-hunting, he shut himself in his library, and a passage of autobiography exemplifies his style as well as his character. 'There happening,' he writes, ' a gentleman of very good worth to stay awhile at my house, who, one day amongst many other, was pleased, in the deadest time of all the winter, with a gun upon his shoulder, to search for a shot of some wild fowl; and after he had waded through many waters, taken excessive pains in quest of his game, and by means thereof had killed some five or six moor fowls and partridges, which he brought along with

him to my house, he was by some other gentlemen
very much commended for his love to sport; and as
the fashion of most of our countrymen is, not to
praise one without dispraising another, I was highly
blamed for not giving myself in that kind of exercise,
having before my eyes so commendable a pattern to
imitate; I answered that though the gentleman
deserved praise for the evident proof he had given
that day of his inclination to thrift and laboriousness,
nevertheless I was not to blame, seeing whilst he was
busied about that sport, I was employed in a diversion
of another nature, such as optical secrets, mysteries of
natural philosophy, reasons for the variety of colours,
the finding out of the longitude, the squaring of a
circle, the ways to accomplish all trigonometrical
calculations by sines, without tangents, with the
same compendiousness of computation,—which in
the estimation of learned men, would be accounted
worth six hundred thousand partridges, and as many
moor-fowles.' Not a sportsman, indeed, but a most
sanguine philosopher; and, assuredly, he had the
laugh the next day! For while he got up early and
broke a young horse, his friend was unable to rise out
of bed ' by reason of the Gout and Sciatick.'

The most important of his tracts is that which bears
the fantastic title, ''Εκσκυβαλαύρον, or the Discovery
of a most Exquisite Jewel . . . found in the kennels
of Worcester streets, the day after the fight.' This
priceless work, which ' serves to frontal a vindication
of Scotland,' is the most extravagant eulogy ever

penned. It is prefaced by a panegyric of the author, 'whose muse,' says the nameless scribe, 'I honour, and the strains of whose pen it is my ambition to imitate.' Presently, Sir Thomas confesses himself his own panegyrist, and declares without a smile, and with a splendid candour, that 'it mentioneth Sir Thomas Urquhart in the third person, which seldom is done by any author in a treatise of his own penning.' Despite the note of unconscious humour, this treatise is a very serious piece of work. It is nothing less than a pæan to Scotland, and its extravagances by no means destroys its value. Above all, it contains the life of Crichton, the Admirable Scot, who is, in truth, the invention of Sir Thomas. Upon this portrait, which will endure for all time, Urquhart expended all the wealth of his imagination ; and whatever opinion we hold of Crichton, we must e'en give the credit to his 'only begetter.' It is evident that the knight's admiration was humble and sincere : he describes his hero's prowess, 'in arms and arts,' with a passionate eloquence, and he shares in every accent the emotion which shook the princess at Crichton's death. 'O villains ! ' thus she spoke, 'what have you done ? You vipers of men, that have basely slain the valiant Crichton, the sword of his own sex, and the buckler of ours, the glory of this age, and restorer of the lost honour of the Court of Mantua : O Crichton, Crichton ! '

His second treatise, appropriately styled the *Logopandecteision*, sets out to be a discussion of the Universal

Language, which he would have equipped with four numbers and eleven genders. Ridiculous it is, of course ; none the less it is lit by flashes of the quickest sense, and shows that, amateur as he was, Urquhart nourished an intelligence far ahead of his time. However, no sooner has he embarked upon his treatise, than he forgets the Universal Language, and proceeds to a set of digressions which might have shamed Rabelais. The real themes of the treatise are his own misfortune and the infamy of Findrassie. So the Second Book is styled *Chrestasebeia, or Impious Dealings of Creditors* ; while the Third boasts for its title *Cleronomaporia, or the Intricacy of a Distressed Successor*. Thus the farce is sustained in a language which for bombast and extravagance has never been surpassed, and with an absence of humour which is nothing less than genius.

Lastly, a word of the *Trissotetras*, a treatise dedicated to his mother, and prefaced by a eulogy of Lord Napier of Merchiston, ' so brave a spark.' The treatise is unintelligible to-day, and probably meant little enough to its author. Moreover, it is written in a jargon which has found no imitators. Urquhart's love of strange words was constant and ineradicable. He declared that a paucity of words was the worst disease of our language, and he set about finding a remedy with a light heart and a quick brain. ' That which makes this disease (the paucity of words),' says he, ' the most incurable is that when an exuberant spirit would to any high researched conceit adapt a peculiar word of his own coyning, he is branded with

incivility, if he apologise not for his boldness with a
*quod ita dixerim, pereant Ciceronianae manes, ignoscat
Demosthenis genius,* and other such phrases, acknowledging his fault of making use of words, never
uttered by others, or at least by such as were not
renowned for eloquence.' Urquhart never invoked
the spirit of Demosthenes or Cicero : he used whatever words he chose to invent, and we are the
richer by such masterpieces as ' pristinary lobcocks,'
' blinkard minds,' 'secret angiports and dark posterns,'
and many another. And with the sublime uncon-
sciousness which always befogged his mind, he declares
at the end of his worst twisted and most turgid mono-
graph that, ' had not the matter been more prevalent
with him than the superficial formality of a quaint
discourse,' he might perchance have been ornate !
Ornate he always was, even though he pretended
a perfect ignorance of himself ; and it was his fine
sense of elaboration which aided him better than any
other quality in the Translation.

A fit companion for these pamphlets is the *Panto-
chronocanon,* in which Sir Thomas, as if in obedience
to his master, has traced his genealogy back to Adam,
the Protoplast. 'Would to God,' says Rabelais,
' every one had as certain knowledge of his genealogy
since the time of the Ark of Noah to this age.' But
Urquhart even improved upon his master, and
carried back his pedigree to the creation of the world.
Assuredly vanity was never thus wedded to courage.
The ancestors of Urquhart come from all countries,

and express their names in all languages. Yet let us
not jeer at the Knight of Cromarty's faith. He
believed whatever he wrote—that is certain ; and
if his sanguine temper be allied on the one hand to
lunacy, on the other to genius, it is not for us to
deplore an alliance, which should do no more than
provoke a sympathetic smile, and which is a lucid
commentary upon his love of Rabelais.

For by the strangest of whims, Urquhart not only
translated Rabelais, but framed his life after the
model of Pantagruel. Not content with his pedigree,
he must needs give himself ' Parresiastes ' for a nick-
name ; and when he did, he assuredly thought of
the Parisians, who thus are called from παρρησία,
' boldness and liberty of speech.' Again he suffered
his life long from the close-fisted usurers, whom
Epistemon saw in hell ' very busily employed in
seeking of nastie pins, and old nailes in the kennels
of the streets.' He defends Crichton against the
Sorbonnists with his master's own rancour. He
discourses as eloquently and as often of debt as
Rabelais himself, and here he is on the side of Pantagruel. He abhors his creditors, though he is less
likely to escape from them before the Greek Calends
than is Panurge himself. Lastly, and before all
things, his death was imitated from the romance
which he gave to English literature. ' He died of
laughter,' says rumour, ' on hearing that Charles II.
was restored to his kingdom,' and you are instantly
reminded of Rabelais' dissertation upon those who

died laughing. Whether death or Urquhart were the plagiarist is idle to inquire. Enough that Sir Thomas could never have found a better fate. Even in his tomb he is linked with the writer whom he interpreted with so splendid a loyalty. And if Cromarty be still a Highland village, if his original treatises move to impious laughter rather than to admiration, the translator is secure of immortality, for with Cotgrave's help he added an imperishable work to the sum of England's masterpieces.

XIII

To turn from Urquhart to Motteux [1] is to travel at a page from the old world to the new, to exchange the fastness of Cromarty for the tobacco and the spilt wine of the tavern. A pert flippancy replaces Sir Thomas's majestic eccentricity; the slang of the coffee-house makes what poor substitute it can for the curious slang of the study; the facile familiarity of the journal comes forth a bitter contrast with the balanced gravity of scholarship. If the sense of Rabelais is followed yet more closely in the books of Motteux's translating, the full humour of the original is attenuated to the taste of a feebler epoch; and while Sir Thomas Urquhart was in spirit earlier than his time, was, in fact, an over-ripe Elizabethan, Motteux

---

[1] Motteux first gave to the world 'The Third Book of the Works of Mr. Francis Rabelais, Doctor in Physick, . . . Now faithfully Translated into English by the unimitable Pen of Sir *Thomas Urwhart*, Kt. and Bar.,' in 1693, and in the following year he published his own version of Books IV. and V.

appears a modern of the moderns, and, being a contemporary of Pepys, writes a lingo that would not have surprised his great-great-grandchildren. Another bond than the love of Rabelais holds them in sympathy : they both express themselves in a foreign tongue ; and while the hesitancy of the Scot is discerned in his weighed and pompous periods, the Frenchman, light-fingered and light-heeled, rattles on with little enough respect for the author he translates, or for the language which he has adopted. His very faults of style and taste give him an interest of curiosity ; and foreigner though he was, he also played his part in the development of our tongue.

XIV

Pierre-Antoine Le Motteux (or Peter Motteux, as England knew him) was born at Rouen when the Grand Monarch sat upon the throne of France. Of his ancestry and boyhood little is recorded, but it is certain that he came of a respectable family, which, while it enriched the city-roll with no great names, was industrious in commerce and staunch in its devotion to the Protestant faith.[1] Mercers by trade, the Le Motteux espoused the daughters of mercers,

[1] Despite its obscurity, the family of Le Motteux is known to have been Protestant in all its branches. Le Nud, Papavoine, Fourgon, the families with which it intermarried, were one and all of the Reformed Church ; and though some abjured, the most of them remained firm in the faith. It is probable, therefore, that Peter Motteux either accompanied friends and relatives to London or found them there. A certain David Le Motteux, for

and grew rich enough to acquire property in Rouen
and its neighbourhood.   The archives tell us that,
in 1662, one Antoine Le Motteux married Isabeau Le
Nud, and of this marriage Pierre-Antoine was born on
Sunday the 25th February 1663.[1]   We may assume
that he followed his father's trade for a while : at
any rate, until the Edict of Nantes was revoked he
remained simple and unknown.   There is no evidence
that he ever practised the craft of letters in France ;
and possibly, had he not been driven from his native
Rouen, he would have lived and died an honest
merchant.   When he was two-and-twenty, the storm
broke.   France, who, in Michelet's phrase, ' si souvent s'arrache sa propre chair,' resumed with bitter
savagery her persecution of the Protestants.   Wanton

instance, married to Marie Miré, is said to have taken refuge
abroad, though his destination is not known ; while one Robert
Miré, married to Madeleine Le Motteux, assuredly sought safety
in London.

[1] There has hitherto been doubt concerning the date of Peter
Motteux's birth.   M. Haag, in *la France protestante*, says he
was born in 1660, while M. Bianquis in his *Révocation de l'édit de
Nantes à Rouen* (1885), gives his birthday as 25th February 1669.
Neither the one nor the other is correct.   M. de Beaurepaire,
the keeper of the archives at Rouen, whose courteous aid I owe
to the intervention of Mr. T. A. Cook, sends me the following
extract from the state papers of Rouen : 'Le dimanche 25 de la
mois Février 1663 fut baptisé. par M. Lemoyne (pasteur de
Rirevolly) le fils d'Anthoine Le Motteux et de Isabeau le Nud,
né le jour susdit, dont le parrain Pierre Le Nut et marraine
Judith Fourgon vefve de deffunct Léon Le Motteux, et nommé
Pierre-Anthoine.'   This document, of course, removes all
doubt.

death and pitiless torture were everywhere inflicted, and the King, as though to celebrate his marriage with the widow Scarron, ordered the pillage of his grave and thrifty subjects. An exodus followed : an exodus of the sturdiest and most ingenious citizens in France —clever artisans, skilled farmers, accomplished gardeners. What was France's loss was Europe's gain. England and Holland, above all, gave welcome to the fugitives, and loyally acknowledge the debt they owe to this plenishing of French blood. The Protestants of Rouen, no doubt, made good their escape without too grave a risk of death or torture. They were already half-way to England ; and, though we know not what became of his parents, tainted with the Protestant heresy, it is certain that Pierre-Antoine himself took refuge across the Channel.

At the age of twenty-two, then, Peter Motteux arrived in London, a stranger in a strange land. In the beginning, may be, he followed the traditional trade of his family ; it is more than likely that he sought the protection of an uncle, already established in the city. Foreigner though he was, he very soon ' commenced author,' as he would have said himself ; and, in 1692, he was already the editor of *The Gentleman's Journal*, a magazine composed upon the model of *le Mercure gallant*, and in England the first of its kind. His adaptability is marvellous : he changes his language as easily as other men change their coats or their opinions ; and though you may condemn his style for a dozen sound reasons, you will

never find this ' Knight of the Quill ' (to use another
favourite phrase) betraying his foreign origin in print.
Moreover, it is clear that by the time he established
his *Journal* he had gained a firm footing in the world
of letters.   Great names sparkle in his pages.   Congreve condescends to send a lyric ; the Person of
Quality contributes his poor little versions of Horace,
his vapid little echoes of Anacreon ; on one page
Nahum Tate discourses in his best manner ' On their
Majesties' Pictures drawn by the Life by Mr. Kneller,'
on another Prior himself proves his amiability in a
copy of verses.   And the minor poet, and the artisan
in fiction, who displays his fancy in short stories, or
' novels,' as Motteux calls them, mindful of his French,
are as inept and tasteless as the minor poets and the
artisans of to-day.   They too dance to the measure
of their betters, and it is a very different measure from
that to which our moderns move their wit.   None the
less *The Gentleman's Journal* lacks neither interest nor
merit.   Behind every page there lurks the figure of
Dryden, already the arbiter and tyrant of letters.   As
his performances are praised, so his preferences are
revered, and it is clear that Motteux early took service
under the great man's banner.   What is more to
the purpose is that the familiar style, which was
the true mark of Motteux and his contemporaries, is
already formed, and it is quite natural that the editor
of *The Gentleman's Journal* should have translated
Rabelais after the motley fashion which we know.
     The *Journal* ran a longer course than is commonly

allotted to such adventures, and survived to puff Motteux and his friends until 1694. Meantime, if we may believe Tonson, Motteux joined the trade of bookseller to that of editor.[1] And, while we are unable to follow that clue, we know that the years in which he directed the fortunes of his review from the seclusion of the Black Boy Coffee-House in Ave Mary Lane were the busiest of his life. He was, in fact, nothing better (nor worse) than an adroit and busy hack. He wrote plays, he composed poems, he translated Rabelais and Cervantes. Nothing was impossible to his apprehensive brain, and few men of his time surpassed him in that fatal facility which depresses all works to a dead level of commonplace. Being before all things a man of his age, he responded most readily to a momentary impulse. When the French laureate indited an ode, *Sur la Prise de Namur*, Motteux was soon prepared with a parody, wherein the ridicule of Louis XIV. was matched with the praise of William III. The death of Mary inspired a foolish dirge, *Maria*,

---

[1] A letter of remonstrance addressed to Dryden concerning the translation of Ovid's *Epistles* in 1692-1693 seems to hint that Motteux published books as well as his review. 'After your arrivall,' says Tonson, 'you showed Mr. Motteux what you had done (which he told me was to the end of the Story of Daphnis), and demanded, as you mentioned in your letter, twenty guineas, which that bookseller refused.' It is just possible that Motteux wished to buy the translation for his *Journal*, but the length (it is 759 lines) should have made it unsuitable; and Tonson plainly describes his rival as 'a strange bookseller.' See Dryden's *Prose Works*, edited by E. Malone, vol. ii. p. 26.

and it was no disloyalty, but a solid conviction, which persuaded the emigrant to insult his persecutors. Thereafter he wrote ' occasional verses ' without number ; he fitted the plays of better men—notably Sir John Vanbrugh's *Mistake*—with prologues or epilogues ; above all, he took part in the life of the coffee-houses, which were rapidly transforming not only English manners, but English literature.

The forty years, which separate the death of Urquhart from the appearance of Motteux's version of Rabelais' Fourth and Fifth Books, witnessed an essential change in the relations which bound writers with readers. The coffee-houses and clubs created a new public and a fresh opinion. In the old leisurely days, when authors wrote to please themselves and their patrons, literature possessed a dignity unknown to Motteux and his friends. These, indeed, the merchant-venturers of the pen, knew that in winning the wits they won the Town, and they made a deliberate attempt to flatter the taste of their many-headed patron. One ancient fashion alone remained—the fashion of extravagant dedication ; but that fashion survived its use, and, where it had once meant patronage or preferment, it was now nothing better than an exercise in adulation. The effect was seen in a debasing of the currency, in the creation of Grub Street, and the sudden growth of a lettered class bent upon popularity and the ruin of its neighbours.

In brief, the battle of the wits had begun, and in this battle Motteux showed a ceaseless energy. He

took sides with what decision he might, and fought
valiantly for his friends and their principles ; nor is it
surprising that he attached to himself firm allies and
fervent enemies. Dryden and Steele cherished a
constant affection for him, praising him with the indiscreet eloquence of friendship, and setting him on
a pinnacle of eminence where he could not long expect
to keep a foothold. Pope, on the other hand, de-
nounced him with all the vigour and venom which he
reserved for the second-rate, and honoured him after
his death with a place in the *Dunciad*. ' Talkers I 've
learned to bear,' he writes in a Satire, ' Motteux I
knew ' ; while in *The Art of Sinking in Poetry*, he
classes the translator of Rabelais among the eels :
' Obscure authors that wrap themselves up in their
own mud, but are mighty nimble and pert.' Nimble
and pert ! It is a just description, which gives us the
best measure of Motteux's strength and weakness.

Presently he fell upon evil days. His plays, despite the amiable criticism of Dryden,[1] were but

[1] Says Dryden, addressing Motteux in his Fourteenth
Epistle :—

> ' Time, action, place are so preserved by thee,
> That e'en Corneille might with envy see
> The alliance of his tripled unity '—

a passage which shows that Dryden, though he misread Chaucer,
knew the rules of French verse, and read Corneille as a trisyllable.
The kindly Genest makes a far juster estimate. Of *Beauty in
Distress* he says : 'It is not a pleasing play—the plot is complicated, but not interesting. The incidents are numerous, but
not well managed.' Damning with faint praise, he declares

poor experiments in mimicry, and could not hope to
keep the stage. When, with the splendid example of
Pope before them, all men thought they had pierced
the secret of the couplet, there was no place for
Motteux's trivial effusions, and he reverted to the
pursuit of commerce, for which, no doubt, his early
experience had well fitted him. So he set up a shop
in Leadenhall Street, stocked it with such treasures
as might delight the most fastidious eye, and bade his
old friends of the coffee-house to advertise his wares.
In all sincerity he might boast that, lessening ' the
number of the teazers of the Muses,' he humbled the
poet to exalt the citizen. Proudly he confesses that
he never looks into any books save books of accompts.
And though he no longer teased the Muses, he confides
his new inspiration to *The Spectator* with an eloquence
which is rarely found in his more deliberate writings.
' Since so many Dealers turn Authors,' thus runs the
letter, ' and write quaint Advertisements in Praise of
their Wares, one who from an Author turn'd Dealer
may be allowed for the Advancement of Trade to turn
Author again. I will not, however, set up like some
of 'em for selling cheaper than the most able honest
tradesman can, nor do I send this to be better
known for Choice and Cheapness of China and

Love's a Jest 'a tolerably good comedy.' The 'dialogue is
well written, but the first four acts want incident sadly, the fifth
has plenty.' And even this appreciation, faint as it is, seems
excessive. The truth is that Motteux's plays are the merest
journey-work, and well deserve the oblivion they have achieved.

Japan Wares, Tea, Fans, Muslins, Pictures, Arrack, and other Indian goods. Placed as I am in Leadenhall Street, near the India Company, and the Centre of that Trade, thanks to my fair Customers, my Warehouse is graced as well as the Benefit Days of my Plays and Operas; and the foreign Goods I sell, seem no less acceptable than the foreign Books I translated, Rabelais and Don Quixote. This the Criticks allow me, and while they like my Wares, they may dispraise my Writing. But as 'tis not so well-known yet that I frequently cross the Seas of late, and speaking Dutch and French, besides other languages, I have the Conveniency of buying and importing rich Brocades, Dutch Atlasses, with Gold and Silver, or without, and other foreign Silks of the newest Modes and the best Fabricks, fine Flanders Lace, Linnens, and Pictures, at the best Hand.' [1] In such terms does he puff his commodity, and we would far rather look into his shop, and buy his samples of China and Japan, 'sold cheap for a quick return,' than con over all the plays and operas that ever he wrote. Nor was Steele content with giving Motteux this generous advertisement in his *Spectator*; a year later he described a visit he paid to 'that industrious Man of Trade, and formerly brother of the quill.' In generous terms he congratulated his friend 'on the humble but beneficial use he had made of his talents, and wished I could

[1] Printed in *The Spectator* under Steele's auspices, Wednesday, 31st January 1712.

be a patron of his Trade, as he had been pleased to make me of his Poetry.' [1]

So for six years Motteux pursued his business, and no more would have been heard of him had he not died a violent and a scandalous death.   The reward of £50 for the discovery of his murderers was unclaimed, and the mist of secrecy which surrounds his sudden end in a house of ill-fame will never be dispelled.   What is certain is that at five o'clock on 19th February 1718 Motteux went off in a coach to White's, that he might procure some ball-tickets for a lady of quality.   He was discreetly habited in a dark-coloured cloth coat, lined with orange-coloured Mantua silk ; and whither he went, or how he spent that afternoon, there was no witness to declare.   At nine o'clock he arrived at White's with a mysterious scarlet cloak about him. He seems to have spoken to no one : and merely ate two glasses of jelly, while a woman waited for him in a coach.   Again there is silence until twelve o'clock, when an apothecary, summoned to a notorious house in Butcher Row, near Temple Bar, found Peter Motteux dead, with a black ring round his neck and bruises about his body.   That he was the victim of foul play there seems no doubt, and his friends did

---

[1] Motteux had dedicated to Steele a poem on ' Tea,' written assuredly in the way of business.   Here is a specimen of the vain effusion :—

> ' Immortals hear, said Jove, and cease to jar !
> Tea must succeed to Wine, as Peace to War :
> Nor by the grape let Man be set at Odds,
> But share in Tea the Nectar of the gods.'

their utmost to bring the malefactors to justice. Two
men and four women were duly arraigned at Justice
Hall, in the Old Bailey ; the men were bullies, and the
women, save Elizabeth Simmerton, who kept the
house, were well known as ' plyers.' The evidence
seemed clear, and the motive of theft was sufficient.
To the general surprise the prisoners were acquitted,
and none paid penalty for Motteux's squalid death.
A strange end, truly, for the martyr of Protestantism
and the translator of Rabelais ! But the French critic
who declares that Motteux lived a ' vie crapuleuse '
is not justified by facts ; and we may easily conclude
that the friend of Steele and Dryden, the industrious
hack, the respectable tradesman, was the victim less
of vice than of accident.

XV

Peter Motteux was not a great writer ; yet he has
a place apart in the history of letters. We may
assume that until he was twenty-two he had little
knowledge of the English tongue. At eight-and-
twenty he was as good a master of a familiar and
flippant style as any of his flippant and familiar contemporaries. It is difficult, indeed, to match this
achievement. His prose, such as it is, shows no sign
of a foreign origin, unless, indeed, we may detect the
insensitiveness of a stranger in his persistent vulgarity.
Words seldom have their correct value to an ear that
has not been attuned to their sound from the very

cradle ; and perhaps we may set down to Motteux's birth Motteux's frequent lapses from good taste.

After this reserve, it may be said that, with the single exception of Hamilton, no man ever mastered a foreign language with the ease wherewith Peter Motteux mastered English. Nor is Hamilton a fair parallel : he was French by sympathy and connection ; he arrived in Paris when he was no more than four ; and, returning to London after the Restoration, he found a court that was French in language as in fashion. How, then, should he forget a tongue which by the habit of childhood he had made his own ? How should he practise an idiom to which he had no other than a birthright ? Beckford, again, belongs to the literature of England rather than of France. *Vathek*, his one experiment in the language of Voltaire, was a triumph to which a wise discretion persuaded him never again to aspire. Moreover, the author of *Vathek* cultivated a French which was classic in form and substance, a French which he might acquire with diligence and compose with accuracy, though it was not of his bone and blood. So Voltaire and Boling-broke aimed at a mastery of either tongue by a scholastic foppery, and even Gibbon himself, to whose mind French was veritably akin, never descended from his desk to the vernacular. He wrote his *Essai sur l'Étude de la Littérature*,[1] as a student might indite an essay

---

[1] Gibbon was hugely proud of his experiment, and knowing naught of Motteux, and ignoring Hamilton, says : 'I might therefore assume the *primus ego in patriam*,' etc.

in the language and manner of Cicero ; and it would have been a vast loss to letters had he chosen for his *Decline and Fall* any other idiom than his own eloquent English.

Now Motteux not only changed his speech after he had grown to manhood : for many years he pursued the trade of hack without betraying his origin ; and it is this use of a familiar speech that distinguishes him from all his rivals. Sophocles is easier to mimic than Herondas, and the English that Motteux wrote was not the English of school or college. It was the rough, unpolished dialect of the news-sheet and the coffee-house. In truth, his rare and curious skill almost deserves the eulogy which Dryden's generous enthusiasm composed for it,[1] and he will always be memorable for an achievement which has commonly baffled the ingenuity and persistence of mankind. On the other hand, while he now and again confesses that what he offers comes from ' a foreign plant,' he does not attempt to excuse himself upon that ground. ' As every Language has its peculiar Graces, seldom or never to be acquir'd by a Foreigner,' he writes in the preface to his *Rabelais*, ' I cannot think I have given my Author those of the English in every place : But as none compell'd me to write, I fear to ask a Pardon,

---

[1] Thus Dryden, in the Epistle already quoted : —

' But whence art thou inspired, and thou alone,
To flourish in an idiom not thy own ?
It moves our wonder that a foreign guest
Should overmatch the most, and match the best. '

which yet the generous Temper of this Nation makes me hope to obtain. Albinus, a Roman who had written in Greek, desir'd in his Preface to be forgiven his Faults of Language; but Cato ask'd in derision, Whether any had forc'd him to write in a Tongue of which he was not an absolute Master? Lucullus wrote an History in the same Tongue, and said, He had scatter'd some false Greek in it, to let the World know it was the Work of a Roman. I'll not say as much of my Writings.' And surely he need not: the reader will find false taste not a little in the works of Motteux; he will search in vain for false English.

The truth is that Motteux's temperament was imitative: his was the monkey's talent; and, having resolved upon the use of English, he handled it with just the liveliness and address which distinguished his contemporaries. With the utmost industry he played the tune of the time: his plays were anybody's plays, his prose was anybody's prose; and the man himself eludes, in his work, the nearest scrutiny. Nor was the age into which he strayed, an unwilling exile, worth the tribute of imitation. The romantic quality of Shakespeare and his contemporaries, faintly echoed under the first Stuarts, was forgotten in a timid classicism. The style had changed with the public, and certain writers, with little enough to say, were pleased to express it in a manner of familiarity which seemed, in their eyes, to shine with the eloquence of Cicero and Horace. In brief, a so-called 'good sense' invaded the literature of Europe, a 'good sense' which has never left us : it became at once a fashion and an ideal to write as you spoke ; and the hacks of the day spoke with the accent of the coffee-house. Moreover, the habit of translating the classics, not as the Elizabethans had translated them, into a noble, personal, coloured prose, but in the language of a vapid simplicity, popularised the worst models. Words began to lose their life and substance : handled by the Elizabethans, they claimed a meaning and a force from their position in the sentence, because the structure of the sentence was infinitely various ; handled by the followers of Dryden they were clear and lifeless.

Thence followed that unification of style which an undue admiration of Cicero has imposed upon the world ; and Motteux and his friends, believing that they were bringing back taste and refinement from a long exile, did their utmost to destroy the character of the English tongue. To such a state of lucidity did they reduce it, that they were forced back upon the use of slang for the common purpose of decoration. Dryden, of course, stood high above this rabble, striding like a Colossus from the old world to the new, with one foot still planted on the rugged mountain of Elizabethan eloquence. They who ran up and down between his feet imitated the worse—the homelier —side of his talent. They dared not attempt to approach his loftier manner,though they might imitate the invective which he lavished on Elkanah Settle or Thomas Hunt. So they were familiar without distinction, diffuse without wit ; and to read their works is to appreciate the task accomplished by Addison, whose timidly correct achievement was a reaction, not against the extravagance of the Elizabethans, but against the vulgarity of his own contemporaries.

Peter Motteux, then, was one of a band which may be described as the small change of Dryden. Tom Brown, Ned Ward, and Durfey were of the number ; they all contributed to *The Gentleman's Journal*, and they all wrote (on occasion) very vilely indeed. Their style was bad-mannered, pert, and riddled with the cheap slang of the hour. With the exception of Roger l'Estrange, they were rarely inspired to real wit or placid dignity. Yet, although their language smelled of the tavern, they were scholars after their own fashion : they knew foreign tongues, and were prepared to turn Latin or Greek, French or Spanish, into English at so much a sheet. Some of them, as Tom Brown, had been to Oxford, and believed themselves the legitimate descendants of the heroes who jested and drank at the Mermaid. The most had picked up what they could of learning in the gutters of Grub Street, and brought into letters a vocabulary which, heard with patience, was disgraced by print.

Such, indeed, was Peter Motteux, to whom we owe the translation of Rabelais' Fourth and Fifth Books— a merry rascal, no doubt, and in his hours the best of bad company. Moreover, when he undertook the Englishing of Rabelais he found a task for which his talents and knowledge should have fitted him excel-

lently. He was a complete master of both tongues,
he understood his text, and he had a genuine sympathy
with the gospel of Pantagruelism. In Urquhart, too,
he had a splendid model ; and since he first printed
the Third Book, as rendered by the knight of Cromarty,
he must needs have studied his forerunner with care
and diligence. But though he pilfers Urquhart's
vocabulary, he cannot emulate his style, and he does
not check his version by the authority of Cotgrave.
None the less, his version has very solid merits of its
own. Though it lacks dignity, it is always near the
original, and when there is no chance of embroidery
you may find passages which are no unworthy echo
of the original prose. Narrative especially encourages
him to a sort of refinement, but the trick of simplicity
soon escapes him, and he falls to a deplorable diffuseness, which might prove the ruin of the austerest style.
And this diffuseness has no warrant either in his author
or in his ignorance. ' Those who accuse the French,'
says he, ' of being as sparing of their Wit, as lavish
of their Words, will find an Englishman in our Author.'
And surely the best method of appreciating Rabelais'
restraint or Urquhart's severity is to contrast a page
of Motteux either with the Frenchman's clear-cut
sentences, or with the sounding eloquence of the
Scottish knight.

And, strangest irony of all, Motteux, in one sense a
master of slang, did not understand the part which
slang should play in the embellishment of style.
Now, slang may be described as a collection of special

dialects, the dialects of the highway, theft, sport, and lechery. The terms which it employs are as technical as are the terms of science or the arts, and their value depends upon the metaphor and imagery which they suggest. Accordingly slang, if it be sincerely understood and discreetly managed, may illustrate a fancy or adorn a tale. And, more certainly than any other artifice of literature, it depends upon a distinguished use. There is no intrinsic merit in the mere collection of strange words, which, for their proper effect, must be so placed as to impart colour or liveliness to a serious statement.

Above all, slang must be suitable, and must chime with the matter in hand. No greater master of the popular speech than Rabelais ever lived. Though he harbours all the outcasts, he never makes his reader conscious of bad company. His specimens of the Bohemian tongue may raise a laugh : they can never inspire disgust. And Urquhart knew as well as his master the proper use of this dangerous material : he too was a curious student of the hedges and the byways ; no phrase was too common for his curiosity, or too vulgar for his sense of style. The effect he produces with words which are common and vulgar is always right, and often splendid. So you may see a gold cup, studded with stones rough and ill-cut, yet noble by the mere force of contrast and arrangement. Motteux, on the other hand, was never artist enough to comprehend these temperate distinctions : his very knowledge of the taverns and streets was a stumbling-block; he has a quip or a proverb ready for any emergency, and he never cares one whit whether his proverb or his quip be in the proper tone. Above all, he did not collect his specimens at first hand. He only knew the coinage after it had passed through the mint of other men's minds. Rabelais, Cotgrave, and Urquhart tracked their slang to its proper sources, and so measured its effect. Motteux listened to the wits who listened to somebody else; or he boldly pilfered from the popular literature of the time. Like all his fellows, he owed a deep debt to the *Travesties* of such men as Cotton and Radcliffe, who found entertainment or profit in dragging the gods and heroes of Virgil or Ovid down to the level of a cheap tavern, and in smearing their august faces with the lees of last night's debauch. In the works of these masters you may match the worst of Motteux's excesses, and the fact that they were an example to him proves his artistic insincerity. For, when he should have been translating a masterpiece of the sixteenth century with what fidelity he might, he was debasing his original with the foolish catchwords of a debased, unknowing age. And the effect which he too often produces could only be matched if the staff of a sporting paper fell to the Englishing of the classics.

For catchwords pass and are forgotten, and much of Motteux' ornament is as dead as last year's pantomime. The true slang, which endures by its sound or by its origin, is as fresh to-day as it was when Shakespeare (say), or Ben Jonson, or Urquhart found it for themselves and used it to give a sparkle to their sober style. Motteux flings down the last periphrasis of his set, and believes that he has made a smart rendering. Wherever the language of these last two Books is obscure, turn to the French, and you will find that it is Motteux' untiring impertinence that causes the obscurity. He cannot long resist the temptation to torture the plain narrative of Rabelais out of shape, and suddenly confronts his reader, against the sense and warrant of his text, with ' as Moss caught his Mare,' or some still viler phrase. Who Moss was may be discovered (perhaps) by an ill-rewarded research; it is evident that neither Moss nor his Mare had the smallest interest for Rabelais, and their introduction is a patent disloyalty. Thus it is that Motteux, closely as in general he adheres to the French, loses the tight-knit concision and humorous dignity which are of Rabelais' essence. What can we say in defence of a translator who, without any excuse, interpolates so foolish a jest as ' His name 's Twyford ' ? which may have been an echo of the theatre or of a comic song. Thus, also, he must degrade his prose with such empty phrases as ' poor Pilgarlic '; thus, too, ' pour quelcque peu nous re-fraichir ' suggests to his nimble mind ' a cup of the creature.' Seldom does he make a genuine attempt to keep his author's images. ' Si la chorde ne rompt ' becomes in his version ' if my cake ben't dough.' Hence it follows that he has no fear of anachronisms, and does not scruple to render ' maitre d'eschole ' by 'the Busby of the place,' with an eye upon Dryden's own pedagogue. His experiments in comic rhetoric are yet more deplorable. To call stones 'St. Stephen's loaves' is but a mean jest ; and in one passage, when he should have written 'at dawn,' he is inspired by Butler, whose *Hudibras* deserved a better fate than the imitation of such witcatchers as Motteux, to the following flight of fancy : 'When day, peeping in the East, made the Sky turn from Black to Red, like a boiling Lobster.'[1] To *Hudibras* the monstrous image is appropriate enough ; it is wholly out of sympathy with Rabelais' epic style.

Thus, as I have said, a raffish familiarity is ever his darling sin. The thought of Panurge persuades him to thrust 'sweet baby' into brackets, while at the mention of Zachée he strikes the note of commonness in 'little dapper Zacheus.' Worse still, 'ce n'est tout ung' becomes in his English ''tis all one to Frank,' and this amiable reference to the Christian name of Maître François is repeated with a kind of unction. Similarly, he doesn't mind cutting and clipping his words out of decent semblance—a true mark of the colloquial style ; so, like the modern journalist, he is base enough to deform 'doctor' into 'doc.' Again, compare his expletives and Urquhart's, and another proof of decadence is evident. 'Ods-bodikins' and

[1] See *Hudibras*, part II. canto ii. :—

> 'The sun had long since, in the lap
> Of Thetis, taken out his nap,
> And, like a lobster boil'd, the morn
> From black to red began to turn.'

'mark ye me' have neither the curiosity nor the gravity which should distinguish the gesture of Rabelais' style. And it is with such gems that he lights up his narrative, thinking the while rather of his time than of his author.

Above all, he is profoundly interested in the slang of the gaol-bird, and had he found a proper opportunity for its use he might have distinguished himself. In the translation of Rabelais this curious speech is out of place, and Motteux uses it to degrade his author and befog his reader. 'Mourir' being the word to render, he breaks out into 'make a worse Figure with a Hempen Collar, and die in the Air,' and, in the same spirit, constrains 'to cut a caper on nothing' to do duty for 'bailler le moyne par le coul.' It is good enough slang, and valuable to the student, but it is not Rabelais; and the conclusion is that Motteux, despite his profound knowledge of pedlar's French, could make no fitting use of it. For slang, as I have said, demands a distinguished and appropriate use, and Motteux comes upon us as an awful warning. Nevertheless, his is the version of the Fourth and Fifth Book which will represent Rabelais in English for all time. It may be edited: it is not likely to be superseded. For it is nearer to the French than even Urquhart's masterpiece in all save spirit; and, while it fills us with a profound regret that Urquhart never finished the task appropriated to him by his genius, we may still thank this amiable, familiar Frenchman for doing after his guise what none else has done better.

PHILIPPE DE COMINES[1]

PHILIPPE DE COMINES was born in 1445 at the Flemish town whence he derived his name. His father, Collart de la Clite, the younger son of the noblest house in Flanders, had already proved himself a valiant warrior and prudent statesman, so that it was foreordained that Philippe should enter, at the earliest moment, into the service of the Duke. Gifted with a superhuman discretion, and a perfect sense of his own advantage, he made an early conquest of prosperity, and he was no more than eighteen when he was advanced to a position of trust about the Duke's person. He accompanied the Earl of Charolais throughout the ill-omened war of the Public Weal, and at the death of Philippe le Bon he transferred a reluctant obedience to Charles, his son. Under the young Duke, Comines found no scope for his adroit and diplomatic talent. He was not of those who are driven into acquiescence by a bold and reckless temperament. Not only did he foresee with many another noble of Flanders the inevitable ruin of

[1] *The Historie of Philip de Commines, Knight, Lord of Argenton.* Translated by Thomas Danett. Imprinted at London by Ar. Hatfield, for J. Norton. 1601.

Charles le Téméraire : he despised the brutal methods
of the Duke as bitterly as he resented the superb in-
tolerance of his behaviour.   Charles, indeed, was incapable of attaching friendship or of guarding loyalty.
Generous and insolent by turns, he speedily alienated
all those whom the new ambition of policy had inspired
to cunning ; and Philippe de Comines was not slow in
shaking off the fetter which trammelled his talent.

An embassy had already made him acquainted with
Louis xi., and it was with complete deliberation that,
in 1472, he changed his allegiance.   The Duke most
justly stripped him of his inheritance, and the partisans
of Burgundy were not backward in denunciation of
the renegade.   Comines is easily absolved from the
charge of treachery.   If he were the vassal of Burgundy, he was also the subject of France ; in deserting
the master for the overlord, he transgressed none of
the rules which govern the conduct of gentlemen.
He recognised that in Flanders he would be ground
to powder under the iron heel of a dying chivalry ; he
knew that at the court of France he would find a
proper scope for those qualities which have given him
immortality.   And it was nothing more than an
honourable prudence which induced him to sell his
talent, not in the highest, but in the most convenient
market.   The King, with a generosity which was half
foresight, did not permit his servant to suffer by the
exchange; and, if Comines was stripped of his Flemish
possessions, he instantly became lord of Argenton, of
Talmont, of Curzon, and many another rich domain.

He married, in the year that he transferred his service, Hélène de Chambes, Dame de Montsoreau, and through his daughter was the ancestor of three illustrious kings. Throughout the reign of Louis xi. his history is the history of France ; if his intelligence prevented his advancement to the highest offices, it encouraged the intimate regard and intimacy of the King ; and as he served his master faithfully throughout his life, so he watched the unwilling breath depart his body, and lived to indite his most loyal panegyric.

At the death of Louis, envy and malice overtook the favourite. Not only was he chased from the court ' with rough and discourteous words,' but he spent eight months in the harsh dungeon at Loches, whose cruelty to others he had often chronicled. And with that perfect dignity, which is the ornament of the historian, he permits a gap in the narrative to tell the disaster, of which he was too proud to complain. Now, the citadel of Loches is a city within a city, a fortress wrapt round with yet another fortress. It looks out upon the fairest plain of France, and the grandeur of its aspect does but enhance the cruelty of its ancient discipline. To-day it remains a monument to the power and implacability of the fifteenth century. Its cages and *oubliettes* attest the ferocity which governed tyrants, when tyranny was a divine right. From his narrow cell at Loches, Comines gazed upon the larger air he might no longer enjoy. Unable to walk more than two bent paces, he was forced to reflect upon the faithful service he had rendered his master ; and so strange was he to ill-nature, that he remained faithful to his ideal of kingship. Rumour has it that he scratched upon the wall of his cell this legend : *Dixisse me aliquando pænituit, tacuisse nunquam.* But rumour is a careless guide, and no doubt the inscription was the work of a more learned and less subtle statesman than Philippe de Comines.

While imprisonment crippled his talent for intrigue, his wife moved heaven and earth for her husband's enlargement, and at last won him permission to plead his cause in Paris, where disgrace forbade him to find an advocate. He was not one to fail for lack of eloquence, and so well did he defend himself—though his service needed no embellishment—that he found not only freedom but an honourable employ. He attended Charles viii. in his journey to Italy, and faithfully recorded the triumphs and failures of the expedition. He was no less resolute in his devotion to the King who had imprisoned him in a loathsome dungeon than to the King who had advanced him to be his chamberlain. The journey to Italy was his last exploit; the remaining years of his life were devoted to an honourable leisure and the composition of his *Mémoires*; and when he died—in 1509—he was not only the father-in-law of René de Bretagne, Comte de Penthièvre, Vicomte de Bridiers, Sieur de Boussac, but the foremost historian of France to boot.

A statesman and man of letters, he was yet so little of an egoist that he left no record of his person and

disposition. His book remains to attest his genius ;
his actions are part of French history. If we would
gain a knowledge of himself, we are driven perforce to anecdote and report. Surely his modesty is
unparalleled : a man of action, who had a perfect
command of his pen, he was yet artist enough to
understand that the central figure of his history was
not himself, but his King. Of opinions he is prodigal :
he is prepared to invent a whole system of government,
but upon the character and attainments of Philippe
de Comines he is strenuously silent. And this well-
intentioned silence was broken by so few of his contemporaries, that we know less of him than we know
of Plutarch, of Livy, or of Polybius, to the last of
whom a later age most diligently compared him.
In a brief half-century his qualities were frozen into
a legend, and all his biographers have precisely the
same tale to tell. Jean Sleidan is our earliest and
most trustworthy authority, and his statements have
been echoed by a long line of translators and commentators. Whether the description be accurate or
not it is impossible to discover ; since it does not contradict the slight sketch which may be drawn from
the *Mémoires*—since, moreover, it is the consistent
portrait of a blameless official—it may be accepted
for truth in default of a better.

Philippe de Comines, then, was of tall stature and
a goodly person, fit by his courage for any enterprise,
and by reason of his prudence foremost in the council
of his King. Though he was a man of affairs rather

than of letters, he was educated above the habit of his time. He had a perfect command of Italian, German, and Spanish, and he never betrayed his Flemish origin by a faulty pronunciation of French. His active memory was richly stored with the histories of the past, and, if it was his lifelong regret that he had no Latin, his own policy was founded upon the example of the Romans. Above all he abhorred idleness; and so fierce was his energy that he could, after the fashion of Cæsar, dictate to four secretaries at a time. Neither bookworm nor pedant, he learned most of all from the discourse of others, especially of such as were of a foreign nation. Two mottoes, says the gossiping biographer, governed his life. In prosperity he would murmur this text against idleness: 'He that will not work, neither let him eat'; while he would solace adversity with this pious reflection: 'I sailed into the deep of the sea, and a sudden tempest o'erwhelmed me.' These indications of character are slight enough, for Sleidan gathered only such anecdotes as were authentic, and as seemed, in the judgment of a friend, to illumine a distinguished career. It was Matthieu d'Arras, wrote Sleidan in 1548, a man of great honesty and knowledge, who furnished the meagre details. And Matthieu d'Arras, an aged citizen of Chartres, had known Comines in his youth, and had even been chosen to instruct his grandson, the Duke d'Estampes. The only other evidence that remains is the portraits, which show us a quick-eyed, sharp-nosed, strong-jawed, prim politician, who measures his own ambition, and knows well how he shall attain it.

It is his book which gives the best measure of the man, whose temperate zeal was plainly at variance with his age. His fortune was to chronicle the decline of savagery, and the savagery of the fifteenth century declined in a prolonged access of fury. Louis xi., discovering a miscreant hired to poison him, not only had him hanged, flayed, drawn, and quartered, but ordered that the house wherein he was born should be burned to the ground. When Villon sang, and mankind was preparing for the joyous emancipation of Rabelais, the world was a prison, and vengeance his privilege who could take it; yet Philippe de Comines was as humane as the ancients, almost as wise as Tacitus himself. He witnessed—perhaps approved —the callous slaughter of whole cities, and was still a gentleman and a man of the world; the supreme folly of Charles the Bold moved him to no more than a grave regret; his own demeanour was so constantly serene that he endured a miserable imprisonment without chagrin, and with scarce a word of protest. His imperturbability is beyond belief, and it was derived less from lack of feeling than from a perfect sense of history. His theme is the superiority of intelligence over brute force, the triumph of astute policy over a chivalry already moribund. The contrast, ready to his hand, might have been invented with dramatic intent, and never once does he allow his subject to override his judgment. Despite his inevitable preoccupation, he remains until the end the same philosophic, impartial historian.

Though he sets out as the panegyrist of Louis xi., though he left the service of Burgundy because he could not approve the tactics of the Duke, he never depresses the scales to one side or the other. Again and again he praises the great qualities of Charles the Bold, condemning only his lack of wit. 'Undoubtedly,' he wrote of the man who was once his master, 'he was endued with many goodly virtues: for never was Prince more desirous to entertain noble men, and to keep them in good order than he. His liberalitie seemed not great, because he made all men partakers thereof. Never Prince gave audience more willingly to his servants and subjects than he. While I served him he was not cruel, but grew marvellous cruel towards his end: which was a sign of short life. In his apparell and all other kind of furniture he was wonderfull pompous, yet somewhat too excessive. He received very honorably all ambassadors and strangers, feasting them sumptuously, and entertaining them with great solemnitie. Covetous he was of glorie, which was the chiefe cause that made him moove so many wars: for he desired to imitate those ancient Princes, whose fame continueth till this present. Lastly, hardy was he and valiant, as any man that lived in his time: but all his great enterprises and attempts ended with him selfe, and turned to his own losse and dishonor; for the honor goeth ever with the victorie.' Thus, with perfect justice, he appreciates the enemy of the King, his master, glosing his violence, and detecting in his pride a noble generosity. He achieved even more than this : a French historian, he dared to applaud the English, and to declare that Edward IV. was the handsomest and most munificent prince that ever he had seen.

His justice is the more astonishing, because, for the most part, he describes events whereof he was a witness. Now, for the historian who depends rather upon documents than upon experience, a show of impartiality is the most obvious virtue. A writer who records that which he saw is tempted either to regard himself as the central point of the universe, or to exaggerate his chosen hero into a fantastic deity. Comines avoided both the one and the other temptation. Had he been so minded he might have composed a private journal ; he might have revealed his own pleasures and his own ambitions ; he might even, with a half-justified vanity, have proclaimed himself the saviour of his country, and taken unto himself the credit of the King's wisdom. He did none of these things : he seems to have interpreted the historian's duty so strictly that he would seldom embellish his recital with picturesque or romantic details. Although he left the mediæval chroniclers leagues behind, although he discarded the arid accumulation of details, which served Matthew Paris and the others for history, his *Mémoires*, save only where Louis XI. is concerned, are lacking in that personal quality which his knowledge and resource might have imparted.

And this defect is the more to be regretted, because, not only did he possess a sense of humour, as is proved by the account of the ill-starred battle of Montlhéry, wherein either side was so bitterly attacked by fear that it retired as far as possible from its opponent, but he was also quick to see whatever was beautiful in art or nature. His picture of Venice—'the most triumphant city that ever I saw'—is a masterpiece, drawn from the life with all the enthusiasm of an artist, to whom strange sounds and fresh sights are an enduring pleasure.

His reticence and severity are instantly explained when you remember that, after the glorification of Louis XI., the object of his book was the exposition of a political philosophy. He lived at a moment when all the world was busied with brand-new theories of state-craft. Though it is not recorded that he and Machiavelli ever met, he spent two years in Italy, and it is certain that he knew by report the author of *The Prince*, who was then making his entry into public life. At any rate, it is a strange circumstance that, though the careers of these two philosophers over-lapped, their works had no point of contact. Comines died in 1509; his *Mémoires* were published in 1523. It was in 1513 that Machiavelli wrote his *Prince*; and, though Nifo's perversion of that work saw the light in the same year as Comines' *Mémoires*, it was not printed in its proper form until nine years later. However, these are puzzles which it is impossible to resolve; it is enough to note that Machiavelli and

Comines were engrossed at the same epoch in a similar speculation.

' I perswade my selfe,' wrote Comines in his Third Book, ' that rude and simple men will not busie their braines about the reading of this historie : but Princes and Courtiers shall finde in it good lessons and advertisements in mine opinion.' So it was composed for the better fashioning of the Perfect Prince. In Comines' cosmogony God comes first : an overruling Providence, a superior Louis xi., whose first interest is the career of princes, and whose treatment of meaner mortals is controlled by the same cunning which was the peculiar glory of the King of France. According to the historian, there is no event wherein this strange Deity does not profess a close and partial interest. In one passage he explains with what eloquence he may the value of archers to an army ; and straightway declares, as if to discount his own wisdom, that ' God shows battles are in his hand.' Literature does not afford a stranger mixture of simple faith and cunning forethought. Not only does he permit his Providence to play the part of an Ancient Chorus, but he constantly interrupts his narrative with astounding digressions, in which with God's guidance the true Philippe de Comines reveals himself. His philosophy is the philosophy of prudence and of the world. For the narrow morality of modern times he knows neither respect nor tolerance. ' It is not to be held for counsel, that is given after dinner,' says he, in anticipated contradiction to Prince Bismarck, and merely because he is thinking of his own experience. The master quality in his eyes is wisdom: *J'aimerais mieux vivre sous les sages que sous les fols*, says he, because, while there are many ways to avoid the displeasure of the wise and to recover their lost favour, with the ignorant a man can devise no shift. Wherefore he left the service of Burgundy for the more intelligent diplomacy of France.

After God the Prince ; and though he never formulates his theory, it is possible to deduce from his pages a consistent policy. He regards a prince as a strange beast, who is not ruled by the common impulses, nor restrained by the common code. So, for the guidance of this megatherium, he would devise, under God's providence, a particular morality. Upon one point his judgment never wavers : 'Two Princes,' he writes, 'that desire to continue in friendship ought never to come together, but to imploy vertuous and wise men between them, who will encrease their amitie, and repair all such breaches as shall happen.' Thus he strikes the note in the First Book ; and he plays the same tune with variations until the end. It is only when youth and hot blood persuade two princes to share their pleasures that he would permit an interview. Afterwards, it is plain that their sole ambition is to encroach one upon the other, and this ambition converts every meeting into a danger. He has at his finger-ends a hundred instances to persuade the doubtful, and he resumes the question in his most adroit and characteristic passage : 'Wherefore we thinke that two great Princes ought never to meet together. The occasions of troubles that arise at these assemblies are these : their servants cannot refraine from talking of matters past, and words will easily be taken in evill part. Secondarily, it is impossible but that the train of the one should be in better order than the other, whereof scoffes arise, which they that are scoffed stomacke. Thirdly, if they be two nations, their language and apparell differ, and that that pleaseth the one, displeaseth the other. Last of all, it commonly hapneth that the personage of the one Prince is comlier and better to be liked than the other ; wherefore he is praised, and rejoiceth and glorieth to heare his owne commendation, which cannot be without the dispraise of the other. And notwithstanding that three or fower daies peradventure after the assembly ended these matters be communed of covertly and closely in men's eares : yet by use they fall in time to open talke at dinners and suppers, and so are reported to both the parties, for fewe things in this world can be concealed, especially tales and reports.'

Cynical as are this vanity and distrust, they are firmly established upon princely, if not upon human, nature. Moreover, the argument gives Comines an occasion to enlarge upon the virtue of prudent ambassadors. Here, doubtless, is a suspicion of egotism. The historian, proud before all things of his diplomacy, remembers the triumphs of policy he might have won, had he been allowed. The King, however, whose distrust of Comines was at least as great as his affection for him, preferred to employ humbler and less intelligent instruments, and Olivier le Mauvais was better to his purpose than the Sieur d'Argenton. But Comines was ready with a complete theory of ambassadors, even more cynical in effect than the distrust wherewith he would separate princes. At the outset, he would discourage embassies altogether, well knowing their danger to states, whose amity is but short. Yet, if the presence of an ambassador be imperative, he would have him well received in peace or war. A prince, should he be of a comely presence, must himself give audience to the emissary of a neighbouring state. (And if a prince be not comely, the less he be seen of men the better.) The emissary, moreover, should be well lodged and laden with presents, and surrounded by persons of great honour and respect, not only with the hope of a profitable flattery, but that he should be guarded against the approach of light-headed discontents, who might betray the realm. When once audience was given, the enemy's messenger should be despatched with all possible speed, for it is a perilous matter for a prince to harbour in his house the plotter of his own destruction. On the other hand, no country may lag behind the zeal of its enemy : ' For one ambassador they send to you, send you two to them : and though they be weary of your ambassadors, and forbid any more to come, yet send still.' However, the interchange and entertainment of public embassies were methods of policy too simple for a courtier bred in the diplomatic school of Louis XI., and, while Comines recognised the necessity of such demonstrations, he trusted rather to the secret service of spies. 'A wise Prince,' he declares with a perfect trust in the code of his epoch, 'must always endeavor to have some secret friend or friends about his enimie, and beware as neere as he may (for in such cases men cannot always do as they would) that his enimie have not the like about him.' And, as for the ambassador himself, he would have him a mild and simple man, who should obey his master's behests without scruple of his own opinion, and uncomplainingly accept the fury of a hostile monarch.

Thus he expounds his political theory, still convinced that a king in his essence is superhuman. Once he confesses, with a sort of chagrin, that 'men they are as we be'; and elsewhere he asserts that, princes' imaginations being strange, it is idle for common men to prate of them as though they understood. He would urge every statesman to be properly subservient : he never yet knew a man who achieved success by keeping his master in fear or subjection. His argument is based always and openly upon self-interest. He worships victory however it be attained ; and he urges learning upon all men, because learning is folly's strongest antidote. Before all created things, princes have need of knowledge, for since their experience is curt, they can guide their conduct only by the example of the past. Despite his admiration of authority he is fierce in his denunciation of a stupid

king. ' Thinke you,' he asks in a rare passage of in-
dignation, ' thinke you that God hath established the
office of a King or Prince to be executed by such beasts
as glorie in saying : I am no scholar, I trust my
Councell well ynough, and refer all matters to them,
and so without further answer depart to their sports
and pastimes ? ' Moreover, he would encourage suspicion as the better part of wisdom. He holds that
it is no shame that a king should keep an eye upon
those that pass to and fro, but a great shame to be
deceived and undone through unpardonable folly.
Even this opinion he would hedge, regarding a prince
that never was deceived as a beast, who under-
standeth not the difference between good and evil.
And, with all his praise of valour and armaments, he
distrusts the efficacy of war, which may be too easily
begun, and may only be ended by the contrivance of
the subtlest treaties.

Nor does the protest of princes avail, for it is God,
the greatest of all kings, that holds the scales of
destiny, which He declines, when He will, upon the
side of war. Now wars and divisions, says Comines,
are permitted of God for the chastisement of princes
and evil people. To every state is appointed its
proper prick or sting—to France England, to England
the Scots, to Spain Portugal. And these stings are
very necessary for the furtherance of morality and the
support of wisdom, since even kings are assailed by
misery and wickedness. ' I knew this mightie King
[Louis XI.],' writes Comines in his tragic epilogue,

' and served him in the flower of his age, and in his
great prosperity; yet never saw I him free from toile
of bodie, and trouble of mind'; so that the conclusion of his work is vanity and disappointment. Travail
and distress are the inheritance of sovereignty;
misery dogs the footsteps of success; and neither
Louis nor Charles the Bold knew, after they came to
man's estate, more than a few broken days of pleasure.
The *Envoy* of the Sixth Book, whereat the author
should have stayed his hand, is nothing less than a
pious lament. Here is an end of philosophy and
cynicism; here is a frank confession that the highest
policy is but a delusion. The great personages, that
toiled so mightily, and purchased honour at the price
of immitigable sorrow, shortened their lives and, peradventure, imperilled their souls. And for what?
For the brief and thankless renown of an empty day.
Thus he cannot refrain from adorning his tale with
a piteous reflection. 'What goodlier examples can
we finde,' he says, 'to teach us that man is but a
shadow, that our life is miserable and short, that we
are nothing, neither great nor small? For immediately after our death all men abhorre and loathe our
bodies, and so soone as the soule is severed from the
body, it goeth to receive judgment; yea, undoubtedly
at the very moment that the soule and body part, the
judgment of God is given according to our merits and
deserts, which is called the particular judgment of
God.'

No less remarkable than his Machiavellian policy

are the temperance and accuracy of his narrative.
Only one enemy, the Flemish critic, Jacques Meyer
('Esprit aigre' is the comment of Lenglet du
Fresnoy),[1] was found to attack his conclusions; and
the sobriety of his judgment equals his consistent and
instinctive accuracy. His style is at once simple and
dignified. Though he wrote as one wholly 'unlettered,' though he delights to remind the reader
that he *n'a aucune littérature*, he yet contrived to
handle French like a practised historian, and to con-
fine his rhetoric to the digressions he loved so well.
Montaigne's appreciation, pencilled in his copy of the
book, is as true to-day as when it was written. 'In
him you shall find a pleasing-sweet and gently-gliding
speech,' thus the passage runs in Florio's version,
'fraught with a purely-sincere simplicitie, his narration pure and unaffected, and wherein the author's
unspotted-good meaning doth evidently appeare, void
of all manner of vanitie or ostentation speaking of
himselfe, and free from all affection or envie speaking
of others : his discourses and perswasions, accompanied
more with a well-meaning zeale, and meere veritie, than
with any laboured and exquisit sufficiencie, and all
through, with gravitie and authoritie, representing a
man well-borne, and brought up in high negotiations.'

    [1] It is to the Abbé Lenglet du Fresnoy that we owe the most
useful edition of Comines' *Mémoires*, fortified with all the documents and correspondence which can throw light upon the period.
It bears this legend upon its title-page : 'A Londres, et se trouve
à Paris, chez Rollin, fils, Quai des Augustins. 1747.'

Indeed, he never lacked praise, and his work was no sooner published than it became a classic. Even before it got into print, it had become, as he wished, the handbook of princes. The Emperor Charles v. carried it with him continually, and Francis i. of France esteemed it so highly that he was bitterly displeased by its publication, esteeming it the property, not of the world, but of reigning monarchs. *Dignus omnibus Alexandris hic Philippus* : thus Justus Lipsius, and the panegyric was echoed by a hundred writers. No less a poet than Pierre Ronsard wrote Comines' epitaph, in the form of a dialogue between *le Passant* and *le Prêtre*, wherein History and Truth deplore the death of a writer who surpassed Titus Livius himself :

> ' pour sçavoir égaler
> La vérité du fait avec le beau parler.'

So to a chorus of approval he passed through many editions. The first—(' Achevé dimprimer le xxvie jour de avril mil cinq cens xxiii pour Galliot du Pré ') —contained but the first Six Books, and it was not until five years later that the expedition to Italy was added. The addition was an artistic mistake ; for, with the death of Louis xi. and the consequent morality, the history, as designed by Comines, comes to an end. The author led up to his climax of misery and regret with the greatest skill, and, for all his professed indifference to the result, set a seal upon his work with his concluding homily. The last two books, therefore, must be regarded as an afterthought, or as

the fragment of another design. The dedicatory
epistle addressed to the Archbishop of Vienne estab-
lishes the point. 'I send you here a memorial,'
writes the author, 'as agreeable to truth as I can
possibly call to mind of all the acts and doings that
I have been privy to, of King Louis xi., our master
and benefactor, a prince worthy of perpetual memory.'
Here is no word of Charles viii., his ill-fated expedition, and his hapless death. Comines declares that
he set forth the character and achievements of
Louis xi., whom he knew better than any man of his
time—that and no more. Meanwhile he frames the
modestest judgment of his own performance : he
sends his work, all penned in haste, to the Archbishop,
hoping that he would find a corner for it in some
Latin work. The Archbishop disappointed this plain
ambition ; within fifty years Jean Sleidan, by translating the *Mémoires* into Latin, had given Comines
the consecration which he so ardently desired ; and
it is by an ironical destiny that, while the Archbishop and Sleidan and the Latin version are all forgotten, the work of Comines lives in wellnigh every
European tongue, and has become part of the world's
literature.

The drama of Philippe de Comines has but one
motive and one hero. The motive is the glory of
wisdom, the hero is Louis xi. And Louis is more
than the hero of the piece : he is the sole personage
who is permitted to play a grand part. The folly of
others is but a foil to his excellences ; and as death

approached, from which he shrank in horror, you feel that the curtain is falling upon the last act, that the one interesting character leaves the stage. Neither the grace of women nor the joyousness of life interrupts the stern pursuit of war and intrigue. If a princess appear by way of incident, it is because she is compelled to make a treaty or a war with the King of France. Now, Comines understood his master as profoundly as he reverenced him. He approached him with the frankness of a Boswell—of a Boswell determined to substitute high policy and craft for the trivialities of private life. He found in the King both virtue and vice, and he made no attempt to belittle the one or to extol the other: he detested flattery as he loathed ignorance, and he solemnly concludes, in defiance of an inveterate superstition, that of all his contemporaries Louis was the least addicted to profligacy. Moreover, the King was well educated for his century and station; even as a child he had studied grammar and logic; above all, he had enriched his mind with a knowledge of history, and knew well how to profit by the examples of the past. His bearing was prudent, yet familiar. Neither proud nor disdainful, he gave audience to whomsoever came into his presence; and while other princes controlled their conduct by the dying dogmas of chivalry, his perfect acquaintance with his own people and other countries enabled him to establish his policy upon the hard rock of knowledge and experience.

His liberality was lavish, if interested; and, while

a free and scathing tongue was his worst indiscretion, he was never slow, when it suited him, to repair by an honourable amend the biting offences of his wit. Naturally fearful, he chose to conquer by policy rather than by arms, and he understood, says Comines, the art of separating allies better than any man that ever lived.   Proud as he was, he would yet humble himself at the call of wisdom, for, said he with a shrug, ' when pride rideth before, shame and damage follow after.' Never arrogant in prosperity, he bore adversity with a perfect carriage, and, knowing when and whom to fear, he was free from the danger of sudden panic.   If he loved revenge, and countenanced cruelty, he resembled therein the most chivalrous of his contemporaries ; and many an act of ferocity, for which he has been reproached, was but the proper punishment of unpardonable treachery.   His implacable pursuit of the Constable Saint-Pol is not only intelligible, but easily justified.   Saint-Pol had been the King's servant and his friend ; he had been advanced to great offices in the state, and magnificently rewarded.   And deceit was so frankly manifest in him that, twice forgiven, he must yet turn traitor a third time on the very day of the King's clemency.   His death, therefore, was a just punishment.   Just also was the execution of Nemours ; and if the cruelty of his dungeon whitened his hair in three days, if he was carried to the scaffold hideously racked, he did but pay the same penalty he would have extorted from his enemy.

So little wanton was the King's cruelty, that his arduous life was wholly devoted to the profit of France and the support of the kingly ideal. With these ambitions he surrendered the splendour of courts for the pilgrim's staff, and turned his reign into a succession of journeys. Michelet calls him a 'Revolution en vie'; yet surely this 'beggar-king' was the sternest of conservatives, the legitimate fore-runner of Louis XIV. He was called to the throne at the very moment when the nobles, proud in the exercise of chivalry, were encroaching upon the sove-reign power; and it needed all his strength of purpose and his unwearying energy to confer permanence and distinction upon his office. With a marvellous intelligence he foresaw that he must invent and develop a new power to check the ambition of the cultured bandits, who would have broken France in pieces for a formula; so he turned from the nobles to the cities, chose his instruments from the people, and converted the burgess into an influence.

With this intent he avoided splendour; and, since it was his wont to symbolise a policy in his costume, the crowning at Reims may be said to represent his reign in little. There he appeared humble and peni-tent, yet withal contemptuous of the great princes, who came in the glory of their state to do him honour. And it is typical of the sovereign who afterwards employed servants so base as Tristan l'Hermite and Olivier le Dain, that, at the supper which followed the coronation, he laid his crown upon the table, and talked only to Philippe Pot, who was set behind his chair. What sympathy could so grave a statesman feel for the Count of Charolais, who turned the victory of Montlhéry into a defeat, because, rather than take advantage of his triumph, he still stayed upon the field, throwing down his gauntlet, and crying aloud that he would fight the bravest hero of the retreating army ? No, Louis preferred to conciliate the citizens of Paris, to let dissension and folly fight his battles, and to buy, with fresh-coined crowns, an advantage which bravery would not always give. When the English came to France, they not only fared sumptuously, but went home with their pockets full of gold pieces. And as he treated the English, so he treated his God : he made Him presents. He was less religious than prudent : the reward of one victory was a silver image of himself, and when news was brought him of Burgundy's death, he vowed, were it true, that the iron lattice which enclosed the reliquary in the Church of St. Martin of Tours should become a lattice of silver. But, on the other hand, he flouted the Pope, and caged the sacred person of a cardinal. His craft equalled his mercenary superstition : there was nothing he loved so well as hostages, and he would pack his house with those whose lives might some day find their value. This craft was never selfishly exercised ; and, though he did not scruple on occasion to butcher his enemies, he was never guilty of so preposterous a slaughter as was inspired by the prudish mother of Charles the Bold, and carried out by Charles himself.

The hatred of his enemies was expressed in ill-veiled compliment : the Duke of Burgundy sadly confessed that Louis was always ready, and might have added that he was always ready because he knew how to wait. Even at the end of his long career he was still young, perhaps because he was born old. At any rate the years had but little effect upon this abstract calculation, and he could write to Dammartin, at the zenith of his power, ' nous autres jeunes.' Not a comely figure, may be, but a great sovereign : great in wisdom, great also in the ambition of creating a vast empire and of emulating Charlemagne, whom he believed himself to resemble, and whom he would actively imitate. With all his toil, with all his self-denial, he triumphed only at the end, and death was already upon him when he witnessed the success of his vast schemes, and when the author of the *Rosier des Guerres* saw the proper victory of wisdom and statecraft.

His appearance was a vivid index of his character. A slyness and contempt are mingled in the forceful superiority of his face. The doggedness which never let him rest is evident in every feature. But none of the portraits suggests the niggard temper, which has been a constant and ill-founded reproach—constant because one historian has echoed another, ill-founded because he was parsimonious only for himself. So long as his guard was perfectly equipped, what mattered it that the King, the friend of the people, went meanly clad ?   When he would lavish a fortune upon the purchase of a province, he could not afford to buy him a new coat, and it is solemnly recorded that he went everywhere with an empty pocket. The Earl of Lodesme, on a visit to France, crossed the river in a boat, the sail whereof was cloth of gold, and his buskins were thick encrusted with precious stones. And Louis, in the phrase of Danett, ' wore his apparell very short, and marvellously uncomely, and was clad in very coarse cloth, besides that he wore an old hat, differing from all the rest of his company, and an image of lead upon it, whereat the Castilians jested, saying that this proceeded of miserie.' That was far from the truth : it was merely Louis's policy, which persuaded him always to subordinate his own pleasure to the glory of France.

As Comines presents his hero as astuteness and energy made concrete, so there is no reason to believe Comines' judgment at fault, especially as the *Mémoires* receive abundant confirmation. And Louis xi. has always been the scarecrow of history, a bogey where- with to frighten the terrified democrat. For the misappreciation of modern times Sir Walter Scott is largely responsible. The necessity of his romance compelled him to paint the King in the darkest light, to portray him as a monster of evil-minded cunning and common debauchery. All the light-hearted sins of the *Cent Nouvelles Nouvelles* were freely ascribed to a monarch who gave his life to an intolerable labour, and who spent his leisure in the fearless hunting of the boar.   And even this ascription proceeded only from a misunderstanding.   It is now certain that Louis XI. neither told one of the famous stories, nor took part in their libertine pleasantries.   The Monseigneur of the *Cent Nouvelles Nouvelles* is not the King, but Charles of Burgundy ; and Mr. Wright,[1] in a lucid preface, has set the matter at rest for ever.   That the King was a model of purity, of course, is impossible. The strong men of the fifteenth century did not conform their lives to a standard of puritanism.   But Comines is precise in the unsolicited vindication of his master from the charge of profligacy, and prejudice may no longer seize this excuse to belittle a great man.

The charge of political villainy is yet more easily rebuffed.   Success, not morality, was the end of Louis's ambition.   He was not an egoist working out a private theory of virtue : he was a strong king building up a kingdom.   Even if he stooped to steel and poison, he did not infringe the code of his day, and the crime of Guienne's death has never emerged from the uncertainty of suspicion.   To say that morality is an affair of latitude is the commonest of commonplaces ; and it cannot be too often reiterated.   Twenty years before the time when Cesare Borgia was discussed, not as a criminal, but as a politician, Louis XI. was free to employ whatever means his end required. ' On ne voit de juste ou d'injuste qui ne change de

---

[1] *Les Cent Nouvelles Nouvelles*, publiées d'après le seul manuscrit connu avec introduction et notes par M. Thomas Wright.   Paris : P. Jannet, 1858.

qualité en changeant de climat,' wrote Pascal; and Pascal lacks not the support of all the ages.[1] Moreover, when to climate you add the lapse of time, it is evident that you cannot judge the France of the fifteenth century by a standard which will presently become obsolete. To hurl the reproach of suspicion at a king who lived surrounded by the spies of his enemies, is the climax of unreason; and, if Louis XI. was infamous to assert that the king cannot reign who knows not how to dissemble, then the game of government has never been played with clean hands.

He left France in peace, and marvellously increased her borders—this is the end and substance of Philippe de Comines' legitimate panegyric; before the exaggerated contradiction of Louis's character, his steadfast loyalty is the more astonishing. And while Comines presents the graver pursuits of his King, the other biography, the so-called *Chronique Scandaleuse*, shows him in his more intimate relation with his own city of Paris. Whoever was the author of this Chronicle,[2] which never justifies its scandalous title,

[1] Lord Acton's Introduction to Mr. Burd's *Il Principe* (Oxford: at the Clarendon Press, 1891), where the materials are given for a full discussion of the question. To prove that modern politicians are of the old opinion, Lord Acton quotes Walpole's statement that 'no great country was ever saved by good men, because good men will not go the lengths that are necessary'; and Lord Grey's confession to Princess Lieven: 'I am a great lover of morality, public and private; but the intercourse of nations cannot be strictly regulated by that rule.'

[2] This *Chronique* has hitherto been ascribed to Jean de Troyes, but M. Auguste Vitu has made it exceedingly

he was an eye-witness of many events both trivial and important; and, especially, he records those very episodes which the graver historian is apt to pass over in silence. Thus he tells us how, on the eve of Charles VII.'s death, a very long comet appeared in the sky, a notable presage of the new King's ambition; and how at Louis's entry into Paris three beautiful and lightly attired maidens ' disoient de petits motets et bergerettes.' And it is plain throughout that though he might behave with nonchalance to hostile princes, the King never neglected his good citizens of Paris. He kept them informed of his projects and policy, and on the morrow of a battle would return to his capital and declare his success or failure. Thus after Montlhéry he arrived in Paris late, and went forthwith to sup at the hotel of Charles de Melun, where he met ' plusieurs Seigneurs, Damoiselles et Bourgeoises.' To them he recited the hopeless mis-adventure with ' moult beaux mots et piteux, de quoi tous et toutes plorèrent bien largement.' Is not this rather the familiarity of a *pater patriae* than the vulgar pleasantry of a monarch inspired only by a taste for low company ? What wonder is it that, if besides these condescensions he remitted the taxes laid upon the people by his father, the citizens followed him with cries of ' Noël! Noël!' and lit joyous bonfires

probable that the real author is Denis Hesselin, and has pre-sented the argument with considerable ingenuity in his pamphlet: *La Chronique de Louis XI. dite* ' Chronique Scanda-leuse,' *faussement attribuée à Jean de Troyes, restituée à son véritable auteur.* Paris: Librairie des Bibliophiles, 1873.

at the street corners! But the King, indeed, was mindful of all. When the Earl of Somerset visited him at the Bastille, he gave the Englishman a black velvet cloak, because a shower was passing over the sky ; and he rarely supped with the citizens of Paris without thanking them for their courage, and thus assuring himself of their eternal loyalty. Under his reign Paris was a city of gaiety and splendour. When the Queen's barge sailed up the Seine, such a pageant was prepared as had rarely been witnessed. Not only did the officers of the city meet her, ' tous honneste-ment vestus et habillez,' but the children's choir of Sainte Chapelle sung ' beaux virelais et autres chansons moult mélodieusement,' while certain ' Damoiselles' offered her a ' beau cerf fait de confiture,' with the Queen's arms hung about its neck.

Though the reign of the nobles was over, there is no trace in all this amiable history of prudery or intrigue. So well did the King understand his people and their strength, that he even flattered them with jousts and tourneys, whereat the *damoiselles* and *bourgeoises* of Paris were the queens of beauty, and the victory rested with the brave citizens. The smallest excuse was sufficient for a pageant, and this tyrant, who has been described as a monster of penury, never sent an embassy away without bestowing upon its seigneurs goblets of fine gold or presents of strange beasts. And then, exhausted with high policy and incessant travelling, he would go off to his fastnesses in Touraine, and find sport or repose at Plessis-les-

Tours, that ruin of which scarce a trace remains ; at Amboise, where the hapless Charles VIII. met his death, and where a cavalier may still ride on horseback to the roof ; or at Loches, where were hidden his darkest dungeons and his fiercest *oubliettes*. There he lived, wisely distrustful of his own countrymen, and attended only by his gallant Scots Guard. The faith he professed in the integrity of these champions was loyally repaid by Lord Bernard Stuart, ' the charbunckell, chief of every chevelrie,' whose elegy is eloquently chanted by Dunbar,[1] and who would scarce have lent his honourable sword to a black-hearted rascal.

But popular opinion is not to be gainsaid. Though the *Chronique Scandaleuse* is the necessary complement of Comines' more palatial portrait, though the one picture confirms the other, the world is still incredulous. Those who condemn the King's life for a masterpiece of villainy see a culminating horror in his death. And truly it was no horror, but a great and tragic spectacle. Louis, at last worn out by excess of toil, fell into a lethargy alternating between insensibility and suspicion, between superstition and the devoutest piety. He retired within the utmost recess of Plessis-les-Tours, which he fortified with iron bars and sharp spears. There also he built watch-towers of iron, and set therein forty crossbow-men, who were bidden to shoot any man who should approach the

[1] See *The Poems of William Dunbar*: Edited by John Small, and published (1883-1884) by the Scottish Text Society, pp. 59-64.

castle after the shutting of the gates.   Meanwhile he
neglected no enterprise which might be of good omen.
He adorned churches, he set free his enemies, he
lavished upon his physician thousands of crowns.
Now he would bid the Holy Man of Calabria to Tours ;
now he would demand that the sacred vial be brought
from its sanctuary at Reims.   It was a stern fight for
life, fought by a King who could relinquish pleasure,
and who clung with ferocity to his declining power.
Wherefore he caused himself to be spoken of in every
corner of his realm, lest men should think him dead.
He despatched emissaries to every part of Europe,
hoping that thereby he might convince his rivals of his
health and strength.   Above all, he caused beasts to be
bought for him in all places : ' Dogs he sent for round
about, into Spaine for a kinde of Spanish greyhound,
called in French *Allans* ; into Britaine for little
beagles, greyhounds, and spaniels, which he paied
deere for ; into Valence for little rugged dogs, which
he made to be bought above the owners owne price :
into Sicily he sent for good mules, especially to some
officer of the countrie, for the which he paied double
the value ; to Naples for horses, and for divers strange
beasts into divers countries, as into Barbarie for a
kind of little lions, no greater then little foxes ; . . .
into Denmarke and Sweden for two kind of strange
beasts, one of the which were called Helles, being of
shape like a Hart, and of the greatnes of a buffe, with
hornes, short and thicke ; the other Rengiers, being
of the bignes and colour of a buck, save that their

horns be much greater.' And when these rare beasts arrived at Plessis he made no more account of them. In being sought and paid for they had achieved their purpose. Thus the most Christian king lay dying, and none knew his desperate straits. Though his strength ebbed fast, he neither relaxed his vigilance nor forgot his duties ; indefatigably he sent messengers to foreign courts ; and it is one of the humours of history that a few months before his death he exchanged letters of courtesy with Richard III., his only rival in hatred and ability. At the outset he wrote promising friendship, and Richard replied, by Blanc Sanglier, with a demand that English merchants should receive protection in France. Presently Richard became more familiar, and asked the dying King for ' aucuns vins du cru de Bourgogne et de la Haulte France pour moi et la reine ma compagne.' [1] There is a strange irony in this peaceful interchange of good services, and the correspondence proves that, even in August 1483, Richard had no inkling of Louis's imminent doom. Not even this fantastic fear of forgetfulness availed to dull the French King's wit. He shuddered less at the approach than at the presence of death. He would, if he could, have exercised a terror from beyond the grave. Wherefore he sent for the Dauphin, whom he already called His Majesty the King, that he might shape his future

[1] See *Letters and Papers Illustrative of the Reign of Richard III. and Henry VII.* : Edited for the Master of the Rolls by James Gairdner. 1861.

policy. Comines, who never left his side, and was ever a faithful witness, declares that in all the time of his sickness he never once complained of his suffering as do other men. In brief, his death was not the last fight of a coward, hungry for decrepitude; it was the unwilling resignation of a statesman who foresaw the ruin of a favourite policy. And how shall he be cleared from the common charge of timidity?

When Comines wrote his Chronicle, he hoped no more for it than that the Archbishop of Vienne should turn it into Latin; and within a century it was part of four literatures! Moreover, so great is the superiority of a living over a dead language, that, while the Latin version of Jean Sleidan is forgotten, the English of Thomas Danett is a masterpiece untouched by age. It possesses all the virtues of majestic speech: written at the time when all men handled English prose with freedom and strength unparalleled, it is distinguished by the rich cadences and the wealth of imagery which are the glory of our Authorised Version. To criticise it were superfluous, since it carries its virtues upon the surface. It satisfies the wisest canons of translation: it is neither slavish nor diffuse; the English is no mere echo of the French, and the sentences are faithfully turned from one idiom into the other. In one respect Danett embellishes his original: the style of Comines is at times restrained unto dryness, and the translator, by the deftest use of words, has put colour where before there was but a uniform grey. If Comines is disposed to write like a well-groomed conscience,

Danett shows a perfect sense of history by amplifying the manner of the conscience into the style of a full-blooded man. He changes the metaphors at will, or invents images where the French gives him no warrant. Thus he renders ' qui en ce temps-là estoit encore un petit orguilleux ' by the infinitely more expressive phrase : ' Whose peacock feathers were not yet all pulled.' When the Duke of Burgundy is ' mis en doute,' Danett prefers to put him ' in a dump ' ; and if the ministers of justice ' firent plusieurs pièces ' of some ' humblet ' or ' by-fellow,' Danett thus embroiders his misfortune : ' They hewed him in to a number of small gobbets.' Above all, the Englishman dislikes the common, inexpressive adjective. On one page ' meschans ' appears as ' unthriftliest,' on another as ' lewd and naughty persons ' ; while the expansion of ' plus mécaniquement ' into ' yea, after a much beastlier sort' throws a curious sidelight upon Danett's character. Though he is as adverse to slang as Comines himself, there is one turn he cannot resist ; and, in rendering the simple ' gagnent ' by ' win the garland,' he anticipates an odious catch-word of the present day. But it is not so much in separate phrases that Danett declares his superiority, as in the sustained picturesqueness of his narrative. You may read his history from end to end with a pleasure which comes rather from the music of the phrase than from the simple statement. For he is a true Elizabethan in his preference of a fat, sonorous prose to the stern and careful elegance of Philippe de Comines.

Of his life little is known.[1] He lives in his works, and we can discover no more of his career than may be gleaned from a scanty preface. He dedicated his translation in 1596 ' to the Right Honorable my very good Lord, the Lord Burghley, Lord Treasurer of England, Knight of the Honorable order of the Garter, and Master of hir Majesties Courte of Wardes and Liveries.' The manuscript, so he tells us, presented to my Lords of Burghley and Leicester in 1566, was permitted to lie hid for many a year, until it was perused anew at the request of Sir Christopher Hatton. ' Since his death,' thus proceeds the preface, ' certaine gentlemen to whose hands the booke happened to come, tooke so great pleasure and delight therein, that they determined to put it to the presse, supposing it a great dishonour to our nation, that so woorthie an historie being extant in all languages in Christendom, should be suppressed in ours.' For a while Danett was in doubt; like Francis i., he thought that the secrets of princes should not be

[1] In a letter addressed by Sir W. Cecil, Secretary of State, to the Earl of Rutland, on 12th June 1563, and printed in *The Manuscripts preserved at Belvoir Castle*, vol. i. p. 87, there is a probable reference to Danett. ' The French demand Newhaven,' says Cecil, ' by an express man named Dallvy. We answer hym that so we may have Calliss he shall have his request. . . . Dallvy is retorned, and I thynk Mr. Dannett shall goe to doo the lyke for us in France, and to demand Calliss.' It was to Cecil that Danett gave, in 1566, his manuscript version of Comines, and thus we may fairly believe that the translator had a more intimate knowledge of embassies than is given by the study of books.

published in the vulgar tongue. His scruple was
overborne, and his book was popular enough to pass
through several editions. He followed the later
French impressions in supplementing the Life of
Louis XI. with the last two books, and he called his
book a *Historie* and not *Memoirs*—the title subsequently adopted. Nor was he satisfied with the work
thus complete. He must needs break the silence,
rigorously kept by Comines during the years of his
disgrace, with a ' Supply,' wherein are mimicked both
the style of the author and his habit of moral reflection.

Danett was no mere translator : he was an accomplished historian as well. Not only does he rigorously
correct his author's text; he supplements the narrative with a set of admirably lucid notes. He had
the literature of his time and subject at his finger-
tips, and, before all things, he was determined to
expose the spiteful heresies of Jacques Meyer, the
Flemish scoundrel, who dared to belittle Comines
and his master. No man of his time was better inspired with the critical spirit, and he had the courage
to specialise in an age devoted to vast enterprises and
the acquisition of universal knowledge. His other
two works prove the steadfastness of his temper ; for
the one is a *Description of the Low Countries gathered
into an Epitome out of the Historie of Lodovico Guicchar-
dini* (London : 1593) ; the other nothing less than
a further supplement to Comines : *A Continuation
of the Historie of France from the death of Charles the*

Eight, where Comines endeth till the death of Henry the Second (1559), 'Collected by Thomas Danett' (London : 1600). However, it is not as an original historian that Danett is remembered : the fashion of narrative and the changing habit of research have left his poor experiments in obscurity. Neither fashion nor pedantry can stale this worthy translation of a masterpiece, unique alike in observation and philosophy.

A TRANSLATOR GENERALL[1]

I

PHILEMON HOLLAND, 'the Translator Generall in his age,' was born at Chelmsford in 1552. From the Grammar School of his native town he passed in proper course to Trinity College, Cambridge, of which august foundation he was successively scholar and fellow. Thereafter he gave himself to the study of medicine, graduated M.D. in 1595, and settled at Coventry in the same year to the practice of his profession. Materials are lacking wherefrom to compose an accurate biography; anecdote for the most part supplies the place of fact; and it is in his works that we must seek the securest evidence of his talent and dignity. From these scanty branches we may throw the vague shadow of a rarely amiable career.

We know not what pursuits or ambitions engrossed him before the year of his arrival in Coventry. Perhaps

---

[1] '*The Historie of Twelve Caesars, Emperours of Rome*, written in Latine by C. Suetonius Tranquillus, and newly translated into English by Philemon Holland, Doctor in Physicke: Together with a Marginall Glosse and other briefe Annotations there-upon, 1606.'

he was of those whose mind and character are not hastily shaped. He was past forty when he commenced the practice of physic ; and it was not until he had completed his tenth lustre that he found the real task of his life. He could not have found a better theatre for his gifts than the Coventry which he loved so well, and which in return generously acknowledged the honour conferred by his presence. It was not then the tourist-haunted city of bicycles and of Peeping Tom ; the houses, now the antiquary's delight, were then all fair with fresh stucco and painted beam ; in the narrow roadway, shadowed by the upper stories, from which the inmates might exchange handkerchiefs and messages of love, passed the staid scholars and gay adventurers of Eliza's glorious age ; and upon all smiled—as they still smile—the lofty steeples of Trinity and St. Michael's. It was the Warwickshire of to-day—the land of Shakespeare, and Shakespeare still inglorious ! Down the stately avenues, less stately then, but already avenues, went Philemon Holland to the unruined Kenilworth, late witness of Amy Robsart's beauty, and to the enduring splendours of Warwick. Wherever he paid his visits he was welcome, for was he not the scholar of whom all the county was proud ? Was he not the kindly physician, who healed not for money, but for healing's sake ?

So he tended the sick in charity, and grew poor. Wherever the pestilence raged, or fever burned, there went Holland, bringing with him the comfort of medicine and good counsel. His worldly wisdom

was not equal to his skill, and his reputation dwindled
as his generosity increased. The great houses which
received him as an eminent wit and renowned scholar
were not disposed to trust his knowledge of physic,
and Holland, still meeting the attack of poverty and
disease, was driven for his own safety to another profession. He became an usher, and for thirty years
he instructed the youth of Coventry in sound theology
and polite learning. The building wherein for so long
he worked and taught still stands, though turned to
baser uses ; and the mere fabric, which now echoes to
the raucous sound of popular psalmody, helps us to
reconstruct the life of the ancient scholar. With the
outward seeming of a Gothic church, the old school
preserves its character of austere simplicity. Once
were ranged within its walls the worn benches of poor
and patient scholars. There in a corner stood the
priceless library—now fallen into unutterable decay—
whose volumes, then consulted by learned men, were
presently torn for fire-lighting and meaner offices, and
whose slim catalogue, written in a princely hand and
bound in vellum, one would like to believe the handiwork of Holland.

Pursuing scholarship, he cherished the fine ambition of making other scholars. Though he was but
an usher in a free school, it was a distinction to be
trained by his intelligence, and we hear of many a
great nobleman whose tottering steps were first
guided by the erudite Philemon. Thus George, Lord
Berkeley, was at the age of twelve placed under his

charge, and Lucius Cary, the great Lord Falkland, was a constant visitor at the school.   Now, Falkland's youth had been wild ; he had been apt, saith report, ' to stab and do bloody mischief ' ; but he, too, falling under the sway of Holland, grew into a grave student. ' I have heard Dr. Ralph Bathurst say '—it is Aubrey who speaks—' that, when he was a boy, my Lord Falkland lived at Coventry (where he had then a house), and that he would sett up very late at nights at his study, and many times came to the library at the schoole there.'   And though Holland did not live to witness his scholar's glorious death, he must have enjoyed a proper satisfaction in training the finest wit and most polished cavalier of his time.

Nor was Lord Falkland ill advised to resort to the library of Coventry School, for it was so well furnished, that it could hardly be matched outside London and the greater cities.   Alas ! the eighteenth century respected not the patience and generosity of the past. The noble volumes, printed at the great presses of Europe, were heedlessly mutilated, and served as missiles for an idle generation of schoolboys, who knew not the example and the severity of Philemon Holland. The few poor relics which survive are a sad proof of excellence wantonly outraged, and if to-day they are beyond the reach of worse mutilation, the harm already done is irreparable.   In Holland's time the books were still fresh upon their shelves, and it is small wonder that in a panegyric of Coventry, presently quoted, he praises the city of his adoption for

' maintaining a faire Librarie, not exampled (without offence to others be it spoken) in many cities of the Realme.'

So for twenty years he taught school, a simple usher, yet dignified high above his common office. In 1612 he received the freedom of the city, an honour not generally conferred upon those who impart the elements. Five years later a yet higher privilege was reserved for him. King James paid a visit to his loyal citizens of Coventry, and Philemon Holland, who had already addressed a pious dedication to his Majesty, was appointed to receive the King in an appropriately pompous oration. That he acquitted himself with glory is recorded in the Annals of Coventry, and assuredly he cut a very handsome figure. He was dressed ' in a suite of black satten,' says the chronicle, and was thus sumptuously arrayed at the cost of the city, which was so little niggardly that it spent upon its representative's apparel the round sum of £11, 1s. 11d. The oration is compact of the familiar commonplaces. The orator compliments his sovereign in the well-known terms of extravagant adulation. He welcomes the King to Coventry on his ' safe returne out of your Noble united Realme of Scotland,' and though the piece lacks its author's characteristic ingenuity, it afterwards made a brave show on the bookseller's list,[1] and at any rate Philemon dressed the part admirably ' in black satten.'

[1] ' A Learned, Elegant, and Religious Speech, delivered unto his most excellent Majestie, at his late being at Coventry.

This was an interlude of greatness, and Holland awaited promotion for twenty years. Indeed, when at last promotion came, it found him unwilling or incompetent, and surely it should not have tarried so long. The doctor, in truth, had been famous beyond the limits of Coventry for a quarter of a century, when the following order of the Council House was signed on 23rd January 1627-8 : ' It is this daie agreed that Mr. Doctor Holland shalbe head Schoolemaister of the free Grammar Schoole, of this Citie, so long as Mr. Maior and his brethren of this house please.' Doubtless Mr. Mayor and his brethren would have pleased until the end, but Holland himself found his new office irksome. The honour, which might have flattered the scholar twenty years earlier, came too late. He was well past seventy ; and however great was his ardour to frame scholars, he could not or would not govern the fortunes of a school. Ten months sufficed to weary him, and on 26th November ' Doctor Holland came to this House '—so say the Annals—' and desired to leave the place of head Schoolemaister of the ffree Grammar Schoole of this Citie, and wished that in convenient tyme this House would provide another.'

By Philemon Holland, Dr. of Physicke, the Right Honourable Recorder his Deputie for the Time. When as his Royall Majestie was graciously pleased to grant and command the erecting of a Military Garden therein : And sithens, to enlarge the aforesaid Cities Charter . . . London. Printed by John Dawson for John Bellaine, and are to be sold at his shop at the two Greyhounds in Cornehill, neere the Royall Exchange. 1622.'

Whether he resumed his ancient office of usher is unknown; it is certain that henceforth he fell upon poverty, and that the declining years of his life were spent in painful embarrassment.

Disabled by age from travelling abroad, he could neither practise physic nor attend his pupils. He had sustained, moreover, a great charge of children, and his straitened circumstances were but the unhappy consequence of his lifelong devotion to charity and sound learning. Coventry came to his aid—in 1632 —with an annual stipend of £3, 6s. 8d., not princely nor even sufficient, but at least a welcome recognition of his worth. Moreover, an appeal to his university was not unheard, and Henry Smyth, Master of Magdalen, and Vice-Chancellor, published in 1635 the strange licence which here follows: 'In consideration of the learning and worthy parts of Dr. Philemon Holland, and in consideration of his want of means to relieve him now in his old age, I have given leave that he should receive such charitable benevolence as the Master and Fellows in every College shall be pleased to bestow upon him.' The Vice-Chancellor was further persuaded to record that not only had Holland translated divers works, but that 'for sixty years he had kept good hospitality, *sit tota Coventria testis*,' and that therefore he was worthy an amiable consideration. One hopes that the appeal was generously answered, and that he who had done so much for learning received from the learned a generous recompense.

And so death found him, a grave and dignified

scholar, full of years, and honoured in an honourable poverty. In the year 1637 ' this eminent Translator,' to use Fuller's phrase, ' was translated to a better life.' Coventry proved her respect by a monument in Trinity Church, and it is to the city's eternal glory that she recognised a great man and worthy citizen in this simple maker of mighty folios. Nor was he ever behind in gratitude, and when—in 1609—he dedicated his *Ammianus Marcellinus* ' to the right worshipful the Mayor, and his Brethren, the Aldermen, etc., of the Citie of Coventry,' he composed such an eloquent tribute to his patrons as nobly repaid their respectful assistance. Therein he applauds the chief magistrate and grave senators of Coventry, first for their wise and moderate government of the place, ' which hath afforded unto him both quiet repose and meanes also to follow his studies ' ; and secondly, for the affectionate love they have always borne to good literature, a love ' testified by courteous entertainment of learned men ; by competent salaries allowed from time to time to such professors as have peaceably and with discreet carriage bestowed their talents among you ; by exhibitions given to poor scholars in the Universitie ; by erecting also of late, and maintaining a faire Librarie, not exampled (without offence to others be it spoken) in many cities of the Realme.' Such the city and such the citizen, well matched in appreciation and attainment, in generosity and gratitude.

A portrait published in a version of the *Cyropædia*

shows us what manner of man was the translator in his old age. White hair and beard frame an oval face, and a large ruff encircles the scholar's neck. Small eyes, a fat nose, a lofty brow, an air of gravity—these are the outward characteristics of Philemon Holland. A quill-pen, held in his right hand, is a proper symbol of his devotion to letters. And as his portrait shows him, so we know him to have ambled through life. Always a recluse, shut up with his pens, which became fabulous, and his books, which were all of serious import, he went seldom abroad ; and though his reception of James I. was a public triumph, his attempt to govern the Free School was, as we have seen, a dismal failure. In brief, he had no talent for affairs : his were the quieter virtues of kindliness and scholarship ; so long as his strength endured, he carried healing and hospitality to the poor ; and even when old age chained him to his bed, he preserved the vigour of his mind. His godson, after the gossiping fashion of the time, confided to Anthony à Wood a sketch of manifest truth. ' His intellectuals and his senses,' wrote Philemon Angel, ' remained perfect until the eighty-fourth year of his age ; and more especially his sight so good, that he never used spectacles in all his life ; he was always of a spare and temperate diet, and seldom drank between meals. And was always of a peaceful and quiet spirit ; and his life so innocent that he was never in all his days either plaintiff or defendant in any suit at law in any court (though he suffered sometimes by it). As a scholar he was a most reserved man, most indefatigable in his study, saying often, that there was no greater burden than idleness.' He drank not between meals, and never wore spectacles—these are the details, so well understood in the heyday of biography, which mark off a man from all his fellows. Indeed, Philemon Holland might well interest the biographers, for he seemed the characteristic pedant of his generation, not dry and crotchety as the pedant of to-day, but ripe and eloquent and quickened by a sturdy love of noble words. Assuredly he was a scholar dear to Aubrey and Anthony à Wood, such a one as for Fuller was a true worthy ; and since he makes no claim upon our interest save by his scholarship, he represents his age and his profession better than North, or any other of his contemporaries.

He was, moreover, a man of clear opinion and wise view. Being a brave and loyal subject of Elizabeth, he was, for all his seclusion, a sound patriot. 'Howsoever I have Faulted,' he writes in the Preface to his *Livy*, ' otherwise by oversight, set against it my affection and desire to do some good whiles I live to my sweet native country.' If he faulted, he faulted generously, and he needs no forgiveness at our hands ; and with these words he strikes the note of love for his country which was struck as well by the captains as by the poets of his time, and which has found its sincerest and most glorious echo in these our own years. Again, he displayed a cunning ingenuity in unravelling the difficulties of dogma, then as now a delicate office. Science and theology were already at war, and though Holland, being a physician and a classic, might have been expected to flout orthodoxy, he deferred in all respect to the authority of divines.

He prefaced his translation of Pliny, the most popular of his works, with an apology for his author's paganism. There is one scruple, he confesses, which troubles him not a little. He fears that Pliny, attributing so much to Nature, may seem to derogate from God, to the heathen ἄγνωστος; and since he would neither corrupt men's manners, nor prejudice the Christian faith, he conferred with sundry divines, who strengthened him in his purpose. Wherefore he resolved to finish the work which he had begun, that he might not ' defraud the world of so rich a gem for one small blemish appearing therein.' Such was his view of theology, a cautious mixture of common-sense and modesty. Nor does it differ widely from the prudence of to-day, which would claim a respect for both the houses. No doubt he himself was ranged on the side of science; but with a wise forethought he saw the danger of disturbing belief, and it was only after taking counsel with eminent divines that he deemed himself justified in dressing Pliny in an English habit.

Before all things he was, in Fuller's phrase, ' the Translator Generall in his age.' North and Adlington are each the heroes of one book. Philemon Holland is a legend : as it were, translation made concrete. He won as great a fame by his splendid versions as have other men by their own invented fables. Epigrams were composed upon his fair achievements; his prowess was celebrated in adulatory verses, and the single pen wherewith he indited a whole work has grown into a sort of fairy-tale. Moreover, the fairy-tale, like every piece of folklore, has its variants. The translator's son informs the world that *Plutarch's Morals* all fell upon paper from one quill, while Aubrey prefers to believe that it was the *Livy* which was thus honoured. Whichever be the truth, the story is found in all the books of anecdotes, further embellished with a quatrain, more curious than accomplished. Thus it runs:

> ' This booke I wrote with one poore Pen
>   Made of a grey Goose Quill:
> A Pen I found it, us'd before,
>   A Pen I leave it still.'

The pen's destiny also is variously described. Aubrey implies that it was presented to the Lady Harington, who ' embellished it with silver, and kept it among her rare κειμήλια '; while Henry Holland declares that it was ' begged by an ancient gentlewoman (mother of a noble Countesse yet living) who garnished it in silver, and kept it as a monument.' Fuller, on the other hand, gives a variant of his own, precise and circumstantial as the others. ' This Monumental Pen,' writes the author of the *Worthies*, ' he solemnly kept and showed to my reverend Tutor, Doctor Samuel Ward. It seems he leaned very lightly on the Neb thereof, though weightily enough, in another sense, performing not slightly, but solidly what he undertook.' If he kept it, you may be sure that he kept it ' solemnly,' and you smile at the moral tag which he as well deserved as Fuller could ill have avoided. Indeed, the pen was something better than a mere piece of folklore; in Holland's hand it was a cunning instrument. Once upon a time there existed in the library of Coventry School a manuscript of Euclid's *Harmonics* in the Doctor's own handwriting. And so beautiful was it, says rumour, that Baskerville, the prince of printers, imitated it for his own peerless Greek fount. To-day it is impossible to confirm the rumour or to admire the caligraphy. For the only trace of Euclid's *Harmonics* is an entry in an ancient catalogue.

' The Translator Generall in his age' ! And thus he lays claim to the genuine spirit of Elizabeth's reign. Thus he played his part in the re-birth of England. He, too, no less than Drake and Raleigh, was a gentleman adventurer; he, too, set sail to cross unknown seas to discover mysterious continents. A literary captain, a scholarly pirate, he plundered strange realms, and never did he return from a voyage without a costly spoil. In his enterprise were displayed the recklessness and curiosity of a valiant generation, nor is it least characteristic of him that he regarded his conquests and the conquests of others as new-made citizens or the prisoners of peace. Livy, said he, has twice been ' enfranchised ' by the French; and, when he offers the proper meed of praise to Sir Thomas

North, ' Plutarch,' he exclaims, ' has newly come to London.' Truly it was no mean task—the task of translation—to which he set himself ; and it needed no apology. Yet he spoke up for it with a wise enthusiasm in his preface to *Pliny*. ' All men,' said he, ' cannot *aut facere scribenda, aut scribere legenda.*' It was not for him to perform mighty deeds, nor to record the deeds of living heroes. So there remained only to give another dress to the works of others, and this he did with an eloquence and a spirit which no man has ever surpassed.

Though his own age accepted the gift he gave, there were yet cavillers, and Fuller was but a mouthpiece when he declared that ' some decry all Translators as Interlopers, spoiling the Trade of Learning, which should be driven among scholars alone.' Fuller himself found a ready answer: ' This opinion,' said he, ' resents too much of envy, that such gentlemen who cannot repair to the Fountain, should be debarred access to the Stream.' So it was that Montaigne, who had no Greek, gave ' prick and praise unto Jacques Amyot ' ; for the wisdom of Plutarch was Montaigne's daily sustenance, and it was only in his compatriot's version that he could read the *Parallel Lives*. And nobly he justified his own lack of knowledge. ' We that are in the number of the ignorant,' wrote he, in a sort of apology, ' had been utterly confounded, had not his book raised us from the dust of ignorance. . . . Even Ladies are therewith able to confront Masters of Arts. It is our breviary.' Thus North's *Plutarch* was a

breviary unto Shakespeare; thus Holland's masterpieces were breviaries unto many generations, and
they have descended to us rich treasuries of sound
English and wise interpretation.

For Holland possessed all the rare and various gifts
of the translator. To him no language was a mystery;
he had a marvellous skill in Latin and Greek, while
Italian and French were as familiar as his own tongue.
So, while North could only rely upon Amyot, Holland
could supplement a loyal study of the original with
the borrowed wisdom of foreign commentators.
Wherefore, with a certain irony, he thus forestalls his
critics. 'Have I varied in some places from the
French or Italian?' he asks; 'censured I look to
be, and haply reproved: but like as Alcibiades said to
one, πάταξον οὖν καὶ ἄκουσον, *i.e. strike hardly (Euri-
biades) so you hear me speake*: even so say I; Find
fault and spare not; but with al, read the original
better before you give sentence.' None knew more
clearly than he that few of his critics could read the
original either better or worse, and he was right to
entrench himself behind the original against the
attacks of French or Italian. And he had a still higher
qualification for his task than a knowledge of Greek and
Latin. He was a master of robust and varied English.
Like the best of his contemporaries, he ignored the
commonness of speech. No man ever spoke as
Holland wrote. Even when he is most familiar his
periods pass like a pageant or march as armed men.

Well as he knew his original, majestically as he

handled his own tongue, he made no attempt to fit the one to the other. His was not the ingenuity which would echo a foreign phrase in native English, and tried by the strictest standard of perfect consonance his translations fail of their effect. He did not put Livy and Suetonius in an appropriate dress ; rather he took Suetonius or Livy, and tricked them out in the garb of his own time. So that he gives us not an accurate reflection of the original, but a quick vision of Livy or Suetonius as they might have been had they been born in Elizabethan England. His commentary upon his own style is an astounding piece of criticism, and at the same time an intimate revelation of seventeenth-century prose. 'According to this purpose and intent of mine I frame my pen,' so he writes, ' not to any effective phrase, but to a mean and popular style, wherein, if I have called again into use some old words, let it be attributed to the love of my country-language : if the sentence be not so concise, couched and knit together as the original, loth I was to be obscure and darke : have I not Englished every phrase aptly ? each nation hath several manners, yea, and terms appropriate by themselves.'

There in a nutshell is Holland's theory of style and translation. He believed (what man ever knew himself ?) that he was writing in a mean and popular style. And so ill-grounded was his belief, that you have but to compare his magnificent periods with the pamphlets of his time to realise the splendour of his manner, the effectiveness of his phrase. His love of old words, on the other hand, is apparent and honourable. Old they were then ! How much older and more dignified do they appear to-day ! And how severe a reproach is this one phrase of an ancient master to those shallow, ignorant critics—loquacious in our midst—who assert that no word is admissible in written English which they themselves do not employ in their ill-done, ungrateful task of journey-work ! When, again, Holland confesses his prose less concise than the original, he puts his finger upon a true quality, whether vice or virtue. Never is he ' knit together ' with the precision of his Latin or his Greek. He embroiders his author with a freedom and liveliness which are delightful and (maybe) in-apposite. When he is at work, Pliny and Plutarch are poured into the same mould, and, different as is the prime material, they both take on the admirable shape of their doughty translator. Thus it is that Holland based his practice upon his theory ; and whether you approve the reasoning or not, you must needs acknowledge the splendour of the result.

In brief, he translated well, because he wrote admirably. His style was so much a part of himself, that he sacrificed in his versions the subtlety of imitation. His prefaces are masterpieces of good judgment and fine English. Here, for instance, is a sketch of Padua, the birthplace of Livy, fashioned with all his plenitude of phrase and sound : ' My purpose is not here to enter into a large field and rhetorical discourse of his praises in regard of any

gifts of fortune wherewith he was plentifully enriched :
namely the place of his nativity, a city more ancient
by 400 years than Rome, flourishing in martial
puissance, able to set out and maintain 100,000
fighting men for the wars ; in stately port at home ;
having a nobility of 400 in number ; in gorgeous
and costly buildings ; in traffic and frequent affluence
of merchants thither ; as also, that Venice was a
Colony deducted and drawn from thence ; and which
is not the least, how at this day the famous University there, affordeth excellent professors in all
kind of learning.'

In such terms he set forth the excellences of Padua,
and it is not surprising that his translations are
brilliant with purple patches. Turn, for instance, to
Hannibal's passage of the Alps, and you will find, not
Livy, but a masterpiece of English. Or, if you be
so minded, glance at Plutarch's essays *On Curiosity*
or *On Superstition*, and you will delight, not in the
cold phrase of Plutarch, but in a piece of learned
English, which seems the near forerunner of Burton's
own *Anatomy*. And thus we arrive at the best
measure of his talent ; with leisure and opportunity
he might have been a Montaigne or a Burton. He,
too, might have woven the woof of research into the
web of fancy. He, too, might have lived in a tower,
or a college room, and eked out a sluggish imagination
with apt quotings from recondite or forgotten authors.
All the materials of an original masterpiece are there
—style, erudition, curiosity ; but he preferred the

pedestrian office of the translator, and he succeeded
so well that in his own lifetime he conquered an easy
fame, and that immortality, the shyest of the demons,
has not remained deaf to his call.

Thomas Fuller, who occupied himself most worthily
with Philemon Holland, declared that 'the Books
alone of his Turning into English will make a Country
Gentleman a competent library for Historians.'
Nowadays it is something of a disgrace in a book
to be indispensable to a gentleman's library; in
Fuller's day, culture was not yet a matter of ostentation, and the compliment was sincerely paid. The
works of Holland might then, and still may, fulfil a
noble bookcase. His originals, as they were admirably turned, were wisely chosen. First came the
monumental *Livy*—in 1600—dedicated in terms of
courtly adulation to Queen Elizabeth. He modestly
describes his performance as the firstfruits of a few
years' 'study,' and he begs the most gracious Lady
to accept them 'for the benefit enjoyed of life and
liberty.' Thereafter he acclaims 'the incomparable
perfections resplendent in your Royal person : the
wonder of the World.' No man had more securely
the gift of Euphuistic English, and his dedications
are one and all noble exercises in the art of adulation.
Within a single year came the vast folio, *Pliny*, whose
bulk alone is an eloquent tribute to the author's energy
and patience. Inscribed in the general phrases of
flattery to the Right Honourable Sir Robert Cecil,
it is prefaced by admirable discourses upon theology

and the art of translation. The author precisely
chimed with the curious spirit of the age, and it is
no wonder that this one of Holland's works was the
most popular.

Then followed a third vast folio, the *Morals of
Plutarch*, addressed in a piece of amazing prose to
James I., whom he describes as his 'dear Lord and
dread Sovereign.' The opening is so fantastic and
withal so characteristic of the writer, that it stands
here as a specimen of Jacobean extravagance: ' In
this general joy of affectionate and loyal subjects,'
thus begins the learned doctor, ' testified by their
frequent confluence from all parts, longing for
nothing so much as the full fruition of that beautiful
Star, which lately upon the shutting in of evening
with us after our long Summer's day, immediately
by his radiant beams maintained still a twilight from
the North, and within some few hours appeared
bright shining above our Horizon, suffering neither
the dark night and confused CHAOS OF ANARCHY to
overspread and subvert, nor the turbulent tempests
and bloody broils of factious sidings to trouble and
subvert our state : I also for my part could not stay
behind, but in testimony of semblable love and
allegiance shew myself; and withal, most humbly
present unto your Highness this PHILOSOPHY OF
PLUTARCH.' In such terms did conscious merit
prostrate itself before the throne of royalty, when
James I. was king ; and that such extravagance is not
permitted to-day is due not to a lofty regard for the

literal truth, but to a pitiful incapacity to frame so grandiose a period.

Holland never fell below the proper level of eloquence, and his *Suetonius* (1606), of which more presently, was dedicated with a rare propriety to the Lady Harington.   Nor even now have we completed the tale of his works.   Such trifles as *Ammianus Marcellinus*, Camden's *Britannia*, and the *Cyropædia* were also Englished after his imperial manner.   And we must not forget his single incursion into what for him must have appeared light literature.   Once even he condescended to translate that strange compost of medicine and superstition, *Regimen Sanitatis Salerni*, or, in his own phrase, ' the Schoole of Salernes Regiment of Health, containing most learned and judicious directions, and instructions, for the Preservation, Guide and Government of Man's Life.'   The book's simple rules, which you may be sure the old scholar followed himself, are translated into a simple doggerel. Here is a sample :

' Shun Busie cares, rash angers, which displease,
  Little supping, little drink, do cause great ease.'

It is poor stuff, and the Doctor too willingly endorses the mediæval nostrums.   But this was the mere diversion of a serious mind, and does not lighten by an ounce the writer's grave reputation.   He still remains the first translator of his age ; and if the Bible is the Shakespeare of translation, then Philemon Holland is the ingenious Ben Jonson of a splendid craft.

II

The *Suetonius* is the finest fruit of his toil, and the reason is not far to seek. Holland did not so much translate as compose an original work upon a chosen theme, and Suetonius was a theme which appealed to his profoundest sympathy. Indeed, the author of the *Twelve Cæsars* was quickened by the selfsame spirit which quickened the biographers of Holland's own time. His genius was a genius of anecdotage, and nothing was essential to his purpose save such facts as appear trivial to the pedantic historian. We may ransack antiquity in vain to find his equal, but we shall easily recognise in the *Athenæ Oxoniensis* the love of scandal and intimate infirmities, which gives a very present life and energy to his immortal book. As we read the *Twelve Cæsars*, we forget that they were emperors; we are persuaded at every line that they were men, and, maybe, monsters of iniquity. For to Suetonius the greatest hero was made of common (or of uncommon) clay; or at any rate he assumed the heroism as familiar, and explained with infinite pleasure and circumstance that emperors are memorable for intrigue, infirmity, and crime. He was possessed, in truth, with the indefatigable curiosity of the modern journalist; nothing was sacred from his prying eye; and he gathered in his facts with the reporter's own superficial love of facts for their own sake, and without the lightest regard to their social or historical import.

And it is not for us to resent the shamelessness of his method. Many a vice is converted by the centuries into a shining virtue, and Paul Pry, an odious figure to-day, may appear to-morrow the fearless benefactor of posterity. Time has the trick of hallowing gossip, and there is no detail so trivial and so impertinent but it appears interesting, nay sacred, in the biography of a man long since dead. Thus we are constrained to admire in the past that which we deprecate in the present; and if the present eavesdroppers make conquest of immortality, our remote descendants will no doubt welcome their indiscretions as an invaluable commentary, though they too will deplore most strenuously their own contemporary reporters.

And there is a perfect logic in the apparent contradiction. We lose the habit of censoriousness with the years; we palliate in the dead those vices and follies for which we would cut a living man. Moreover, the law of libel looks not beyond the grave; and, though at the moment of writing his book Suetonius deserved the pillory, he has won at last an admiring appreciation. It is his conspicuous merit that he drew a series of individual portraits; there is not one of his emperors who is not separated from his fellows rather by the peculiar frailties of his temper than by any public achievement. 'Art,' says M. Marcel Schwob in a luminous essay on biography, 'is opposed to general ideas; it desires only the unique'; or in other words, *il ne classe pas, il déclasse*. Conquest does not set a peculiar stamp upon a man; intellect

defies the resources of skilful portraiture. And these
truths were ever present to Suetonius, who selected
for his illustration the facts which the more princely
historian rejects with scorn. For instance, his
admiration of Augustus is generous and sincere; he
applauds his administration, and gives full credit to
his sense of justice; and, having finished with his
public life, he bids us pay a visit, as it were, to the
man himself, revealing to us not only his thought,
but the ordering of his daily life.

All thought of the politician, the prig, the literary
patron, vanishes in an instant. No longer are we contemplating the hero who found Rome brick and left it
marble; but a Roman citizen of the first century,
whose trivial tastes and fancies seem worth recording.
Thus (we are told) he slept always on a low bed, and
wore no apparel that was not of housewife's cloth,
spun at home by the women of his family. In the
winter he clad himself stoutly against the cold,
putting on as many as four coats, and a waistcoat of
wool; and he had so great a fear of the sun, that even
at home he always kept upon his head a broad-
brimmed hat. Careless of elegance as he was in his
dress, he chose his shoes with much circumspection,
underlaying the soles that he might appear taller than
he was. At table, though he ate little meat, he was a
gross feeder—bread, small fishes, cheese, and green
figs being most to his taste. And it was not his
custom to wait for the meal-time; rather he would
eat whenever his stomach called for food. A small

drinker, he delighted most in Rhætian wine; and, like Holland himself, he seldom drank between meals. He preferred a sop of bread soaked in cold water, or a piece of cucumber, or a young lettuce-head, or some new-gathered apple, sharp and tart.

His appearance, if not precisely handsome, was surely distinguished. 'He had a pair of clear and shining eyes,' says Suetonius in the language of Holland; 'wherein also (as he would have made men believe) was seated a kind of divine vigour: and he joyed much, if a man looking wistly upon him held down his face, as if it were against the brightness of the sun. But in his old age he saw not very well with his left eye. His teeth grew thin in his head, and the same were small and ragged. The hair of his head was somewhat curled and turning downward, and withal of a light yellow colour. His eyebrows met together; his ears were of a mean bigness; his nose, both in the upper part, bearing out round, and also beneath somewhat with the longest. Of colour and complexion, he was between a brown and a fair white. His stature but short.' There he is painted, with all his imperfections, by the hand of a faithful artist, who knew not how to conceal the truth. It may be something of a shock to hear that the divine Augustus saw not well with his left eye, that his teeth were small and ragged; yet it is to his greater glory that he should be drawn as a man, than represented in the guise of a graven image with a marble intelligence and a mechanical gesture.

The portraiture of Suetonius does not cease here:
he heightens the effect by a hundred other intimate
touches. For instance, the celestial bear (says he)
was marked upon the Emperor's breast, and he was
not very sound in his left hucklebone. Moreover,
the forefinger of his right hand was so weak, that
at times he could scarcely write, even with the help
of a finger-stall of horn. And no less curious is
Suetonius when he records the qualities of the
Augustan mind. He saves from oblivion a dozen
tricks of style and speech, which seem to bring the
man even more vividly before us than his limping leg
or failing speech. Thus, when the Emperor pointed
to those who would never pay their debts, he was
wont to say : ' They will pay at the Greek Calends.'
For Augustus, too, loved his little joke. And did
he wish to express the speed of something over-
hastily accomplished : ' It was quicker done,' he
would exclaim, ' than asparagus is boiled.' Again,
he would substitute *baceolus* for *stultus*, *vacerrosus*
for *cerritus* ; and while others employed the phrase
male se habere, he by a euphemism would say *vapide*.
Trivial differences are they all, but it is by trivial
differences of speech that the individual is recognised,
and it is to great purpose that Suetonius has preserved these subtle traits which the more earnest
chronicler proudly despises.

Augustus, amid the manifold duties of an empire,
found time also for the cultivation of literature,
and his views concerning the Latin tongue, if not

always wise, were stoutly maintained. He preferred prepositions to case-endings, we are told, and for the sake of clarity he would repeat his conjunctions very often. So he forestalled the development of language, and by an act of prophecy compelled Latin to initiate a practice which all the modern tongues have followed. Moreover, being a practical politician, rather than an artist in speech, he detested ' the stinking savours of dark and obscure words.' Strange expressions, either new or old, were distasteful to him ; and it was one of his pastimes to gibe his friend Mæcenas, that prince of dilettanti, for his *myrobrechos cincinnos*, and even to compose parodies of his conceited style. Little concern have these entertaining details with politics, but they are the very elements of character ; and so it is that while Pericles is still a splendid abstraction, the Roman emperor appears, after nineteen centuries, an intelligent and wayward human being.

Augustus is treated no better than the rest, and there is not one of the twelve who does not masquerade before us in dressing-gown and slippers. And what a magnificent material did Suetonius choose whereon to exercise his genius ! It was a period of colossal enterprise and savage lust. The old austerity was dead, and the modern world had not yet learned the lesson of restraint. The vastest empire, save one, which a triumphant energy has ever fashioned, had succeeded to the policy of small states. A hundred wealthy colonies poured into Rome a willing tribute. Military

glory was aided by an unparalleled talent for administration.   As no land seemed too distant to subdue,
so none was too wild for civilisation.   The progress
of victorious armies was marked by the longer lasting
achievements of peaceful ingenuity.   The modern
general lays his railroad as he goes; the Roman
warrior, inspired by a similar wisdom, threaded the
desert by an imperishable highway.   Wherever a river
was to be spanned, he threw across it a bridge which
has defied the shocks of storm and tide.   He carried
the gift of pure water from hill to hill on the giant
aqueducts, which attest to-day the Roman omnipotence.   The known world was but a network of
imperial roads, and an army might march without
impediment from York to Jerusalem.   Meanwhile
the wealth of tribute gave the emperors means and
opportunity to indulge their vices and pamper their
appetites.   And surely they rose one and all to the
height of the occasion.   The masterpiece of Suetonius
might bear for a sub-title, 'The Grosser Passions
delineated'; for, in truth, there is no passion, no
vice, that does not find itself personified in one or
other of the Twelve.   To us it appears remarkable
that so much wickedness should be concentrated in
so few monarchs.   But lack of habit accounts for
much, and maybe it is natural that the Romans, for
centuries accustomed to the republican ideal, should
interpret callously the advantages of a tyranny.   Here
were a set of men, trained to believe in equality,
suddenly raised to the summit of divine honours.

And with the aid of that monstrous corruption which is the birthright of Cosmopolis, they grappled vices, as their generals annexed provinces.

So Suetonius spared no single one of the emperors. He lays a blasphemous hand on the great Julius himself. If he does not see in this splendid hero the greatest general, the wisest statesman, the finest historian that the world has known, he yet esteems his virtues, and does all the justice of which his unemotional temper is capable to Cæsar's illustrious qualities. But the chance of scandal cannot be resisted, and Suetonius omits not even the scurrilous verses of the time. However, it is with Tiberius that the biographer reaches his highest talent. The description of the voluptuary's *sæva ac lenta natura* ($\pi\eta\lambda\grave{o}\nu$ $a\H{\iota}\mu a\tau\iota$ $\pi\epsilon\phi\upsilon\rho\mu\acute{e}\nu o\nu$) is nothing less than stupendous. The emperor who appointed a new officer of state, *a voluptatibus*, easily surpassed the Marquis de Sade in ingenious cruelty. Whether the sojourn at Capri be faithfully described or not, it remains an insurpassable record of wild insanity, until at last the emperor ceases to be human. Tacitus himself had no love of Tiberius, yet his loftier portrait is also more easily convincing. The man of weak will and clear perception is a psychological possibility; and while in the page of Tacitus Tiberius is a figure of austere tragedy, in Suetonius he is a strange bogey of disgust, an extravagant epitome of the vices.

So the vain and brutish Caligula, who believed that in gathering shells he was wresting the spoils of

Ocean, who designed a horse for the consulship, and who could scarcely dine without the excitement of carnage, is followed by the stealthy Claudius, who, despite his erudition and tact of government, loved nothing so much as the contemplation of dying gladiators, and who died in a welter of blood. Then comes Nero, fit subject for Suetonius, professional poisoner and amateur of the arts, who delighted in gold fish-nets and silver-shod mules, who sang his own songs ' with a small and rusty voice,' and who really believed that with his death there died an artist. So Galba's misery is matched by the gluttony of Vitellius, and even the wisdom of Vespasian is balanced by a hungry covetousness. Titus escapes easily with the semblance of too fine a virtue ; and, since Suetonius is resolved that the emperors shall be remembered by vice or triviality, Domitian is sent down to posterity as the fly-catcher.

Meanwhile, under Claudius and Nero, the mighty empire grows in strength, and Suetonius does not note it. In his page the drum is not beaten, the trumpet blares not. When he might present to the world a great historical drama, he prefers to play the tragicomedy of cruelty and lust. The triumph of engineers is as little to him as the courage of armies. True, he records without sequence or statistics the mere events of each reign ; but his curiosity is for passion, not statesmanship, and he is only himself when, forgetting the march of empire, he sits him down to enumerate the follies and vices of his heroes. Tacitus, of course, invites a comparison, and in these two—Suetonius and Tacitus—are illustrated the opposing methods of history. The author of the *Annals*, that he may set forth his country's omnipotence with a proper reverence for truth, is deaf to the frail, delightful voice of hearsay. Though he has no ardent love for his empire, yet he understands its strength and its weakness, and he displays its achievements with an absolute regard for the claims of proportion. A rarely wise man, he knows most things, and what he does not know he easily divines. And as you read him, you recognise that he is not only relating the story of one period : he is opening a treasure-house of political sagacity, from which the statesmen of all ages may enrich themselves. More than this, he is a master of style and irony ; with four words he can sketch a situation or enunciate a policy. He who wrote, ' They make a solitude and call it peace,' has nothing to learn in the art of expression, and it is the good fortune of the world that the most puissant writer of all time should have elected to write the history of the most puissant age.

And Tacitus merely affords a general confirmation of Suetonius. His material is so far loftier, that they rarely meet upon a common ground. The one strikes the stars, the other crawls upon the earth. For the very reason that they live and work at different levels, the one supplements the narrative of the other. To doubt the infinite superiority of Tacitus would be to laugh at the truth. One might as well prefer a

common memoir to the Hamlet of Shakespeare.
Tacitus is a philosopher, with a godlike understanding,
who compels conviction while he dazzles the judgment.   He lectures you in the staid and noble dialect
of omniscience, and to miss a phrase is to confuse the
argument.   Suetonius, on the other hand, has no
ambition of politics or philosophy.   He is but a
shambling old gossip, who sits over the fire and enter-
tains the first comer with the stories his grandfather
told him when he was a boy.   (*Sed avum meum nar-
rantem puer audiebam*, says he, in the phrase of the
true gossip.)   For our guidance he provides nothing,
for our amusement much: and it is small wonder
that while we render all our respect to Tacitus, we
turn more often to Suetonius, that he may beguile our
leisure.   We cannot always rest at the cold and
splendid altitudes of thought; it is seldom that we
cannot enjoy a crack across the hearth with a master
of scandal.

The question arises: Was Suetonius moved by
malice or by love of truth in the selection of his
material?   And the answer comes that he is never
convicted of the worse motive.   At the same time, it
is evident that he had a natural love for whatever was
curious and abnormal.   Let us suppose that all facts
are of equal value, and we must confess that the historian's interest is mirrored in his choice.   So
Suetonius found food for reflection in the decaying
morality of the empire, and he reported that which
he heard and knew with a perfect impartiality.   He

held a brief for nobody; and if he ever felt the prick of political animosity, he is careful to conceal the wound. Averse from flattery, he closed his history at the death of Domitian; and there is not a single word in his book that impugns his honesty.

He had, on the contrary, a passion for accuracy, and while he suppresses his judgment he parades his facts. As a writer he is clear rather than distinguished, and his single preoccupation is to explain his meaning with a just simplicity. Where Latin fails him, he falls back upon Greek; and as he was a master of both tongues, he could at will double his vocabulary. Of the man we know little enough, and that little wholly to his credit. By profession an advocate and writer, he discharged the office of secretary to Hadrian, and left behind him one immortal work. His peace was disturbed by an unhappy marriage, on which account he demanded, with faulty logic, the *jus trium liberorum*. These scanty rumours, with two passages in Pliny, complete our poor information. And Pliny's affection may be cited for the confusion of those who are persuaded by Suetonius's outspokenness to belittle his character and flout his sincerity. 'He was my comrade,' says Pliny, 'and the companion of my school-days.' Thereafter, in a letter to Trajan, Pliny declares him the most upright, honest, and learned man that ever he had met, and that he loved him the more the more closely he came to know him. So once again we must separate the man from his work, and feel no surprise that a gentle scholar should have recorded faithfully and without shrinking the vices and frailties of the Roman emperors.

Such the writer and such the book which Philemon Holland elected to translate in the plenitude of his talent. As has been said, he rather transformed than translated it; for, however akin to his own curiosity was the matter of this amazing book, the curt, crabbed, even brutal style of Suetonius was wholly alien from Holland's elaborate eloquence. For Holland (as we have seen) loved to adorn a simple statement, to turn it about in a dozen different attitudes, to trick it out with the rich frippery of Elizabethan English, and he did not scruple to embellish and increase his author beyond recognition. In mere bulk his version must surely double the original. Here is one instance of many : ' Jacta est alea,' exclaimed Cæsar as he crossed the Rubicon. 'The dice be thrown,' translates Holland ; ' I have set up my rest ; come what will of it.' It is magnificent, but it is not the polite echo of the accurate translator. However, Holland's object was to employ all the resources of his own splendid prose ; and he employs them to such admirable purpose, that you may read his *Suetonius* in perfect forgetfulness of the Latin, and in perfect satisfaction with the rise and fall of the majestic periods. The masterpiece is dedicated ' to the Right Honorable and Vertuous Ladie, the Ladie Harington,' and the inscription proves that Holland had no ill thought of the book's outspokenness, though he does presently declare that Suetonius penned the lives of princes

eadem libertate qua ipsi vixerunt. ' If haply in prose-
cuting this point,' says he, ' he hath recorded aught
that may be offensive to chaste and modest minds, ye
shall do well to glance over with your eye such places
lightly, as I with my pen touched unwillingly.'
Furthermore, he tells us that the work was composed
during the last pestilence in Coventry, ' for being
altogether restrained then from free practise of my
profession abroad, and no less impatient of idlenesse
at home, I could not readily think of a better course
to spend that vacation, than in an argument having
a reference to mine old grammatical Muses, and
according, in some sort, with my later studies in
Physic.'

He composed the work for ' the benefit of young
scholars,' and truly the pathology of the Cæsars
might most properly call forth his medical knowledge.
Moreover, he equipped his version with a set of notes
which, if often inapposite, are always erudite with
the quaint erudition of his century.   Alone of the
Elizabethan translators, he can refer with confidence
to original authorities, and sprinkle his pages with
quotations from Josephus and Aulus Gellius.   Nor
does he neglect such more modern writers as Beroaldus
and Casaubon, and he never lets slip a vague chance of
discoursing upon his own art of medicine.   In brief,
author and theme are perfectly matched, and it is
a genuine pleasure to read Suetonius's masterpiece
of familiar scandal echoed thus pompously in the
sounding prose of Philemon Holland.

MONTAIGNE

WHEN Montaigne was at home he betook himself somewhat the oftener to his library.
Thence he could survey at a glance his whole household—his garden, his base-court, and his yard. There
he could read or write as his fancy led him ; or, better
still, he could dream undisturbed. Now, he would
take a book from its shelf, and find in the wisdom of
the ancients a parallel to some misadventure of to-day.
Now, from the wealth of his own experience he would
illustrate the discoveries of Seneca or Plutarch. For
such a quest, no room could be better fitted than
Montaigne's famous library, which played the same
part in his life as the senate or battlefield plays in the
lives of more active citizens. Its very quietude en-
sured the 'idleness and liberty' which were the
essentials of Montaigne's happiness. There he was
secure from the interruption of family or friends ;
there he was both 'at home and to himself.' It was,
he tells us, the third storey of a tower, with no flat
side save that which served for his table and chair,
and he could see at a single glance all his books ranged
about him. Though it was but sixteen paces across,
it had on three sides a rich and free prospect ; and

thus it lacked nothing that might solace and inspire
the poet. Here, then, was Montaigne's throne;
here he was master of both will and mind; here he
achieved the triumphs which have given him a serene
immortality. Nor was Montaigne himself unmindful
of the part which his library was to play in his career.
When, in 1571, he dedicated the balance of his years
to solitude, he placed in the *cabinet assez poly*, adjoin-
ing his library, a solemn inscription, which may still
be deciphered. Therein he declares that, wearied
with the service of the court, and with public employ,
he has retired *in doctarum virginum sinu*, and that he
consecrates his modest house and pleasant retreat to
freedom, tranquillity, and ease.

Moreover, that he might still remember the vanity
of human knowledge, the fleeting insignificance of
our human life, he inscribed upon the beams of his
library such maxims as were a guide unto his footsteps. Still legible, these are the texts upon which
his philosophy is founded, and they afford a clear
proof that his work was more clearly designed than
he would have us believe. *Quid superbis, terra et
cinis?* is the question asked on one side. On another
the timely warning: *Ne plus sapias quam necesse est,
ne obstupescas.* Here is summed up in five words the
gospel of his incertitude: οὐ καταλαμβάνω—ἐπέχω
—οὐδὲν ὁπίζω. There you may discern the confession
of his sympathy: *Homo sum; humani a me nihil
alienum puto.* The choice of these maxims is not
more remarkable than that any maxims were chosen

at all. It was, so to say, a solemn consecration, a plain admission that his library was for Montaigne a scene of labour and enterprise. We picture Julius upon the battlefield of Gaul, Demosthenes in the council denouncing the Macedonian. Montaigne comes to our imagination seated in his turret, now idly turning the leaves of a book, now looking over the wide and fruitful plain, or perhaps surprising an idle serving-man in his base-court. Yet none worked harder than did Montaigne in his twenty years of seclusion, and though the library measured but sixteen paces, it was the field of many a hard-fought fight against ignorance and pedantry.

Of the duties which Montaigne owed to the world he had little to say. Those details of success or failure, which make up the life of the most of men, and which are the staple of the biographical dictionary, were to him of no account. He lived in thought, not in act, and his simple tale is soon told. He was born between eleven o'clock and noon on the last day of February 1533. His father, Pierre Eyquem de Montaigne, a wealthy gentleman, had followed the wars in Italy. His mother, Antoinette de Louppes, was descended from a family of Spanish Jews. With an amiable vanity Montaigne was wont to boast of his noble origin ; but his ancestors were not always lords of the soil, and his great-grandfather had amassed a comfortable fortune by the sale of wine and salt-fish in Bordeaux. However, there lay upon his father no taint of commerce, and Montaigne was educated as became his quality. After some years spent in the College of Guienne, where he played a part in the tragedies of those once renowned poets, Muret and Buchanan, he was put to the study of the law, and at twenty-one he was appointed Conseiller à la Cour des Aides de Périgueux, a post which he held against the grain for fifteen years.

No man was ever less fitted for the practice of the law. His humanity was always stronger than his sense of justice, and the persecution of the Huguenots was a wanton outrage upon the freedom and tolerance which were the passions of his life. However, he made the best of an ungrateful profession, and lightened its weariness by frequent appearances at Court, for the pomp and splendour of which he cherished a secret love, and where, doubtless, he felt those promptings of ambition which he was always eager to suppress. Ever a devoted champion of the throne, he lived upon terms of friendship with more than one king. He presented his *Essays* to Henri III., who took a keen pleasure in their perusal. ' Sire,' said Montaigne, ' then I, too, must please you, since my book contains nothing else than a relation of my life and actions.' Henri IV. he served with the greater willingness, because in so doing he flattered both his reason and his loyalty. Once, indeed, the King of Navarre paid him a visit at his château. The monarch condescended so far as to ask neither ' essai ' nor ' couvert ' ; he slept in Montaigne's own bed ; and, before he left, he hunted a deer in his host's forest. What a meeting must have been theirs! For generosity of thought and hatred of fanaticism they had not their equals in Europe; and we may be sure that, when they wearied of condemning persecution, they exchanged *maintes plaisantes histoires*, for they were as well matched in gallantry as in wisdom. Meanwhile Montaigne had married, at two years below the age recommended by his master Aristotle, Françoise de la Chassaigne. It was a match of prudence, and, though Montaigne had little love of matrimony, he submitted to it, because it agreed with his sense of duty and custom. He regarded it unto the end with the same sad conscientiousness wherewith he regarded the Cour des Aides at Périgueux. 'Had I been left to choose,' said he, 'I would not have married wisdom herself.'

The one important event of his public career was his election, in 1581, as Mayor of Bordeaux. The office disturbed his idleness, yet flattered his vanity. He was proud to think that he had discharged a duty, whose only reward was the honour which it conferred; and he was the more pleased that, as he succeeded a Marshal of France, so it was to another Marshal that, after serving a double term, he resigned the chair. Keeping the example of the ancient Romans always before his eyes, he administered the affairs of his city with justice and moderation, and yet did not escape censure. Once, when the plague was raging in Bordeaux, he suggested that he should not come into the town, 'seeing the bad state it is in,

especially for persons coming, as I do, out of good
air.' For this simple piece of prudence Montaigne
has been saddled, by those who loved not his opinions,
with charges of cowardice and neglect. But no one,
familiar with his work and character, will misunder-
stand either his caution or his candour, and the
theological acrimony, which cast a slur upon his
courage, is by this forgotten.

As I have said, nothing mattered less to Montaigne
than the events which make up the life of other
men. ' The Mayor and Montaigne,' said he in an
immortal phrase, ' were always two by an evident
separation,' and it is Montaigne, not the Mayor, who
has interested the world for three centuries. Moreover, much as he loved Paris, even for her faults,
faithfully as he served Bordeaux, which honoured
him, these cities are not his proper background. If
we imagine him outside his library, it is in Athens
or Rome, discussing high matters with the heroes
of Plutarch. These, indeed, were his real contemporaries, and he seems to have strayed by hazard into
the France of the sixteenth century. Wherefore the
one conspicuous event of his life was his retirement,
in 1571, from the world of affairs. Then it was that
he found the true environment of his energy and
intelligence ; then it was that he took his place among
the books, which were the dearest companions of his
solitude. Of his library he speaks somewhat slight-
ingly ; it was, says he, ' des belles entre les librairies
de village ' ; yet it rose to the number of a thousand,

and included the treasures of his friend La Boëtie.
A village library, says Montaigne, and how precious
that village library would be to-day! After his death
the books were given by his daughter in shameful
carelessness to an abbé of her acquaintance, and only
some seventy-five have been recovered, scored with
notes, and holding in their margin the material of
many an essay.

Montaigne is among the wisest readers that the
world has ever known, and he was wise because he
was never a slave to his books. Desultory in the true
sense, he leapt from author to author, as chance or
fancy bade him. He did not study; he was content
to turn a page here or there; in other words, he tasted
the pleasures of literature, and never glutted a wholesome appetite. The most of men read either that they
may boast their knowledge, or add to their baggage
of superfluous information, and Montaigne was guilty
of no such weakness. Sincere in his study as in his
life, he read only when the mood was imperious, and
only such books as flattered his humour. To busy
himself for more than an hour at a time with the best
of literature was, in his eyes, a wilful interruption of
ease. Once upon a time he set aside all other pursuits
that he might read the *Metamorphoses* of Ovid; but
he was then no more than seven, and with years he
acquired what seemed to him a better wisdom. In
his riper age Tacitus alone availed to tempt him from
his idleness. This author he read through without
interruption, confessing that he had not done such a

thing for twenty years; and so well pleased was he with the effort, that he not only composed a luminous criticism, but summed up the historian's qualities in a phrase, which, for point and concision, could hardly be matched outside Tacitus himself : 'Vous diriez souvent qu'il nous peint, et qu'il nous pince.'

The truth is, Montaigne never forgot that he was a country gentleman, and, being not wholly free from the arrogance of his class, he cherished a kindly contempt for letters, even though they conferred upon him an immortal fame. He loftily declared that to pretend to literature for the sake of gain was a meanness, unworthy the grace and favour of the Muses. Above all, he despised those who distressed themselves in the pursuit of learning—a pursuit which he knew could be as troublesome as another; and, if to be studious were to spoil health and good-humour, study was not for him. He would be master in his library as elsewhere, and he would not sacrifice his gaiety of heart for the erudition of all the ages. Did a passage perplex him, he passed on, nonchalantly observing that nothing was worth deciphering at the expense of toil. It is not strange, therefore, that he hated the pedant, who interpreted life by books, who furnished his soul rather than shaped it, whose restless curiosity could not escape the domination of printed texts ; and so warily did he avoid the common pitfall of scholars that, in his own despite, he died among the most learned men of his time.

However, for all his feigned contempt, he loved

reading as profoundly as he understood it. At the outset he devoted himself to books that he might beguile the solitude of the country, and distract an importunate imagination; he soon found their companionship indispensable. He never travelled without them, either in peace or war; they were, said he, the best munition that he had found for this human voyage. And, more than all, he loved books because they served to awaken within him the faculty to reason, to sharpen his wits, to increase that knowledge of himself, which most he valued. Which were the books he loved best? 'As for myself,' said he, 'I love no books but such as are pleasant and easy, and which tickle me, or such as comfort and counsel me to direct my life and death.' Among the pleasant and easy he counted Rabelais, the Decameron, and the *Kisses* of Johannes Secundus. For this conjunction he has been blamed by the critics, yet unworthily, since Rabelais would have found it a lofty compliment to be read for no other reason than delight in his flim-flam stories. His real game (*gibbier*) was history or poetry, for which he had a peculiar inclination, and in these his preference was all for the ancients. While he quotes but a few of the moderns—Comines, Guicciardini, and Du Bellay, among others—Plutarch and Seneca are ever at his hand or on his tongue. Without the ancients, indeed, Montaigne might have written his *Essays*, but he would have given them another shape and form. In the disciple's regard Plutarch is the

master workman of his kind. Amyot is our French
Plutarch, his splendid versions are ' our breviary,' and
the loyal admiration and profound influence of Seneca
are evident on every page. What a noble array of
poets was mustered upon his shelves ! Virgil and
Horace, Lucretius and Catullus, Lucan and the good
Terence, Ovid and Persius, he knew and quoted them
all. And Homer was the true god of his idolatry ;
Homer, who with Alexander and Epaminondas completed the triad of human excellence ; and, pagan
though he was, he held the Bible in so high a reverence that he thought it should not be generally
used, nor dispersed into many idioms. Such, then,
were some of the books which beguiled his tranquillity, whose pages he turned over with a blithe
gratitude, and upon whose wisdom is based the wisest
of modern books.

Montaigne's own book is a paradox of literature. In
one respect it is a medley of quotations from Plutarch,
Seneca, and the rest ; in another, it is as pitiless a
piece of self-revelation as Pepys's *Diary*. The two
aspects are not opposed. As I have said, Montaigne's true contemporaries were Epaminondas and
Philopœmen, Alexander and Julius, for he places them
all in the same age of discernment, and in revealing
himself he resumed antiquity. He could not check
his own experience by the example of lesser men,
and he found in their braveries a pleasant foil for
his own modesty. Indeed, though his purpose was
to give an account of his own life and actions, he

confessed, in an eloquent defence of Plutarch and Seneca, that his book was wrought wholly from their spoils. In acknowledging the debt, he made an ingenious distinction : 'I did not study,' said he, ' to make a book ; I have somewhat studied because I have made one.' Accordingly, he would not allow himself guilty of plagiarism : true, he pilfered scraps from other men's books, but when he gathered the scraps, he made them his own by an exquisite application. And, with experience, he came to rely more liberally on his own knowledge : while the first essays of the first book might have been the work of many an ingenious author, well versed in the classics, he grows in strength as he writes, until the amazing candour of the third book reveals a master, alone and unmatched in literature.

As he denied that he was a serious student, so he would have all the world know that he was not a professional writer. ' Je suis moins faiseur de livres,' said he, not without a touch of pride, ' que de nulle autre besogne ' ; yet, precisely because he was no maker of books, he has conquered a gracious immortality. He never knew the torture of continuous expression. He wrote as he read, when the humour was upon him ; he spoke to paper as to the first man he met ; and it is this gift of literary intimacy which has given him a unique and honourable place. We read Plutarch and Pascal ; we talk with Montaigne ; and since talk is impossible with a stranger, Montaigne has made him our friend. The impres-

sion of intimacy is heightened by the author's hap-
hazard method of writing.   He put his hand only
to what he calls 'this bundle of diverse pieces'
when excessive idleness overtook him, and nowhere
else than in his own house.   So that it was composed
at leisure, and at long intervals.   When once a passage
was written, he did not correct it, and if he made any
change, it was but to diversify, and not to take
away.   He had no ambition to record events, and,
being asked to write the affairs of his own time, he
would not be at the pains, said he, not for the glory
of Sallust.   In brief, there was nothing so contrary
to his style as a continued narration, and his subject
shifts and changes at a word or thought as easily
as familiar converse.

Now he, who understood all things, understood
perfectly the merit of his book.   He believed, with
justice, that of its kind it was alone in the world,
and that it was, above all, 'a book of good faith.'
How should it not be, since he himself was its subject,
and since he was gifted above all the sons of men with
candour and self-knowledge ?   He wished to be wise
with his own wisdom, and not to go a-begging, even
to Plutarch or Seneca, for intelligence.   With which
purpose, when the melancholy engendered by solitude
drove him first to read and then to write, he found
his argument in himself.   And so the man and the
book grew up side by side.   As he wrote, he discovered his soul, which was the true business of
his life, and he gladly imparted his discovery to the

world. 'I have no more made my book,' said he, ' than my book has made me ; a book consubstantial to its author, of a fit occupation, a member of my life, not of an occupation and end, strange and foreign, as all other books.' And there is one point of modesty he observes. Others, he declares, are emboldened to speak of themselves, because they find the subject worthy. He chose to talk of himself because he found the subject barren and thin, and so he held himself guiltless of ostentation. In other words, he set up a statue, not to adorn market-place, or church, or public square, but for the corner of a library, to amuse a neighbour, a kinsman, or a friend. When the book was written the author had his reward. As for readers, he would be content with a few, with one, with no one. And there is not a library in the world that does not keep a corner for the statue of Montaigne, not a scholar but finds pleasure in his incomparable book.

It is a commonplace of criticism that Montaigne was an egoist, and true it is that he climbed a serene height of self-knowledge inaccessible to other men. But there are egoists good and bad, and the word connotes so many opposing qualities that it is necessary to make a distinction. For instance, there is the fierce and blundering egoist, who is jealous of the past, loathes the present, and fears the future. This one is restless if the limelight of public attention be not always directed to his brow ; he holds that all the privileges of life should belong exclusively to himself ;

because he covers his head, he is indignant that another should dare to wear a hat; and it is not wonderful that he sees himself and all others in a wrong perspective. With egoists of this kind Montaigne has no affinity : he aimed not at selfishness, but at self-knowledge. On the one hand, he was great enough to put no more than the value of a straw upon the opinion of others ; on the other hand, his interest in self did not diminish his kindness towards the world. He was amiable in acquaintance, perfect in friendship, a grave detester of cruelty, and, though sternly centred in his favourite pursuit, he was free both from hatred and jealousy. Γνῶθι σεαυτόν was his arrogant motto, and he essayed with a light heart that most difficult study of all—the study of self. That he succeeded therein beyond any other philosopher was due to his profound scepticism. The most of men take all things on credit, even themselves, and fulfil their paltry functions without thought or hesitancy. They came they know not whence ; they do they know not what ; they go they know not whither. Montaigne, doubting all things, doubted himself most of all, and deliberately set out to resolve the uncertainty, in the same spirit of conquest which tempts adventurers across the seas. And who knows but it is a rarer achievement to find a man than a continent ?

Knowing himself, he knew also the task which lay before him. It was not his purpose to describe his acts, but himself, his essence. 'Other men,' he points out, 'look before themselves. I look within myself; I have no business save with myself. I consider myself unceasingly; I control and taste myself. Others go ever elsewhere, if they think well of it; they go ever forward. *Nemo in sese tentat descendere.* I turn inwards upon myself.' Again he faithfully accepts for his own Plato's great precept : 'Fay ton faict, et te cognoy.' And jealously he guards the privilege of candour. 'My art and profession,' says he, 'is to live. Let him who forbids me to speak of it, according to my sense, experience, and custom, bid the architect to speak of buildings, not according to himself, but according to his neighbour, according to the knowledge of another, not according to his own.' So, descending into himself, and examining the thoughts and motives of his brain, he proved himself the first psychologist in literature. And he differed from his followers in this, that he analysed not the character of hastily-invented puppets, but his own, which from its very proximity would easily have defied a less clairvoyant insight.

He did not underrate the hazard of his enterprise. He confessed that no description was so difficult as the description of oneself. Nor did he undertake the task in a spirit of boastfulness. Acknowledging that his life was 'low and lustreless,' he justly claimed one point of superiority : while most authors present themselves to the people by some strange and special mark, he is the first to reveal himself by his universal essence, as Michel de Montaigne, not as a grammarian, a poet, or a juris-consult. It is, then, with a man that we have to deal, and a man so keenly determined not to exaggerate his traits, that he fell into the other extreme of self-depreciation. He was once asked for what he was fit, and jestingly replied ' for nothing.' Thus his portrait at all costs must be honest ; he must even pierce below the surface, and anatomise body and soul. ' I display myself wholly,' said he ; ' it is a skeleton, wherein appear, at a single glance, veins, muscles, and tendons.' He acknowledged a single limitation : though he told the truth, he did not tell the whole truth, but only so much as he dare, and he dared the more the older he grew.

However, man, according to his gospel, was *ondoyant et divers*, and he mutable as the rest ; so that he could not hope to do more than seize a mood or depict a humour. He, who never maintained a fixed opinion, whose philosophy was incertitude, was least of all disposed to dogmatise concerning himself ; and, as if to prove the impossibility of self-knowledge, Montaigne's spiritual autobiography is full of inconsistencies. Yet the contradiction does not impair the credibility of the narrative, and we may be sure that Montaigne never wrote a sentence that was not unimpeachably true, at least for the moment. He speaks variously of the one subject that engrosses him, because he sees it in various aspects ; and he has nothing to say of himself simply, and solidly, without disorder or confusion, for he knows that to-morrow he will peradventure be other than to-day. And he is of good heart, for from the part you may infer the whole, and each parcel, each occupation of a man, declares him equally with another. But while he never ceased to be busy about himself, while he viewed strange customs and the freaks of fortune with a keen curiosity, he took little interest in the affairs of others, and here he showed himself a very prince of egoists. As nothing pleased him but to write of his own state, his own moods, so he could not hear with patience the state of his fellows. If by an indiscretion another's experience were thrust upon him, he turned his eyes incontinent within himself, to see if he were affected thereby. For the rest, he exclaimed : 'we have lived enough for others. Let us live for ourselves, at any rate this end of life,' and how well he succeeded his book is an eloquent testimony.

For in the vast drama of self which he composed, if drama it may be called, he is not merely the protagonist ; he is almost the only actor. He does not depict the strife of every day ; he is content to record its results upon himself ; and he gives the impression not of one who lives, but of one who has lived. When the energy of his own brain is not quick enough to excite his intelligence, he valiantly pits himself against the ancients, and tries a fall with Plutarch or Cicero. And while his drama dispenses with actors, it dispenses also with a background. There is no change of scene, no rumble of stage-machinery to disturb the quiet action. You feel sure that if he be not reading, or writing, or dreaming in his library, he is jogging along on horseback, as heedless of his goal as of the morrow. There is but one actor, whom he admits upon the stage, and whom he always treats with deference and respect. This is his father, the one other besides himself that Montaigne has permitted us to know, an old Gascon, whom we see almost as clearly as we see his son. He was a small man, yet full of vigour, straight and well proportioned. His expression was agreeable, his skin dark; his demeanour, gentle and modest, grave and stately, was matched by the well-ordered propriety of his dress, whether he went on foot or on horseback. His strength had grown for his son into a sort of legend. Not only was he exquisitely adroit in all noble exercises; he performed feats which might have seemed miracles to acrobats. At the age of sixty, as if to mock at the poor nimbleness of youth, he would leap, clad in furs, into his saddle, or go round the table on his thumb. And his activity is not surprising, when we read that the canes wherewith he trained himself to throw the bar, to put the weight, and to fence, were weighted with lead, and with lead were shod the boots in which he practised running and jumping. He was, withal, religiously inclined, even to superstition, as his son thought, and though he used few words, he spoke ever to the purpose, while he was wont to intermix with his speech ornaments borrowed from ' vulgar ' books, Spanish for choice, and among Spanish books, from Guevara's *Mirror of Princes*. These few cunningly chosen traits mark off Montaigne's father from his contemporaries, and convince us that sympathy permitted the essayist to understand at least one other character than his own.

Pierre de Montaigne, though a man of few words, was distinguished by a rare originality. He gave his son a unique education, and his son profited by it with a unique intelligence. Now, the elder Montaigne, after much searching among the wiseacres of Italy and elsewhere, came to the conclusion that the sole cause, why the men of his time did not attain the skill and knowledge of the Greeks and Romans, was that they gave the best hours of their youth to acquiring languages, which the ancients possessed for nothing. He, therefore, appointed to be his son's tutor a German, who spoke no word of French, but was ready and skilful in Latin. 'There were also joined to him two of his countrymen,' says Montaigne, ' but not so learned, whose charge it was to attend, and, now and then, to play with me, and all these together did never entertain me with other than the Latin tongue.' And this was not all : no member of the household, neither father nor mother, neither man-servant nor maid-servant, was ever permitted to speak to the infant Montaigne, save in the scraps of Latin which they picked up for the purpose. And thus, until he was six, Montaigne knew no more of French or Perigordin than of Arabic. Latin was his mother-tongue, and to his father's wise governance he owed that sound knowledge of the classics which determined his character and his work. Montaigne's father had travelled yet further on the road of humanity than his championship of Latin might imply. He wished also that his son might taste the fruits of duty and science not by force, but by his own will; he encouraged in him an innate love of liberty; and lest a sudden awakening from sleep should distemper his brain, he caused him to be roused every morning by the sweet sound of some instrument. Moreover, though he transmitted to his son an excessive pride in his ancestry, he would not have him guilty of exclusion, and accordingly he sent him from the cradle to be nurtured by humble folk, with the excellent result that his sympathy always embraced those of another class and habit than his own.

As few actors participate in the drama of Montaigne, so it is diversified by few episodes. Once upon a time he suffered a disastrous fall from his horse, and he describes the event and its sensations with a wealth of detail, which suggests that his tranquillity was rarely interrupted. By this reticence we are the gainers. Adventures of a sort are common to all men, and, as it was Montaigne's ambition to paint himself, he selected for portrayal those features wherein he differed from, not those wherein he resembled, his fellows. His method of portraiture, indeed, is the distinguishing mark of his genius. Admirable as are his ideas, they are either borrowed or shared; but in proving himself not a mere philosopher, but a man,

he has achieved a triumph unique and his own.   Of
what aspect, then, and of what habit was he ?   He was
of a mean stature, but strong and compactly built ;
his face was not fat, but full ; his complexion something between the jovial and the melancholy ; his
health, until disease overtook him, was blithe and lusty.
Of accomplishments he boasted none ; he was neither
musician not sportsman, while his hands were so
clumsy that he could neither carve at dinner, nor
write legibly enough to decipher his own script.
Though he passed many years in the country, he
could not tell a cabbage from a lettuce, and the
mechanical arts were as troublesome to him as the
casting-up of accounts.   Yet he boasted with perfect
justice that in events he carried himself like a man,
in conduct like a child.   And for all his shortcomings,
he was not ashamed of his aspect.   ' I have a favourable appearance,' said he, ' both in form and expression,' and he declared, not without a boast, that the
mere sight of him not only exacted consideration
from strangers, but had more than once preserved
him from imminent danger.   Precise in all things,
he was always dressed either in black or in white,
herein following the discreet example of his father.
A gentleman in his own house, he thought, had
no need of finery, since his train and his kitchen
answered for him.   There had been a time, when but
a younger son, he delighted to trick himself out ; and
magnificence became him well, though there are those,
said he, upon whom ' fine clothes weep.'   One piece

of coquetry he retained unto the end : whether walking or riding, he carried a cane in his hand, and aimed therein at a certain elegance.

As has been said, his candour increased with increasing years, and in his marvellous third book he revealed to the first comer the numberless secrets which a puritanical temper refuses to discuss. There were many reasons why he should do this, besides the best reason of all, that he could do it without false shame. Like Rabelais, he knew no other end than to live and be merry. Virtue, he insisted, was a gay and pleasant quality, nor would he ever approve the harsh looks and harsher morals of the censorious. His curiosity, moreover, was boundless, and, as he wrote upon a beam in his library, nothing in mankind (or in womankind) was alien to him. His courage equalled his curiosity, and inspired him to make an unexampled confession, frank, yet never morbid. He was, in his own account, ever a free and inconstant lover. He had fought, not without glory, and when his arms hung upon the wall, he looked back to his victories with some complaisance. Yet even he confessed that he had known defeat : ' I have often wanted fortune,' says he, ' and sometimes also enterprise.' Like Quartilla in Petronius, he could not remember when first he learned the rudiments of the art, but he had studied it so faithfully, that he was emboldened to give to the less fortunate the fruits of his experience. ' He that should demand of me,' thus he counsels, ' what the chief or first part in love is, I would answer, to know how to take fit time ; even so the second, and likewise the third.'

Even more astonishing than the confession of his loves is his patient dissection of the trivialities which he noted in his daily existence. No habit, in his eyes, is too foolish to be recorded, no preference but deserves immortality. So he gravely tells us the likes and dislikes, which we may observe in our friends, but which play too small a part in official biography. When he committed these amazing confidences to paper, he was no longer young, and his habits were fixed beyond change. He could not eat between meals, he explains, nor keep his head long bare, nor cut his hair before dinner. He could dine comfortably without a tablecloth, but not without a napkin, for this astute philosopher was barbarous enough to despise spoon and fork, and to eat with his fingers. For drinking, he despised all material save glass, and that must be of the best. His appetite was strong even to gluttony, and he ate so greedily that he often bit his tongue. As to what he ate, he was indifferent, taking whatever was given him with satisfaction. But if he might choose, he preferred his meat high and little cooked ; he abhorred beer ; he cared for neither salads nor fruits, except melons ; he always drank five glasses of wine, no more and no less ; and it was a matter of conscience with him to eat flesh on fish days. For the rest, he liked to repose himself with his feet higher than his seat, and though he never had the itch, he found much pleasure in scratching. He did not wear spectacles, but, when he read, he put a glass upon his book, to dull the whiteness of the paper. Thus with an ingenious frankness he reveals all those whims and fancies, which, in the opinion of such old biographers as Anthony à Wood and John Aubrey, were the proper delineation of a man.

There is but one personage in history whom we know as well as we know Montaigne—Samuel Pepys ; and though they are separated by a vast gulf of intelligence, they are bound together by a similarity of temperament. They both deemed it a heinous sin to stunt the pleasures either of mind or body ; they both looked upon life with an eye of insatiable wonder ; they both loved whatever was beautiful and of a noble aspect : a pretty face would seduce Pepys from the service of his country, and when the question was put why men should frequent the company of handsome persons, that, said Montaigne, is only to be asked by the blind ; they both yielded to an imperious desire of confession. But nothing could be more different than their methods. Pepys revealed to us what manner of man he was by telling us what he did, and whom he encountered in his passage through life. It was his not to reason but to record. He presents himself to us, half unconsciously, as an actor in a drama, wherein Mistress Knipp and the rest are cast for parts, as well as himself. Montaigne, on the other hand, perforce assumed a solitary rôle. As he is never tired of telling us, he looks within, not without, and presents us not with this episode or that, but with the sum of his experience. In other words, he had no true sense of drama either in life or art. He sat at home in his tower, examining his own character with a discerning eye, while Pepys with a new coat on his back sauntered down Whitehall, rejoicing in the sunlight, and exchanging smiles with beauty as it passed. Montaigne's method was deductive, Pepys's method was inductive. The one gave us the conclusion, and bade us deduce the facts; the other recorded the facts with scrupulous humour, and left the conclusion to us. The one was a system unto himself; the other was a faithful spy upon his own actions. Yet they agree in this: each ' warmed both hands before the fire of life,' and each confessed his indulgence with engaging candour.

Pascal, with a singular lack of humour, blames in Montaigne ' le sot projet qu'il a de se peindre.' The project was not so foolish as Pascal thinks, especially since Montaigne, having given us a glimpse of the outward man, displays with equal honesty and understanding his rare and gifted temperament. He was, above all, of an excellent modesty. ' No one thinks less of himself,' said he in perfect sincerity, ' no one thinks less of me than I do myself '; and so he ranked himself with the common sort, boasting only that, though he was guilty of the basest defects, he neither disavowed nor excused them. Even his plainness of speech, for which others applaud him, seemed in his eyes deplorable; but it was Nature that chose it, not he himself; and in this, as in all things, he bowed

humbly to her dictate.   His kindliness never wavered.
He had a marvellous weakness for pity and humility.
As he hated tyranny, whether of speech or act, so he
was wonderfully patient and considerate towards his
friends ; yet with his habitual irony he descried in the
sufferings of others a bitter-sweet point of pleasure.
He loved idleness as he loved liberty, but he loved
moderation better than either, and he held a crouching and sleepy laziness far worse than a thorny and
painful industry. 'The one pincheth, the other
dulleth me.' Though he thought it a sin to check
his natural impulses, he was no friend of vice, and he
was never a prey to violent passions.   His apprehension was naturally hard, and he encrusted it and
thickened it every day by reason.   For the rest, he
thought that every one should be the loyal servant
of his prince, that ceremony was necessary to an
elegant life, and that not even reason herself should
disturb our dignified and respectable traditions. Yet
he was loath to take a part in the civil wars which
tore his country asunder, and it is characteristic of his
humane temper that he declined to shield his house
from the prevailing violence.   Nor was his confidence
misplaced : his house escaped when many garrisoned
castles fell before the fury of the enemy.

In friendship, as I have said, he was perfect.
Neither time nor circumstance could turn his loyalty
nor weaken his attachment, and it was with a regretful
pride that he recorded this generous talent. 'I am
very capable,' he wrote, 'of acquiring and keeping

rare and exquisite friendship,' and his affection for La Boëtie was the one romance of his life. He never ceased to think of his friend, he never ceased to mourn his loss. Many years after the death of La Boëtie, the memory of him would bring tears of grief to Montaigne's eyes, and he has paid a tribute to him exquisite alike in pathos and eloquence. As the friendship was based upon no interest, so it defied a reasonable explanation. 'If I am pressed to say why I loved him,' wrote Montaigne, 'I can give no answer but this : ' parce que c'estoit luy, parce que c'estoit moy." ' And bitterly he deplored the separation : ' I do but languish, I do but sorrow : and even the pleasures still offered me, instead of yielding me comfort, do but redouble the grief of his loss. We were co-partners in all things. Methinks I have stolen his part from him.

> ' *Nec fas esse ulla me voluptate hic frui*
> *Decrevi, tantisper dum ille abest meus particeps.*

I am so accustomed to be always his double, that methinks I am but half myself.'

Though his friendship was rarely given, his companionship was free and open. He delighted in the liberal exchange of opinions, in the loud-voiced contest of opposing talkers. For him conversation was the most fruitful, most natural exercise of human wit ; and we can imagine with what eloquence and resource he conducted an argument. Now, talk is always more daring than literature : it escapes the petty restraint,

which a misguided convention has placed upon the
printed page ; and, bold as Montaigne was when he
held a pen in his hand, no doubt he surpassed his own
freedom when he faced an adversary at the fireside.
There was nothing he could not say, no hidden place
that he could not discover. He did not share the
puritan's fear of words. Moreover, he possessed this
signal good quality: he cared not what was the subject,
nor which side he took ; it was talk for its own sake
that he loved—talk candid, intimate, and unrestrained.
Despite his treacherous memory, he had command of
all the curious knowledge of his time, and the author
of the *Essays* must perforce have been apt in illustration and swift in repartee. Above all, he practised a
strong and manly familiarity ; he delighted in a sharp-
ness and bitterness of communication. Gentlemen,
he thought, should be able to endure the sturdiest
expressions from their friends ; and so great was his
toleration in the battle of intelligence, that he was
astonished at no proposition, he was wounded by no
belief, he thought no fantasy too frivolous or extravagant, if only it struck a spark of humour, or lit up the
dull corner of an argument.

Of this sport he never wearied. He could talk all
day, if only the discussion were conducted with
method and sincerity, if only eloquence were not
employed for competitive parade. But no talker ever
won his approval who did not freely give himself to
the controversy. Why should he concern himself
with those who do nothing but by the book ? 'I

would rather my son learn to speak in a tavern,' said he, ' than to prate in the schools.'   In fact, he hated a pedant worse than a fool.   He made an admirable difference, which Rabelais would have approved, between an abecedarian ignorance and a doctrinal ignorance.   The simple peasants, he thought, were honest folk, and honest folk also the true philosophers ; those who came between he regarded as dangerous, inept, and importunate.   Their half-knowledge made them obstinate and ardent in the defence of an opinion, and obstinacy and ardour were, in Montaigne's eyes, the surest proof of folly.   ' There is nothing,' said he, ' that is so certain, resolute, disdainful, contemplative, grave, and serious as the ass.'

And after talk he best loved travel.   He voyaged in thought, even in his library, and when he went abroad he carried his wits with him.   For he travelled for travel's sake, and once afoot he cared not whether he came back.[1]   He did not set out in order to return,

---

[1] Montaigne has given us his theory of travelling in his *Essays*. In his *Journal* of a voyage through Germany and Italy, discovered and published in 1774, we have a specimen of his practice.   The *Journal* is eminently characteristic of its author, even when a secretary and not Montaigne holds the pen.   It is life rather than art that engrosses him, and he always spares us the pedantry of the guide-book.   Wherever he goes he is content, if apt to show a lack of regard for his own country.   Nothing puts him out, save an encounter with Frenchmen, whom he found living together at Padua and elsewhere to their great detriment.   He appreciated the wine and food of foreign countries with a discriminating palate, and adapted himself with scrupulous loyalty to strange customs.   He notes that on one

but merely to be in motion, and on one occasion he
would have gone from Rome to Cracow or Greece,
had he not been hampered by his companions. Now,
we read Montaigne discoursing upon his journeys
with the greater regret, because to-day the art of
travelling is dead, or dying. Tourists we have, but
no travellers. Men are hustled from end to end
of Europe for the sake of pride. They see nothing
of foreign countries ; they bring back naught save
a tangled memory of strange dishes. Truly that
courier was not mistaken who said, with a sad glance
at his mob of followers : ' They think they travel, but
they are wrong; it I is who travel.' Montaigne,
however, was singular even in his own age. He, too,
deplored the folly of his countrymen, who were out
of their element if they were out of their village, who,
should they meet a compatriot in Hungary, feasted
that good fortune, and joined with him in scorning
as many barbarous fashions as they saw. ' They
travel close and covered, with a silent and incom-

occasion they had white hares for supper, that at Lindau the
fish were excellent, though they ate only the liver of the trout.
The most vivid memory which he carried away from Lucca was
a memory of setting dogs. Wherever he went, he observed the
women with an admiring eye, and this accomplished traveller,
who wisely abstains from chattering of the fine arts, thinks it
worthy of record that at Florence the courtesans stand at the
doors of the houses to attract lovers, while at Rome and Venice
they sit by the windows. The *Journal* is not a great book ;
indeed, it is not a book at all ; but it will always have a value as an
undesigned commentary upon the *Essays*, and it bears the marks
of authenticity upon every page.

municable wit, defending themselves from the con-
tagion of some unknown air.' Montaigne's plan was
far other than this. He changed his diet and his
habits with his sky. He would do and eat in Germany
what the Germans did and ate. A new custom was
more pleasing to him than a fine building, man more
curious than stones, and life superior to the art even of
Italy. And like the perfect traveller that he was, he
went abroad with a sense of irresponsibility. The
care of his house no longer irked him ; he recked not
what overtook him in his absence. He knew only
that about him was food for wonder, that the sun was
high in the heaven, and that he was on horseback,
where best he could think, where most he was at his
ease. Why, then, should he ask whither he was going,
or what he came out to see ? A true voyager, he had
neither plan nor aim, and he delighted every morning,
because he knew not where that night he would lay
his head.

Despite the interest of his life and character,
Montaigne is pre-eminently the man who thinks. He
tries all things, questions all things, doubts all things.
Distinguo is a word ever on his tongue and in his mind.
Que sçais-je ? he asks, and with perfect frankness
answers 'Nothing.' This attitude of mind seems
the more admirable when we remember the time in
which Montaigne lived. He had seen his country
torn asunder by the fiercest fanaticism. The news
had been brought to his solitary tower of the massacre
on St. Bartholomew's Eve. And he sternly declined

to take part in the orgy of blood, and by refusing to
fortify his house, he gave a practical proof of his
indifference. Maybe he would have spoken out with
greater freedom, maybe he would now and again
have substituted France for Athens or Rome, had
not the savagery of his age counselled prudence. But
he knew well that men believe nothing so firmly as
that of which they have the least knowledge, and, as
he said, it is putting a high price on our conjectures
to make them an excuse for burning a man alive. So
he kept his mind open upon either side: while he
was disposed to distrust miracles, he thought it a
singular impudence to declare dogmatically that no
miracle was ever wrought. He reserved his fiercest
scorn for those who persisted in an untenable opinion,
and was himself always ready to abandon a *mauvais
party*, or to correct his judgment, wisely recognising
that many things which yesterday were articles of
faith are to-day nothing better than fables. And,
as he would guard his own conscience free, so he
would accord a like liberty to others. To give every
man the right to hold his own opinion was, in his
eyes, to mollify asperity and to win an easy respect
for the laws. He was, indeed, as faithful a pupil of
Pyrrho as his dislike of systems permitted him to be.
That is to say, he was a sceptic, who doubted even
scepticism itself. His philosophy was as free as air,
as free as Shakespeare's own. He would bow the
knee neither to this one nor that, and, though he
cherished an enthusiastic admiration of Socrates, he

surveyed even that great man's teaching with a critical
eye. However, Pyrrho's doctrine responded most
accurately to his taste, and, if he would not, like the
master, refuse to avoid the obstacles he met in the
road, he found a pleasure in the science of ignorance,
and practised indifference as an art. Why, he asked,
in a world where all was uncertain, should he insist
with frenzied ardour upon this dogma or upon that?
He could, said he, sustain an opinion, but not choose
it. The incertitude of his judgment was generally
so nicely balanced, that he would have been content
to leave the decision to the drawing of lots or the
throwing of dice. While he esteemed truth the
highest of the virtues, the very foundation of human
intercourse, he knew not where to surprise it. 'Truth
and falsehood,' said he, 'have the same visage, the
same port, taste, proceedings. We behold them with
the same eye.' Moreover, the world is not merely
uncertain; it is also illusory. Is not man *divers et
ondoyant*, a botched and a parti-coloured work? So
life of itself is neither good nor bad; it is the place
of good and bad, according as we prepare it for them,
and since troubles enter within us by no other road
than our own brain, we can despise them or convert
them into blessings. Or, in the words of Hamlet,
'there is nothing either good or bad, but thinking
makes it so.' Nor does our existence hold aught that
is strange or new. If you have lived a day, you have
seen all: one day is equal to eternity.

It was this doctrine of incertitude and illusion that

inspired Montaigne to his exquisite moderation. He
could not but play the part of a spectator in the
drama, of whose very progress he was doubtful. He
could not cherish anger against those who disagreed
with him, when he was convinced that all the appearances of the world were but the fruit of his fantasy.
But he hated excess with all the ardour of a sceptic's
soul. He loved temperate and modest natures, and
he declared that virtue would become vice, if it were
embraced with too fierce and violent a desire. And
so it was that he looked with a cold eye upon science.
What folly is it to teach children the motion of the
stars when they know not their own souls! Copernicus has discovered that the earth moves. How
long will it be before the conclusions of Copernicus
are upset? While on every side the professors of
science are insisting upon finality, new continents are
floating into our ken, and the very form of the earth
is as yet unknown.

When science failed, and even his trusted reason
deceived, Montaigne turned to Nature for a guide.
Our great and puissant mother can neither injure
nor betray us. She, indeed, is superior to the teaching of history, to the wisdom of the philosophers.
The instinct which she has implanted in our breast is
coeval with the life of man, and perfectly adapted to
his use and profit. Nature, in brief, can do all, and
doth all. Yet it is not given to every man to hear
her voice, or to divine her laws. It is a more difficult
emprise to live according to our natural condition

than to subdue the world.　In this respect the animals are our masters.　If we go about to imitate them, we soon discover how weak is our art, how grievous our shortcoming.　Nor can ignorance easily discern the force and purpose of Nature.　' If the frost chance to nip the vines about my village,' says Montaigne, ' my Priest doth presently argue that the wrath of God hangs over our heads, and threateneth all mankind; and judgeth that the pip is already fallen upon the Cannibals.　A vain and presumptuous conclusion! But whosoever shall present unto his inward eyes, as it were in a picture, this great image of our mother Nature in her entire majesty; and in her visage shall read so general and constant a variety; who shall view himself therein, and not himself, but a whole kingdom, as the part of a very delicate point, he only can value things according to their just proportion.' In this eloquent passage Montaigne reveals both his worship of Nature and his own humility; and in his unquestioned obedience to natural laws he shows a far nobler sincerity than ever was attained by Rousseau and the other antics of his inspiration.

While he worshipped the ancient mother of us all, Montaigne did not flout the achievements of art. He recognised that the France of the sixteenth century was not the garden of Eden, and that it would be a mere blasphemy to ignore the work of the centuries. In other words, he was the loyal defender of custom and tradition.　A sound conservative, he would if he could have put a spoke in the wheel of progress; he

was disgusted with novelty, whatever face she wore ;
but he did not complain, nor regret that he was not
born upon all fours, and protected by a hairy covering.
His respect for the law was profound and logical.
' The laws,' he said, ' maintain their credit, not because
they are just, but because they are laws ; and he who
obeys a law because it is just is obedient on a false
ground.'   If only the anarchs of to-day would accept
this excellent theory, the world would be a pleasanter
and safer dwelling-place.   Montaigne, lover of liberty
as he was, never forgot the allegiance which he owed
to society and to his prince, and though laws were
the work of men, and often of fools, they had a
mystical foundation in custom, and rightly claimed
the reverence of all.

    Despite his indifference, there was one object which
Montaigne thought worth the strife, and that was
pleasure.   A true epicurean, he declared his preference without shame or hesitancy.   ' Whatever they
may say,' he wrote, ' even in virtue itself, pleasure
is our final aim.'   He liked to beat the ears of the
crowd with this word ' pleasure,' for the world heard
it unwillingly, being hypocritically in love with grief
and misery.   And Montaigne was gay even in his
irony.   To laugh, in his judgment, was always better
than to cry, not merely because it was more amusing,
but because it was also more disdainful.   For him
the true mark of wisdom was a constant joyousness,
and he boasted that he was exempt from sadness and
passion, which he neither loved nor esteemed. ' There-

with they adorn wisdom, virtue, and conscience : a
base and foolish ornament.' Youth and high spirits
never failed to delight him, and he feared the encroachment of age so bitterly that he anticipated its
sorrows, and owned himself old at forty. Not even pain
could disturb his serenity : when the stone afflicted
him, he cheerfully declared that he was naturally in-
sensitive, and scanned the disease with an impartial
eye. He even discovered in it a certain dignity,
which pleased him ; and he applauded the restraint
wherewith it played its game apart, and let him play
his after his guise. In truth this contempt of pain
was part of his gospel of pleasure, and doubtless the
good-humour wherewith he endured a constant agony
recalled the sturdy spirit of the ancient Romans.

If he were pagan in his desire of pleasure, he was
doubly pagan in his contempt of death. He lived
his life that he might be prepared at the first call to
leave it. What came after was of small interest to
him. He only knew that life was a gift, of which
we might make the best, and which we should lay
down without sorrow or remorse. To this theme he
recurs again and again, as though the mere thought
of it fortified him to meet the inevitable change with
courage and composure. None reflected oftener that
the end of our career is death. None knew better that
what happens once, and takes so brief a time, is but a
light affliction. ' The premeditation of death,' said
he in his old Roman fashion, ' is the premeditation of
liberty : he who has learned to die, has learned not to

be a slave.' He saw with impatience the grief which the apprehension of fate inflicted upon others. ' We trouble death with the care of life,' he wrote sorrowfully, ' and life with the care of death. The one annoys, the other affrights us.' For himself he was always booted and ready to depart. He knew how suddenly the summons might come, how insecure was his tenure. The knots which bound him to life were all undone, he had taken his leave of every one, save of himself. ' The longest of my designs,' he wrote, ' does not extend to a whole year : now I apply myself only to make an end : I shake off all new hopes and enterprises : I say a last farewell to all the places that I leave : I dispossess myself daily of what I have.' So, while he loved life, he had no fear of death. He even contemplated suicide with a benignant tolerance. He thought the hour of death had come, when life held more evil than good, since death is the remedy of all ills, and the more voluntary it is, the fairer it seems. Life depends upon the will of others, death upon our own. Nevertheless, ready as he was, he feared the trappings of death. A bed, surrounded by his friends, on this side the physician, whom he bitterly distrusted, on that ' the other doctor of the soul,' was a vision of perpetual disgust. If he might choose, he would rather die on horseback, away from his house, and far from his friends. Or if this boon be denied him, he would that death should surprise him planting cabbages, ' careless of her, and still more careless of my unfinished garden.'

Such are the views concerning life and death held by one of the wisest among the sons of men. With that fine candour which made it impossible that he should lie even to himself, he exposed to others his thoughts and his impulses. He scorned to hide what the world might call his 'vices' as bitterly as he scorned to extol what the world with equal effrontery might call his 'virtues.' His impartiality considered neither vice nor virtue : it was content only with the truth. And what is remarkable even in him is his universality. Like a greater than he, he 'held the mirror up to Nature,' and in painting himself, he painted all men. None can read his book without uncovering some of the secrets which lurk hidden in his own soul ; there is no circumstance of life, whose tangle these *Essays* may not unravel. As a French critic has said, there is something of Montaigne in each one of us, no matter what his pursuit or predilection may be. He saw himself in so many aspects, he was, in his familiar phrase, so *divers et ondoyant*, that he may be taken as an index of the human race. 'It is not in Montaigne, but in myself, that I find all that I see in him,' said Pascal in a luminous phrase, which Montaigne himself might have written, and no man is so little an egoist but that he may discover in the *Essays* of Montaigne, what Montaigne discovered in the literature of ancient Rome, a revelation of his own soul.

His style was equal to the demand made upon it. It was, in Sainte-Beuve's phrase, 'the instrument of his charm, the true wand of his enchantment.' For he wrote not as a maker of plain prose, but as a poet. There is scarce a sentence in his book which is not brilliant with imagery, and his fancy is so rich in metaphor, that the variety and colour of his writing are inexhaustible. Yet, with a rare lapse from knowledge of himself, he affected to despise his style. He declared that his language had nothing of care or polish, and that he wrote *à peu d'hommes et à peu d'années* ; had it been a lasting matter, he would have employed a firmer language. Here, once more, he misjudges himself. If his syntax is not scholarly like the syntax of Rabelais, it is three centuries nearer Latin than the syntax of to-day, and his vocabulary is as vital and diverse as his thought. That, indeed, is his conspicuous merit ; he makes the dead words live, even as Homer made them live ; and accordingly his book, which he destined for a brief and inglorious career, is read by thousands, and will die only with the death of intelligence.

In this matter of style Montaigne is uncertain and contradictory. At the outset he had made up his mind that he was not a writer, but a landed proprietor with something to say. He regarded his *Essays* in the spirit wherein Congreve regarded his comedies, as trifles beneath him. Like the author of *The Way of the World*, he desired to be accepted on no other footing than that of a gentleman, and there was no Voltaire to administer the reproof that, had he been so unfortunate as to be a mere gentleman, he would

not have been worth a visit. He held, maybe, that,
while a country squire might honourably tell the
truth, he fell below his position if he involved himself
in the intricacies of style. Therefore he pretended
that, as Tom Nash said of the Devil, ' he had left
form and was all for matter ' ; and he formulated his
theory in a piece of admirable prose, of itself a sufficient contradiction. ' I do more willingly wind up
a notable sentence,' he wrote, ' that I may sew it
upon me, than unwind my thread to go fetch it.
Contrariwise, it is for words to serve and to follow ;
and if the French tongue cannot reach it, let the
Gascon. I would have the matters to surmount, and
so fill the imagination of him that hearkeneth, that he
have no remembrance at all of the words. It is a
natural and simple speech that I love, written as it is
spoken, and such upon the paper as it is in the mouth,
a pithy, sinewy, short, and compact speech, not
so delicate and combed as vehement and piercing.
Rather difficult than tedious, void of affectation,
free, loose, and bold, that every member of it seem
to make a body, not pedantical, not friar-like, not
lawyer-like, but, as Suetonius calleth that of Julius
Cæsar, soldier-like.'

This passage, better than any other, expresses Montaigne's early view of style. And even here it may be
noticed that, in spite of protest and asseveration, he
is already engrossed with the manner of his writing.
Why, if words are only fit to be forgotten, should he
aim at a pithy and sinewy speech ? Why should he

keep before him the soldier-like quality of Julius
Cæsar? The truth is that Montaigne, like every
other great writer, was a conscious artist. The more
he wrote, the more obediently he fell beneath the
sway of words. It is impossible to overlook the
malicious satisfaction wherewith he puts upon paper
the *mots humiliants*, as Sainte-Beuve calls them, which
are generally banished from literature, nor the delight
wherewith he marshals his metaphors, and adorns his
thoughts with all the trappings of a figured style.
This is not the conversation which by a whim he was
pleased to think it; this is not talking to paper as to
the first man he met; and Montaigne was artist
enough to know that another medium, and another
audience, demanded a separate style and treatment
of its own.

Presently Montaigne changed his theory. 'It is
my humour,' he wrote, 'to look rather at the form
than at the substance, rather at the advocate than
the cause.' Every day it pleased him to read such
authors as had no care of their science, and to seek
therein their manner, not their matter. The latter
pronouncement is doubtless the more sincere; and,
though something may be allowed for a changing
humour, the appetite of style comes in writing; and
Montaigne, having once set pen to paper, delighted
in choosing his words and shaping his sentences.
His criticism of other writers is just and acute. He
saw the strength of Tacitus, as he exposed the weakness of Cicero. In one essay he has compared the

Latin poets, and found the right phrase for each of them ; in another he has set Plutarch and Seneca side by side, as one who was their faithful and intelligent companion. But poetry was the passion of his life, though he himself composed haltingly in verse, and though he confessed that poets were the best judges of their art. 'Here is a wonder,' said he : ' we have many more poets than judges and interpreters of poetry,' a piece of ingenious and far-sighted criticism. Still more remarkable, he saw the beauty of simple folk-songs in an age which was beneath the spell of the classics. As in science, so in poetry, he hated only the leaden mediocrity. He could admire the songs of the people as readily as he forgave an abecedarian ignorance ; and he quotes an amorous canzonet of the Cannibals with the approval which he might have given to Anacreon or Horace. ' Adder stay, stay good adder, that my sister may by the pattern of thy parti-coloured coat draw the fashion and work of a rich lace, for me to give one to my love.' The beauty of such simple poesy is amply appreciated to-day, but Montaigne's judgment was prophetic, and enforces his claim to a place among the great critics.

His influence was immediate, and is universal. He crossed the Channel in the English of Florio as early as 1603, and passed into the very substance of our literature. Rumour has it that he carried English blood in his veins, and assuredly there is a quality in his masterpiece which instantly won him the sym-

pathy of our poets. A copy of Florio's translation,
now in the British Museum, bears the name of
William Shakespeare, and when, the better to guard
this precious treasure, a second copy was bought,
there was found inscribed upon its title-page : ' Sum
Ben. Jonsoni liber.' A strange coincidence ; and
amply warranted by the appreciation of these two
great poets. The author of *Volpone* declares that his
contemporaries stole out of *Pastor Fido* ' almost as
much as from Montaigniè,' while Shakespeare, by a
passage in *The Tempest*,[1] has made his debt clear
beyond argument. But did Shakespeare's debt begin
and end here ? That is a question which has agitated
the indiscreet critic as violently as the Baconian heresy.
One writer has gone so far as to urge that Hamlet
is Montaigne, and that Shakespeare's tragedy was
written in order to confute the essayist. Such folly
is unspeakable, and need not detain us an instant.
Nor is it in general a fruitful enterprise to estimate
Shakespeare's debt to this writer or that. Those who
delight in parallel passages will find no difficulty in
confronting Shakespeare and Montaigne, but when
the passages are neatly numbered and docketed, a
positive conclusion is still impossible. Though the
same reflections concerning life and death, the same
deploration of man's mutability, may be found in
either writer, the similarity proves nothing. In the
first place, they are also found in works to which both

[1] A passage from the essay *Of the Cannibals* is paraphrased in
Gonzalo's speech, Act II. Sc. i. of *The Tempest*.

Shakespeare and Montaigne had access ; [1] in the second, they are part of our human birthright. And there is a third reason why these two writers should arrive at the same thoughts. They were both great enough to be commonplace ; they both dared to interpret the obvious ; they both rose above the sad necessity of being original. How, then, shall we apportion to each his share of intellectual discovery ? Is it not wiser, refraining from ingenuity, to acknowledge the free paraphrase of *The Tempest*, and for the rest to recognise in Shakespeare and Montaigne a regal kinship ? Though Plutarch was the breviary of each, each could draw upon his own wealth, each could rest upon his own authority, and we are better employed in reading both of them without guile than in fastening a fanciful debt upon the author of *Hamlet*.

Montaigne prayed that he might die on horseback, or planting cabbages. His prayer was not granted. He died, like a good citizen, in his bed, fortified by the sacraments of the church, and surrounded by his friends. So long had he pondered upon death, that it had no terrors for him. As he said, he had long been booted and ready to depart. And while death, which set free his soul from slavery, held no secret, the riddle of his life was still unsolved. ' I have seen

[1] For instance, in Boethius' *Consolation of Philosophy* you may find the following sentiment: *adeo nihil est miserum nisi cum putes*, which suggests that in one oft-quoted instance Shakespeare did not borrow from Montaigne, but that both put their hand in the same cupboard.

no monster or miracle in the world,' he wrote in one
of his last essays, 'more manifest than myself.'
Erasmus had already expressed his wonder at the
miracle of human life. Sir Thomas Browne was
destined to echo it. And though the riddle was unsolved, Montaigne abandoned life with a good heart.
'We are richer, each one of us,' said he, 'than we
think,' and with this confidence upon him, who would
not face death ?

THE LIBRARY OF AN OLD SCHOLAR

THERE is a personal intimacy in a library which does not belong to any other possession of man. To look upon the books of scholar or poet is to see the place in which he sharpened, if he did not forge, his thought. When he has scored the margin with comment or reflection, he has imparted something of himself to the printed page; but even when the page is virgin-white, you cannot forget the sentiment of him whose hand has touched it. The copy of Florio's *Montaigne*, with Shakespeare's name scrawled on the first sheet, will always affect the beholder more poignantly than a copy to which no legend is attached. And if the mere accident of possession sanctifies a book, the use and comment of a great man might make it priceless. What would we not give for Shakespeare's *Plutarch*,[1] annotated or scored by his own

---

[1] In the Greenock library there is a copy of Plutarch's *Lives*, which some suppose to have been Shakespeare's. It bears upon the title-page the following inscription: 'Vive : ut Vivas : W. S. : pretiū 18s.' But apart from the fact that there is no evidence that the W. S. of the title-page is Shakespeare, the book could throw no light upon his Roman plays, as it was not printed until 1612, by which date *Julius Cæsar*, *Coriolanus*, and *Antony and Cleopatra* were already written and acted.

careful hand? It might reveal the process of his work more clearly than a month of argument; it might show us how he turned the noble prose of North into impassioned verse. And what is true of a single book is ten times true of a collection. A man's temper is touched at many points of interest, and by his choice and preference you may know him. The library of Samuel Pepys, for instance, is the best index of his many-sided mind. The careful arrangement of the books, nicely adjusted according to their height, is as familiar as the methodical taste which dictated their selection. There they remain for all time, as Pepys intended they should remain, in the cases which he designed for their reception. If physical immortality were possible, surely it could best be attained by this artifice of Samuel Pepys. For as you stand in the room, which he himself might recognise, and gaze upon the books ordered by his will, you may easily believe that he still haunts the place. It is not a museum filled with the indiscriminate spoils of a lifetime; it is a living library, such as he, the pious donor, might have inhabited. And not only are the treasures disposed according to the fancy of him who gathered them; they are such treasures as best illustrate his curiosity. In one press lies his music, written much of it by his hand; and there you may still find the manuscript of the famous song 'Gaze not on Swans,' or of the yet more famous 'Beauty Retire,' which Knipp herself was wont to sing. Or you may turn over the collection of ballads and broadsides which he made for his amusement, and which to-day is priceless to the student of popular literature. Or you may recall his zeal for the Navy, which he served so faithfully, by contemplating the documents wherein is set forth the prowess of our fleet. Wherever you look, you see the hand of Samuel Pepys, and you would not be disconcerted if he descended sudden from Kneller's canvas and pointed out to you his own cherished possessions. However, few men were ever so thoughtful of the future as the benefactor of Magdalen College, and the library of Pepys remains a unique episode in the history of letters.

As we look at their libraries, we find it hard to believe that Samuel Pepys and William Drummond of Hawthornden were in a sense contemporaries. In truth their lives overlapped, since Pepys was entered at Magdalen College a few months after the death of Drummond. Yet this overlapping brings the men no nearer one to the other; for while Pepys, a true child of the Restoration, was ahead of his time, Drummond lagged always in the past. In taste, sympathy, and style he was an Elizabethan, who by an accident of survival, had estrayed into the reign of Charles. His library, in the care and bequest of which he rivals Pepys, was already old-fashioned when he presented it to the University of Edinburgh. It is all the more interesting on that account. For his books reveal the predilection of an old scholar, who was seventeen years of age when James united the thrones of England and Scotland, and who lived to

see the head of Charles fall to the headsman's axe.
And his library displays far more of the man than do
his works. When he wrote, he could never shake off
the habit of pedantry ; when he purchased books, he
purchased those which the whim or fashion of the
moment commended ; and he who turns over his
treasures, now safely housed in the University of
Edinburgh, may transport himself in fancy to the
study of Hawthornden, where Drummond and
Jonson met over a bottle and wrangled of poetry.

The two libraries are divided by more than time.
Pepys's books are kept in the 'new building,' for which
he himself subscribed, and which he designed for their
reception. Drummond's books are put away, separate,
it is true, but in a bookcase to which no romance can
be attached. Moreover, a too zealous librarian, to
whom they were once entrusted, put them in new
covers and planed them down with a Procrustean in-
exorability. The result is that many a fine copy is
spoilt, and the most are defaced, by bindings upon
which Drummond's eye never lighted. The deface-
ment is an eternal regret. But it must be remembered that the laird of Hawthornden was no cox-
comb. He did not, like Pepys, insist upon the decent
housing of his books. It was not his own library that
he was sending down to posterity—it was the library
of Edinburgh's University. So far from insisting
upon a separate maintenance, he did but add his books
to the general stock, and set his name below those of
Clement Little and other benefactors. None the less,

he was desirous that his and the other names should be properly preserved, 'which,' said he, 'as it can be no disadvantage to the living, may serve to the dead as a kind of epitaph.'   That is written in the proper spirit, and Drummond has achieved the epitaph he valued most highly.   'Here lies a pious benefactor,' so it might run, 'who, in enriching his University, bequeathed to the world a picture of his mind.'

For the books, presented to Edinburgh in 1627, and afterwards increased, are Drummond's mind laid bare.   They do not form the library of a specialist, curious to exhaust a single subject, but rather of a dilettante, to whom no subject comes amiss.   They are bounded, then, neither by language nor by a narrow taste.   Drummond, being a true Scot, spoke the vernacular, and found all other tongues of equal difficulty.   Spanish and French, maybe, came as easy to him as the English, which he always wrote with the pedantic accuracy of an accomplished foreigner.   Nor did the seventeenth century know the hard dividing lines which in our day separate the literature of one country from the literature of another.   In the first place, Latin was the common speech of scholars ; in the second, the cost and hardship of travel gave a studious solemnity to the grand tour.   And so we find Drummond expressing a polyglot sympathy after the fashion of his age.   So we know from his manuscripts that in one year he read Tasso and Guarini, Bembo and Petrarch, Sanasar's *Arcadia* and Henri Estienne's *Defence d'Hérodote*,

as well as Spenser's *Faery Queene* and a treatise by
Scaliger.   Of this catholicity his library is a yet better
proof.

Being a scholar, he perforce knew the classics, and
being a gentleman, he filled many a shelf with dull,
heavy, respectable volumes.   Here you find the
Greek grammar of Johannes Varennius, there a fine
example of primitive archæology entitled *Petrus
Ciacconius Toletanus de Triclinio*, which, despite its
curious cuts, is not likely to tempt a modern reader.
The masterpieces of Greece and Rome he collected
as the humour took him, and without any ambition
of completeness.   He possessed not a few pretty
editions, which any bibliophile might proudly
treasure, if only they were tall copies.   But for the
most part he seems to have read the classics in languages not their own.   For example, he studied
Thucydides not only in the Latin of Laurentius
Valla, but in the French of Claude de Seyssel, and one
wonders that he did not add thereto the version of
Thomas Nicolls, goldsmith of the city of London,
who also knew more of Seyssel's French than of the
original Greek.   So, too, he read the *Carmen Sæculare*
in Greek, Ovid in Spanish, and Herodotus in Italian ;
indeed, were it not for an occasional Xenophon, a slim
volume of Lucian, the Aldine Plautus and Virgil, and
the blameless verses of Apollonius Rhodius, you might
almost believe that Drummond borrowed his learning
at second-hand.   Nevertheless, the curiosity is un-
deniable ; and since Drummond lived before the age

of exact scholarship, you reproach him as little as he
could have reproached himself.

Before all things Drummond was a poet, and in
duty bound he gathered the masterpieces of his fellow-
craftsmen.   In his library you may still see the first
editions of Shakespeare and Ben Jonson, as they might
have come hot from the press.   It is true that Ben
Jonson told Drummond that Shakespeare wanted art ;
but long before the poet's tramp to Hawthornden,
Drummond had read and judged Shakespeare for himself.   Here, among his books we find *Romeo and
Juliet*, as it was printed in 1599 by Thomas Creede for
Cuthbert Burby, *Love's Labour Lost* in the small quarto
of 1598, as well as ' *The Most Lamentable Romaine
Tragedie of Titus Andronicus*, . . . at London.   Printed
by J. R. for Edward White, and are to be solde at
his shoppe, at the little North doore of Paules, at the
Signe of the Gun.   1600.'   Of his friend Drayton,
he had the splendid *Battaile of Agincourt*, and therewith the works of Daniel, that other poet who wrote
of wars, ' and yett hath not one batle in all his book,'
while Joshua Sylvester's ' *Lachrimæ Lachrimarum, or
the Distillation of Teares Shede for the untymely Death
of the Incomparable Prince, Panaretus*,' a book surrounded, like his own *Mœliades*, with black bands of
mourning, doubtless captured his fancy.   Of course
he treasured the works of Spenser, to whose preciosity
he owed a profound debt, while for the better passage
of his leisure he kept and thumbed Turberville's
Tragicall Tales, translated ' in time of his trouble '

out of Bandello and Boccaccio. Possibly it was
patriotism which urged him to purchase David
Murray's portentous *Death of Sophonisba* (1611); he
may not plead so good an excuse for the acquisition
of *Humours Heav'n on Earth, with the Civil Warres of
Death and Fortune*, by John Davies of Hereford. But
even this fantastic work has a certain curiosity to
commend it, and assuredly it lives up to its profession. ' O ! 'tis a sacred kind of excellence,' says the
title-page, ' That hides a rich truth in a Tale's pretence '; and whatever ' rich truth ' the tale contains
is effectually hidden from our knowledge. On the
other hand, he esteemed *Astrophel and Stella* so highly
that he kept its sonnets in manuscript, a compliment
which he paid to no other poet except Donne. Moreover, he followed the fashion of the hour, and collected
plays, as a modern reader might collect novels, and he
had better luck than the luckiest of the moderns.
For here we find *The Spanish Tragedy*, there the
Comédies Facésieuses of Pierre de l'Arrivey, while, like
a true Elizabethan, Drummond boasted the possession of such popular masterpieces as *Volpone*, *A Game
of Chesse*, and *Two Wise Men and all the Rest Fooles*.
Now, if the most of these are not beyond our reach,
on our shelves they would figure in neat little re-
prints, with neat little notes. And we are no more
likely to discover the small quartos, which their own
creators first contemplated, than we are to study
arithmetic (with Drummond) in the treatise of
Chauvet, or to consult for a dictionary Florio's im-

mortal *Worlde of Wordes,* which Drummond read in its first edition of 1598. Yet if I had my choice of the library, perhaps I would take the beautiful black-letter translation of Gawin Douglas. This, indeed, was a masterpiece, which no Scot could lack, and which truly it is more easy to look at than to read. But the type has a rugged splendour all its own, and the title-page might serve at once as a biography and a criticism of Gawin Douglas. Thus it runs : ' The xiii Bukes of Eneados of the famose Poete Virgill Translated out of Latyne verses into Scottish metir, bi the Reverend Father in God, Mayster Gawin Douglas, Bishop of Dunkel and unkil to the Erle of Angus. Every buke having hys perticular Prologe. Imprinted at Londō, 1553.' ' Unkil to the Erle of Angus ' ! That touch of pride reminds you of the famous couplet—

> ' The great Dalhousie, he, the god of war,
> Lieutenant-colonel to the Earl of Mar.'

But the *Virgill* is a fine book, and, were it mine, I would not exchange it for the *Essayes of a Prentise in the Divine Art of Poesie,* by James vi. himself, which doubtless was highly esteemed by the loyal Drummond, nor for J. Derrick's *Image of Ireland* (1581), of which Hawthornden's copy is reputed unique.

Drummond's library was not wholly devoted to humaner letters. Theology, with astrology, its entertaining vice, also engrossed him, and he added Hebrew to his long list of conquered languages. Moreover,

he appears to have read such religious books as were
his with zeal and attention. His copy of *Chrysosto-
mus de Ecclesia* has its slender margins thickly
scrawled with notes, a tribute of interest which he
does not often pay to secular literature. For the rest,
his theology is varied in doctrine, and expressed in
many tongues. A metrical version of the Psalms in
Spanish, made by Juan le Quesne (1606), jostles an
ill-printed chap-book, entitled *A Briefe Instruction,
by way of Dialogue, concerning the Principal poyntes
of Christian Religion,* by the Rev. M. George Doulye,
priest (1604). Then there are the Latin poems of
Franciscus Bencius, the Jesuit, and five volumes of
sermons by Bernardino Ochino, the revolted Catholic,
whose famous *Tragedy* may have influenced Milton.
Nowadays there is not much desire to read the
reply of Villagagno, ' Eques Rhodius,' to Calvin ; but
the tract of D. Gregorius Nazianzenus, ' adversus
mulieres se adornantes et excolentes carmen satyri-
cum,' is still apposite, and should contain many
useful reflections. On the other hand, Drummond
consulted the stars as well as the orthodox guidance of theology, for he possessed not only one
of the works of Raymond Lully, but a far more
secret treatise, *De Elementis et Orbibus cælestibus,* an
ancient and erudite book written by Messahala, the
most highly vaunted astrologer among the Arabs,
whereto he added the yet more mysterious *Alcabitii
ad magisterium judiciorum astrorum Isagoge.* So he
was curious concerning precious stones and their pro-

perties, a lore closely bound to mediæval occultism, and he studied the matter in Conrad Gesner's Latin work on Fossils, Stones, and Gems, which the title-page assures us will prove useful and pleasant not only to doctors, *sed omnibus rerum Naturæ ac Philologiæ studiosis*. Thus the inquisitive Scot packed his head with mysteries, and put a humble faith in the literature and learning of an age earlier than his own.

Once in his life this man of books embarked upon an adventure which had nought to do with poetry or politics. Being a true child of his age, he devoted himself with a sanguine mind to the simple discovery of the impossible. The seventeenth century was a season of restlessness and research; the England of Elizabeth was dead, and the England of Anne, which was presently to be chilled by the cold douche of common-sense, was as yet undreamt. Meanwhile all the eager spirits were busy with miracles; they knew vaguely what problems awaited solution; they knew too little to recognise that the most were insoluble; and, when Drummond was granted the Royal Patent of an inventor, he proved himself as reckless and fantastic as the vainest of his contemporaries. To find a just comparison for his extravagance, you must go to the works of Sir Thomas Urquhart and the Marquis of Worcester, who both in style and project resemble the laird of Hawthornden. While the knight of Cromarty was prepared to deduce his pedigree from Adam or to square the circle, while the philosopher of Raglan would anticipate the steam-engine or revolutionise the martial arts, Drummond asked leave to fabricate ' various machines, which may be of use and profit to the State in the affairs both of peace and war,' and to solve the great problem of perpetual motion.

The ambition, no doubt, seemed modest in 1626, and no doubt Drummond deemed it essential to protect himself against the encroachment of rivals. Wherefore he composed a document, to which Urquhart himself might have set his name, and in which, after Urquhart's own fashion, he gave high-sounding Greek names to his warlike engines of attack or defence. But, like his rivals, he does no more than sketch his ambition ; he artfully refrains from explaining his inventions. For instance, he tells us that he has devised a cavalry weapon which will enable one warrior to perform as much in battle as five or six can do with the common arms. And the name of this weapon is Βακτροβροντηφον, or the Thundering Rod. No more precise in its details is his Λογχακοντιστης, or Shooting Pike, a murderous implement, wherewith one foot-soldier may do the work of six *sclopetarii*. Moreover, he would explode his enemies with burning-glasses ; he would invent a boat called the 'Εναλιοδρομος, or the Sea Postillion, which seems to foreshadow the paddle-boat of modern times ; he would construct a repeating-gun called the 'Ανωξιβαλιστρον, or the Open Gun, ' by which without fail in the same space of time in which hitherto one ball has been discharged, there may be discharged four or five, and that whether in naval or in land engagement.' After these exploits, maybe, a machine of perpetual motion, appropriately styled 'Αεικινητος, seems tame enough ; and the whole scheme is chiefly interesting because it illustrates the temper of the time. To us it is incredible that vague and wandering schemes such as these should need protection ; but Drummond was secured against all competition for twenty-one years, and the patent was signed and sealed at Hampton Court.

The hare-brained inventor, of course, is still in our midst—the poor, hopeless, hopeful maniac, who believes that the chasm between thought and fact may easily be crossed ; yet never did the hare-brained inventor thrive so fantastically as in the Britain of the seventeenth century. Urquhart and Drummond and Worcester were all possessed by that enchanting spirit of mad enterprise which distinguished their age and country, and they pursued their aim with so single-minded a purpose that it is not surprising that the ' scantlings ' of the Marquis of Worcester have been ascribed by more than one historian to the translator of Rabelais.

The keen interest which Drummond professes in the arts of war is mirrored in his library ; and he was as curious in the healing as in the giving of wounds. He possessed, for instance, ' the *Sclopotarie* of Josephus Quarcetanus, Phisitian, or His booke containing the cure of wounds received by shot of gunne or suchlike Engines of Warre,' in the English edition of John Hester (1590), and it is to the pages of this strange work, no doubt, that he owed some of his own ingenious notions. Moreover, that rare book, the *Pallas Armata*, was his, and right valiantly does it justify its sub-title, 'the Gentleman's Armorie, wherein the right and genuine use of the Rapier and of the Sword, as well against the right-handed as against the left-handed man, is displayed : And now set forth and first published for the common Good by the author' (1639). This work, of which but few copies exist, does not precisely touch upon the palatial art of the battlefield ; none the less, it is such as no warlike gentleman of the age could spare, and on its merits it is worth examination. For it is equipped with a set of cuts, which represent fencers, naked as when they were born, and among its dedications is a set of verses by no less a poet than Richard Lovelace himself. Thus Drummond treasured the literature of all such subjects as engrossed his active intelligence ; and if his ingenious projects were secure, not only against the privilege of twenty-one years, but against all time, they find a brilliant reflection in his books.

For, indeed, Drummond interpreted his library in no mean spirit. Though by the accident of his century he possessed a goodly collection of masterpieces, he did not cherish a peculiar love of rarities, and the few books, which to-day are unique, were not then read to shreds. But hear his own wise pronouncement : 'Libraries are as forests, in which not only tall cedars and oaks are to be found, but

bushes too and dwarfish shrubs ; and as in apothecaries' shops all sorts of drugs are permitted to be,
so may all sorts of books be in a Library : and, as they
out of vipers and scorpions, and poisoning vegetables,
extract often wholesome medicaments for the life of
mankind, so out of whatsoever book good instructions
and examples may be acquired.' That is a liberal
saying, and it explains the presence in Drummond's
library of many a book which the pedant of to-day
would dismiss with contempt.   Indeed, he had room
on his shelves for the anthology of jests and the
common chap-book, as well as for stately editions
of classics, while among his ' dwarfish shrubs ' are
not a few such as time seldom spares.   The sturdy
oak of literature easily survives the shock of centuries,
but the poor low-growing bush, whose leaves are
within the reach of every defacing hand, is speedily
torn to pieces.   So that while the Aldine Homer may
now and again be recovered, where shall we find those
slim pamphlets which pictured the crimes and criminals
of the seventeenth century ?   Yet they have their
fascination—these ragged, ill-printed books—a fascination rather of life than of letters.

In 1612, for instance, the name of John Selman was
on every tongue, and doubtless the ' flying-stationers '
of the time sold a rude woodcut of his features at every
street corner.   Drummond, at any rate, treasured a
stately, whimsical account of his exploits and dying
speech, wherein you know not which to admire the
more, the rhetoric of Sir Francis Bacon or the elo-

quence of the culprit. *The Arraignment of John Selman*, so runs the title, '*who was executed neere Charing-Crosse the 7 of January* 1612 *for the Fellony by him committed in the King's Chappell at White-Hall upon Christmas day last in presence of the King and Divers of the Nobility.*' That a miscreant should commit so base a crime on such a day, in such a place, before so august a company, might well seem monstrous; but Sir Francis Bacon's eloquence is humorously overcharged. 'The first and greatest sinne that ever was committed,' said the mighty lawyer, 'was done in Heaven. The second was done in Paradise, being Heaven upon Earth, and truly I cannot chuse but place this in the third ranke.' Even the obscure Selman, set side by side with Lucifer and Eve, must have felt amazed; but he too rose to the occasion, and his 'last speach' reflects vast credit on his ingenuity or on the prison-chaplain's literary sense. 'I am come (as you see),' he murmured on the scaffold, ' patiently to offer up the sweet and deare sacrifice of my life, a life which I have gracelessly abused, and by the unruly course thereof made my death a scandall to my kindred and acquaintance.'

After this little masterpiece Samuel Rowland's *Humours Looking Glasse* (1608) seems but sorry stuff, and argues that the cheap jest-book was not much better then than now. In the same category we must put '*A Chrystall Glasse for Christian Women. Containing a most excellent Discourse of The Godly Life and Christian Death of Mistriss Katherine Stubs, who*

*departed this life in Burton upon Trent in Stafford-
shire, the fourteenth of December* 1625 ' ; despite its
pompous title it is but a poor specimen of popular
theology.   Far more exhilarating in subject and treatment is the *Hymnus Tabaci* (1628), a dwarfish shrub
in the forest of books.   Its author, one Raphael
Thorius, modestly compares his work to the famous
Syphilis of Fracastorius, and appropriately illustrates
the title-page with Bacchus and his attendant satyrs
encircled with the fumes of tobacco.   Moreover,
being a doctor, he declares that his work ' non delectat
modo sed et docet,' and but for the slur cast by the
book upon Drummond's loyalty, which should have
compelled agreement with his hero James, we might
congratulate him without reserve on the possession
of a rare and trivial work.   However, it was not only
by such toyish books that he proved his curiosity.
The colonies over sea also entertained him, as is
attested by Captain John Smith's *Virginia and New
England*, and the treatise of Fernando Cortes, *De
Insulis nuper inventis*.   And that no human knowledge should seem amiss to him, he studied in French
the art of growing mulberry-trees and of making silk.

Such were some of the books which Drummond
presented to the University of Edinburgh with dignity
and circumstance.   He gave them at several times, and
he fitted them with varying inscriptions.   On the
title-page of one is written in a bold and elegant hand :
' Ego donatus sum Academiæ Edinburgenæ à
Guilielmo Drummond.'   Others bear his name alone,

almost faded to illegibility, and now, alas ! all are cut and clothed afresh.   There they were in the library of Hawthornden, when Ben Jonson paid his celebrated visit to Scotland ; and the facts that Drummond received his august visit in their midst, and that Ben himself possibly hooked some of them off the shelf to verify a quotation or enforce an argument, assuredly lends them an added interest.   For Ben Jonson's visit was the golden event of Drummond's life, and happily for us he has left a full and particular account of the conversations which were held across the table or at the fireside.   The journey itself is ever memorable, since Jonson made it on foot, for which the Lord Chancellor Bacon reproached him, saying that he 'loved not to see Poesy goe on other feet than poeticall dactylus and spondæus.'   The making of journeys was the fashion of the time, and Taylor, the Water Poet, was not many months in advance of Jonson. Indeed, Jonson found him at Leith, and gave him two guineas to drink his health withal, which, however, did not hinder him from telling Drummond that 'Taylor was sent along here to scorn him.'   And nothing could have been further from the truth, since Taylor tramped to Edinburgh, like an American journalist, with no worse object than to prove that he could cover four hundred miles without money or beggary.

Of Jonson's voyage we know but little, except that at Darlington his boots were worn out, that he pur-chased a new pair, and that he made it a point of

honour to make them last until he should see Darlington again.   Arrived at Hawthornden, he was met
with the immortal 'Welcome, welcome, honest Ben,'
which he instantly countered with 'Thankee,
thankee, Hawthornden.'   And then began the un-
equal duel of wits.   On the one side was the Scots
laird, by nature a gentle prig, by training an amiable
pedant.   On the other side gloomed the careless
swashbuckler, determined to fight the good fight of
letters even in the Mermaid's mouth.   Now, Drummond was always tinged with the vices of the *petit-
maître*.   Look at his portrait, and you will see that
he was no fit antagonist for Jonson's sturdy wit.
The lofty forehead, sure index of an overgrown in-
tellectuality, the mignard moustache, the elegant
ruff prove that the laird of Hawthornden was plea-
santly absorbed in the bubbling trifles of existence.
Moreover, he pursued literature, not because he must
or because his genius clamoured for expression, but
because, being a squire delicately tinctured with polite
learning, he found in the Muses a fashionable dignity.
The great names which were bandied up and down
Grub Street had been vaguely echoed in his ears;
his curiosity had tempted him to the purchase of
Shakespeare, Heywood, and Drayton as they reached
Scotland from the booksellers; and he expected the
arrival of Jonson as the Eastern Jew looks towards
sunrise for the fulfilment of prophecy.   Moreover, as
his timid respect for the professors of literature counselled him to silence, so he was prepared to listen with

reverential awe to the man who had shaken the hand
of Shakespeare, and had presided in his arrogance over
the parliament of poets.   And Jonson appeared, burly
and travel-stained, with no glow of fear or reverence
left in him, and prepared, after the first greeting was
over, to demolish the pretensions of every poet, except-
ing one, that ever climbed the slope of Parnassus.

How, then, should the two men have understood
one another ?   If Jonson were not profoundly interested in Drummond, Drummond could not help
listening with open mouth to him who had frequented
the Mermaid Tavern.   And Jonson, after the second
bottle, was ever eager to disparage all his contemporaries. 'What do you think of Shakespeare ? '
lisped Drummond in wholesome fear.   ' Shakespeare
wanted art,' retorted honest Ben, though he would
not have endured a hostile word levelled by another
at his friend and master.   Thereafter Ben, with light
and genial disdain, led Drummond over the wide
battlefield of literature, and showed him the heaps of
slain and wounded.   Sharpham, Day, and Dekker were
all rogues ; Donne (whom, by the way, Jonson reverenced), 'for not keeping of accent, deserved hanging';
' Daniel was an honest man, but no poet ' ; Drayton
(Drummond's especial idol) ' feared him, and he
esteemed not of him ' ; ' he beat Marston and took
his pistol from him.' So Jonson repeated the gossip
of the Coffee House, and Drummond trembled at his
insolence. How in truth should he stomach the vio-
lation of all his shrines ?   To Jonson the recklessness

of criticism was nothing ; he would not be held in the morning to the opinions which he expressed over-night ; he knew all the gods, and knew, moreover, that their feet, if not their heads, were made of clay. Worse still, the great man thought little enough of Drummond's own exercises : ' they smelled too much of the Schools, and were not after the fancy of the time : for a child (says he) may write after the fashion of the Greek and Latin verses in running.' Then, wearied with poetry, he turned to scandal, told intimate anecdotes of Gloriana herself, covered with shame the most of his contemporaries, and left Drummond gaping in terrified amazement.

Destiny never planned a more amusing situation, and most worthily did Hawthornden take advantage of it. For the gentle laird had a pale glimmering of Boswell's genius, which gave immortality to another Johnson, and he understood, better than most, the importance of trifles. So he jotted down the splendid trivialities of his guest, and the result is a precious document, bearing upon it the vivid marks of truth, from which we can get a clean and clear glimpse into the great age of English literature. That Drummond understood Jonson is unlikely ; that he disliked him is certain : the professed man of letters will seldom meet the polished amateur without distressing him by what appears (and is not) a common blasphemy. And when Jonson, having blackguarded all his friends, took up his cudgel again and went upon the tramp, poor Drummond sat down in the reaction which naturally followed this debauch of Rhenish and talk, to give his opinion of Jonson. Why not ? True, Jonson had spoken in the excitement of hot blood, while Drummond wrote in the composure of reminiscence ; but Drummond was dealing with material which he only half understood, and it is easy and just to find excuses for him.

Hitherto he had known none more intimately connected with literature than Andro Hart the Edinburgh printer, and Alexander the Edinburgh poet, so that Jonson's proud condemnation of all the world inflamed him to anger. ' Jonson,' he complained, ' is a great lover and praiser of himself ; a contemner and scorner of others ; given rather to lose a friend than a jest ; jealous of every word and action of those about him, especially after drink, which is one of the elements in which he liveth ; a dissembler of ill parts, which reign in him, a bragger of some good that he wanteth, thinking nothing well but what either he himself or some of his friends and countrymen hath said or done ; he is passionately kind and angry ; careless either to gain or keep ; vindicative, but, if he be well answered, at himself.' There you see the true man of letters sketched by the amateur. ' Given rather to lose a friend than a jest '—that is Ben Jonson's temper, and the temper of many a poet who lived either before or since. ' He was jealous after drink '—and you may be sure that the most of Ben Jonson's dogmatic opinions were delivered a very long way after drink. Yet Drummond's offended vanity is, in spite of itself, truthful and sincere. Old Ben could never have taken his host seriously. The memory of Hawthornden vanished with the taste of the last stoup ; for Ben most properly took up a far larger space in Drummond's imagination than Drummond could ever take up in his. And you readily forgive the aspersion as Jonson himself would have forgiven it—with a laugh of good humour. But Gifford, Jonson's biographer, unhappily inspired, has rated Drummond like the pedant that he was. He has also been betrayed by his partisanship into manifestly false statements. He declares that Drummond decoyed Jonson into his house that he might jot down notes, which he never intended to publish, and which were not printed until seventy years after Jonson's death. The charge is too foolish to demand refutation, and Jonson would be the first to flout the crazy loyalty of his biographer. Jonson, who had the humour which Gifford lacked, would have known that you cannot fetter the opinion of a host, and that Drummond had a perfect right to confide to his commonplace-book whatever wayward and casual views he chose to entertain. Indeed, he deserves a universal gratitude for exhibiting an admirable comedy played in the seventeenth century by the poet and the amateur—a comedy the more admirable, because the amateur that jotted it down guessed not of its excellence.

This, then, was the supreme event which passed in Drummond's library, and which throws a lustre upon the books now treasured in the University of Edinburgh. And the books have another interest, because Drummond, above all writers that ever held a pen, was the product of his library. He wrote English, as he wrote Latin, as he might have written French or Italian, like a foreign tongue. His very correctness proves the want of habit, and suggests that his language came straight from books. His verses leave you cold, because they are with few exceptions exercises upon a given theme. When he writes a sonnet, he thinks of Shakespeare, from whom also he borrowed his boldest images. The comparison of night to a reeling drunkard, for instance, might suggest a touch with life did we not remember that *Romeo and Juliet* was before him. In fact, he was a worthy imitator, who played the game of a past age more elaborately than any of those to whom the game was a natural heritage. He was, like his library, an Elizabethan who had wandered into the age of Charles ; he was prepared to fit the commonest idea with a symbol, and to turn the plain facts of life into metaphysical conceits. To say that he was a bad poet is more than any durst ; he suffers rather by being too good—by smelling, in Ben Jonson's immortal phrase, ' too much of the Schools.' He wrote few verses that you can criticise, fewer still that quicken your admiration. To say of Phillis, ' her hand seemed milk in milk, it was so white,' was to play the tune of the time without expression ; and it is perchance a bitter indictment to declare that such a line as 'the stately comeliness of forests old' strikes an odd note of freshness and sincerity. The truth is, Drummond was merely a poet in the sense that they are poets who dabble in Pindaric Greek. As I have said, he wrote a foreign language with all the ease and circumspection that an acquired knowledge demands. For all that, he was an accomplished versifier, and as good a specimen of the symbolist as our literature affords.

Now and again he attempted the austerer medium of prose, and strangely enough it is in prose that this bookish gentleman won his real triumph. His *Cypress Grove* is touched here and there by the rare quality of distinction. The obvious praise, which must be bestowed upon it, is none the less because it is obvious. It suggests and participates the sounding prose of Sir Thomas Browne. In thought it is but an echo of the prevailing Platonism ; in expression it is vastly better than the most of contemporary prose, and there are passages at least in which Drummond forgot that English was not the vernacular, that his style was masquerading in fancy dress. Take, for instance, the following : ' If thou dost complain that there shall be a time in the which thou shalt not be, why dost thou not too grieve that there was a time in the which thou wast not, and so that thou art not as old as that enlifening Planet of Time ? For not to have been a thousand years before this moment is as much to be deplored as not to be a thousand after it, the effect of them both being one : that

will be after us which long long ere we were, was.'   Or
again, this other passage : ' One year is sufficient
to behold all the Magnificence of Nature ;   nay,
even one day and night ;   for more is but the same
brought round again.   This Sun, that Moon, these
Stars, the varying dance of the spring, summer,
autumn, winter, is that very same which the Golden
Age did see.'   That is prose, not too sternly subdued
to the fashion of the ancients, yet stately and dignified.
And then again, when he tells you that ' life is a
journey on a dusty way ;   the furthest rest is Death,'
you have a momentary impression that he is writing
his own language ;   but when he proceeds that ' swift
and active Pilgrims come to the end of it in the
morning, or at noon, which tortoise-paced wretches,
clogged with the fragmentary rubbidge of this world,
scarce with great travel crawl into at midnight,' you
are brought back to the printed page, and you remember that after all Drummond was the child of
his library.

And to be the child of a library is no mean heritage,
since it assures the one supreme comfort of this life.
Drummond shows us what it is to be born of books ;
infinitely worse is his plight who is born without
books.   For books are the friends which can inflict
neither failure nor disappointment.   They grow old
with your blood, and buckle their friendship to you
with the passing years.   Of your nearest intimates
you may say what a wise lover of books said of
Plutarch : ' He is so universall and so full, that upon

all occasions, and whatsoever extravagant subject you have undertaken, he intrudeth himself into your work, and gently reacheth you a help-affording hand, fraught with rare embellishments, and inexhaustible of precious riches.' So it is that when men speak of taste, you may disregard their argument, and cling close to those well-worn friends, who have become yours by industry and usage. So, you can isolate yourselves in the tower of your library, and defy the world of fashion and displeasure. And it is for this that you love old Drummond, who has not only left a library, unique in history, but who found the true source of his inspiration in books—the kindest companions which man can encounter on this earthly pilgrimage.

ROBERT BURTON

R OBERT BURTON, *Democritus Junior*, made
his first entrance upon the stage of this
melancholy world on the 8th of February 1576. He
came of a gentle family, anciently established at
Falde, a pleasant village in Staffordshire; his grandfather, by marriage with Elizabeth Herdwick, had
acquired the manor of Lindley, situate at the foot of
Oldbury Hill, not far from Bosworth; and it was at
Lindley that Robert Burton was born. Of their
birthplace both he and his brother ever entertained
a kindly opinion, and well they might; for it was
favoured by art as by nature. It stood upon Watling
Street, at an equal distance from four flourishing
market-towns, and the soil, though a kind of woodland,
was yet apt for pasture and corn, and ' long ago it hath
had the praise for good sydowe pease (as they term
them '). Better still, it shared Ireland's immunity
from adders and other venomous snakes, which,
seen in ' all the bordering confines,' dared not trespass
upon the lordship of Lindley.[1] There it was that

---

[1] The Burtons, both William and Robert, professed a lively
interest in their family and lineage. In William Burton's
Description of Leicestershire (1622) much information may be
found concerning his ancestors, while a fourteenth-century

Robert Burton grew to boyhood, until he was old enough to become a grammar scholar at Sutton Coldfield in Warwickshire, ' *loco ingrato et sterili,* but in an excellent air, and full of all manner of pleasures.' The excellence of the air, however, did not compensate for the irksomeness of learning, and the cruelty of the harebrain schoolmaster, *Ajax flagelliferus,* who presently convinced Burton that there is ' no slavery in the world like to that of a grammar scholar.' From Sutton Coldfield he proceeded to Oxford, where, henceforth unto the day of his death, he led the calm, placid life of research, which best suited his temperament. Entered a commoner at Brasenose College in 1593, he was elected student of Christ Church, ' the most flourishing college in Europe,' and there, *augustissimo collegio,* he passed from youth to age,

volume of *Statuta Angliæ,* which belonged to Robert Burton and is now in the Bodleian Library, contains a curious series of notes. The first entry is made by William Burton, standard-bearer to Henry vi., who fell on Towton Field, and from whom Robert Burton was descended in the fifth degree. Of Burton's father we know little. Of his mother, Mistress Dorothy, we get an amiable picture in *The Anatomy.* She had excellent skill, as her son allows, 'in chirurgery, sore eyes, aches, etc., and such experimental medicines as all the country where she dwelt can witness'; and she did 'many famous and good cures upon divers poor folks that were otherwise destitute of help.' Once being at Lindley in the vacation time, Burton found her attempting to cure an ague with an 'amulet of a spider in a nut-shell lapped in silk,' and thought there was no warrant for her remedy. But when he discovered the same medicine recommended by Dioscorides, Matthiolus, and Aldrovandus, he bowed to authority and gave credit to his mother's amulet.

until, in 1639, death overtook him. It was from his
'studie in Christ Church' that he addressed to the
reader his conclusion of *The Anatomy*; it was to
Christ Church that he bequeathed such of his books as
Bodley's Library rejected; and the ancient and noble
foundation, to which he paid so high a reverence,
honoured itself and its alumnus by celebrating his
achievements in imperishable stone.

At the outset he looked for preferment in the Church.
He bustled abroad, tiring himself, and troubling all
his friends. Nor did he bustle in vain, since he found
bountiful patrons and generous benefactors. His
college conferred upon him the Vicarage of St.
Thomas in Oxford, 'to the parishioners whereof,'
says Anthony à Wood, 'he always gave the sacrament
in wafers,' while Lord Berkeley presented him with the
Rectory of Segrave in Leicestershire, which town, he
tells us, 'I am now bound to remember,' and which
is 'sited in a Champaign at the edge of the Wolds,
and more barren than the villages about it, yet no
place likely yields a better air.' Ecclesiastical eminence, however, was not the end of his ambition; he
was a scholar before he was a divine; and had he not
been content to remain *Democritus Junior*, to live a
silent, solitary, private life, *sibi et musis*, he would
surely have been caught up in a tangle of disappoint-
ments. For, though he confesses that, were there
no buyers, there would be no sellers, he knew well
enough that the Church suffered from griping patrons,
that covetousness and ignorance persuaded men to

traffic in livings. So, in single-minded content he
resolved to devote himself to humane letters, remembering full well that their pursuit, also, was not
without its miseries. Even if learning did not make
men mad, it availed them little. The scholar, who
escaped melancholy, was always richer in ridicule than
in pence. He lost his wits, neglected health, wealth,
and all worldly affairs, became no better than a
dizzard, merely that he might pierce profitless
mysteries, or confer immortality upon another. His
very knowledge was useless to him, since it did not
help him to pay court to a lady, or make a congee, like
a common swasher ; and he must perforce live out
his life either a parasite, ' crouching to a rich chuff
for a meal's meat,' or wearing the ragged livery of the
Muses.

Nevertheless Burton deemed himself fortunate in
the choice of a profession, nor did learning and
poetry ever find a more eloquent champion. Great
men are more beholden to scholars, he declared with
a proper arrogance, than scholars are to them. And
he would never join in laughing at the follies of his
kind : though he confessed readily enough that a mere
scholar was a mere ass, he recognised that the faithful
servant of learning was an ' honest, upright, innocent,
plain-dealing man.' 'What was Achilles without
Homer ? Who had known the Cæsars but for
Suetonius and Dion ? ' And with perfect sincerity
he gave a practical proof of his allegiance to scholarship. He lived penned in his study, and knew the

larger world only through the friendly intelligence
of books. But, if adventure and romance were
denied him, he was both a zealous student and a keen
spectator. For more than forty years he worked,
read, and talked in Oxford, well satisfied with the
gifts of fortune. There was a time, it is true, when
he felt the goad of ambition, when he would have
gone abroad to engage in the strife of wits, but the
desire of place and wealth passed; and 'now as a
mired horse,' he wrote, ' that struggles at first with
all his might and main to get out, but when he sees
no remedy, that his beating will not serve, lies still,
I have laboured in vain, rest satisfied, and, if I may
usurp that of Prudentius,

> ' Inveni portum; spes et fortuna, valete,
>   Nil mihi vobiscum, ludite nunc alios.
>
> .   .   .   .
>
> ' Mine haven's found, fortune and hope adieu!
>   Mock others now, for I have done with you.'

In bidding farewell to hope and fortune, he found
peace. ' I have little, I want nothing; all my
treasure is in Minerva's tower,' said he in a fine, characteristic phrase, and how rich was that treasure he
has proved in the parti-coloured wisdom of his book.
Henceforth, then, he did little else than read, write,
and laugh. Though he, too, like Montaigne, was a
desultory reader, he was desultory for another reason.
Montaigne skipped from book to book, because an idle
temper made close application impossible. Burton

was so greedy in the acquisition of knowledge, that he could not read fast enough, and confusedly tumbled over divers authors in his haste to make their wisdom his own. He was not in any sense what to-day we should call a specialist. It was his aim to have an oar in every man's boat, to taste of every dish, to sip at every cup. Though he disclaimed with an excessive modesty any profound learning, he boasted that he had a smattering in all things, and truly he made good his boast. The superficies of his knowledge can only be measured by the erudition of his time, and if he cannot lay claim to original research, the research of no scholar, ancient or modern, escaped his vigilant eye. Anthony à Wood handsomely sums up his accomplishments in a simple sentence : ' He was an exact mathematician,' says he, ' a curious calculator of Nativities, a general read scholar, a thro'-paced Philologist, and one that understood the surveying of lands well.' And, though he carried in his head so vast a baggage of other men's learning, no man was ever less of a pedant. Even when he quoted dead words, he seemed to inspire them with something of his own abounding life ; though he dwelt in a monastic seclusion, *ipse sibi theatrum*, though he never travelled but in map and card, he professed a vivid interest in the great drama, unfolding about him, wherein he played no part.

Now and again, however, he would go into the city, like Diogenes, to observe the fashions ; he would listen for a while to the chatter of the market-place ;

and with his quick apprehension would learn more in an hour than a clodpate in a year. And, even when he did not stir abroad, at least an echo reached him from the outside. The common-rooms were then, as now, the centres of amiable gossip, and in Burton's own words, ' a vast confusion of vows, wishes, actions, edicts, petitions, lawsuits, pleas, laws, proclamations, complaints, grievances, are daily brought to our ears.' Nor did he neglect any source of information. Grave scholar as he was, he loved the popular literature of his day, and when he died, he left behind him a priceless collection of chap-books, almanacks, and plays, ' now tragical, now comical,' such as Bodley had excluded from his library, lest it should be said that they had ' stuffed it full of baggage books,' and which nevertheless are to-day among that library's rarest treasures. Truly it was these very baggage-books which kept Burton's mind and diction fresh, and which saved him from falling, under the weight of learning, into the pit of pedantry.

Like many another great man, Robert Burton has eluded the biographer. Of his life and character we know no more than we may gather from his book and the genial anecdotage of tradition, which, though sometimes false in letter, is often as true in spirit as truth itself. Like the genuine scholar that he proved himself, he was at once simple and absent-minded, as Hearne testifies in his *Reliquiæ*. ' The Earl of Southampton went into a shop,' writes the Antiquary, ' and inquired of the bookseller for Burton's

Anatomy of Melancholy. Mr. Burton sate in a corner of the shop at that time. Says the bookseller, My lord, if you please, I can show you the author. He did so. *Mr. Burton*, says the earl, *your servant*. *Mr. Southampton*, says Mr. Burton, *your servant*, and away he went.' The pointlessness of the story is its point, and it gives us a vision of the ambling, fantastic scholar, whose mind was in his books, even when he went abroad.

Though he was by all accounts a 'melancholy and humorous' person, he could be, if he chose, the liveliest company. Anthony à Wood heard 'some of the Antients of Christ Church often say that his company was very merry, facete, and juvenile.' And we can easily imagine the excellent stories which this broad-minded, bold-tongued devourer of books told his colleagues in the common-room. Yet there were times when even the politest converse palled upon him, and then he would go down to the bridge-foot in Oxford [1] and hear ' the bargemen scold and storm and swear at one another, at which he would set his hands to his side and laugh most profusely.' There

[1] Such is the story told by Bishop Kennett, and it is matched by what Burton himself says of Democritus, 'that sometimes he would walk down to the haven and laugh heartily at such variety of ridiculous objects which there he saw.' Of course it may be said that Burton in going down to the bridge-foot was but imitating Democritus, but you are sure that Burton yielded to an imperious desire when he listened to the bargemen, and that the similarity of recreation is merely another tie which links Burton to his hero.

you get a glimpse of the real Burton, whose humanity was never quenched by scholarship, and who, feeling at times the inevitable reaction from books, could only cure his boisterous temper by a boisterous remedy. Indeed, if we do not picture him delving in the pages of a mighty folio, we see him, in our mind's eye, shaking his sides with laughter at the bargemen's scurrility.

' A little wearish old man '—in these words Burton describes Democritus, with a glance, no doubt, at his own mirror, for Burton too was little, wearish, and old. If we may trust his portraits, there shone in his face a kindly, sly intelligence, which his book does not belie, and for once at least, we find aspect and talent closely matched. Something of a precisian, too, he seems, one whom study has gifted with a serene insight into men and things. And though he gave his days and nights to research, he was scarce heard of in the world of letters, until the publication of his *Anatomy* made him for ever famous. His name is rarely met in the annals of his time. Apart from sundry sets of verses,[1] we can ascribe nothing to him,

---

1 The curious will find two sets of verses signed ' Rob. Burton, S.T.B., ex Aede Chr.' in Camden's *Insignia* (1624), while a tract entitled *Death Repeal'd by a thankful Memoriall sent from Christ Church in Oxford, celebrating the noble deserts of the Right Honourable Paule late Viscount Bayning of Sudbury*, contains a quatrain by Burton, both in Latin and English. The Latin is inelegant, and the English is no better than the doggerel which does duty for translation in the *Anatomy*. For the rest some dozen specimens of Burton's Latin muse survive. Marriages

save a Latin comedy called *Philosophaster*, which was acted at Christ Church on February 16, 1617. Though it first saw the light in 1617, it was written some years earlier, as the author is careful to explain, and with good reason.[1]   For in the meanwhile Ben Jonson had lashed in the *Alchemist* the same impostors as inspired the satire of Burton, who justly defended himself against a possible charge of plagiarism.   The play itself, though we should not pay much attention to it, were it not for the authorship, is far fresher and more sparkling than the most of such performances.   Its scene is laid at Osuna, in Andalusia, whose Duke attempts to revive the glories of an ancient university.   He, therefore, invites men of learning to his city ; and his appeal is answered by a mob of quacks in poetry, science, and philosophy, whose pretensions are an admirable excuse for Burton's satire.   Now and again the satire assumes an air of prophecy, and the author sketches in imagination a bridge which shall unite Dover and Calais, and dreams that the Mediterranean is made a fish-pond.

and funerals were his best inspirations.   On the one hand he deplores the deaths of Prince Henry and James I.   On the other he sings an Epithalamium to Charles I. and Henrietta Maria. But it is evident that he was an unskilled poet in either tongue.

[1] The *Philosophaster* was lost for many years, and was not printed until 1862, when Mr. Buckley edited it for the Roxburghe Club.   Two copies exist in manuscript, of which the one belonged to Burton's brother, the other was Burton's own. On Burton's copy it is stated that the play, written in 1606, was 'alterata, revisa, perfecta Anno Domini, 1615.'

Meanwhile he was composing his masterpiece, nor did his labour end in the composition. With unfailing diligence he saw the book through the press, correcting 'many letters mistaken, misplaced, added, omitted . . . false points, etc., which are in some copies only, not throughout.' And even after the first edition had astonished the world, his work was not done. He still increased, polished, and corrected, until in 1639 death gave the last cure to his melancholy, and then he bequeathed to the printer a sheaf of emendations. Thus unto the end he remained faithful to the pursuits of a melancholy scholar, and it is not surprising that gossip declared him a suicide. Surely, said the popular voice, he who writ of madness, must needs be mad himself, and how should madness end, save by the rope? Mr. Robert Hooke told Aubrey, who was not one to waste a piece of scandal, that ' he lay in the chamber of Christ Church that was Mr. Burton's, of whom 'tis whispered, *non obstante* all his astrology and his books of Melancholy, that he ended his days in that chamber by hanging himself.' And there was another reason why the credulous should believe that Burton hastened his end. It was whispered that, having calculated his nativity, he had foretold the day of his death, and ' rather than that there should be a mistake in the calculation, he had sent up his soul to Heaven through a slip about his neck.' Here gossip is at fault. So sane, facetious, and humane a man as Burton died, one is sure, at his appointed time. Nor was he of those who, like Montaigne, believe that every one has a right to rid himself of a vain and tedious life. He condemned suicide with a determined eloquence. ‘God and all good men are against it,’ he wrote. ‘He that stabs another can kill his body, but he that stabs himself kills his own soul.’ And while he condemned the sin, he excused the sinner. ‘God’s mercy,’ said he, ‘may come betwixt the bridge and the brook, the knife and the throat. Who knows how he may be tempted. It is his case, it may be thine.’ However, for this sin Burton needs no forgiveness, and Christ Church paid him the honour that is withheld from those guilty of self-slaughter. He was buried in the north aisle of the Cathedral, where a comely monument with a ‘bust painted to the life’ marks his grave, and beneath the bust is this inscription, which none save he could have written : *Paucis notus, pauci-oribus ignotus, hic jacet Democritus Junior, cui vitam dedit, et mortem Melancholia.*

That melancholy gave him death is a rhetorical artifice. That melancholy gave him life the fame of his *Anatomy* is a certain testimony. For Burton, like Rabelais, like Montaigne, is the master of a single book,[1] from which his fame can never be dissociated

---

[1] The First Edition of Burton’s book, *The Anatomy of Melancholy*, was published at Oxford in 1621, a quarto, which was subsequently enlarged to a folio. Its success was immediate, and Anthony à Wood says that the bookseller got an estate by it. It is attributed on the title-page to Democritus Junior, and Burton sternly reproves the curiosity of those who would discover him. ‘Seek not after that which is hid,’ says he ; ‘if the

in the minds of men. In one sense, at any rate, melancholy has marked him for her own. Moreover, his choice of a subject was as natural as it was fortunate. Not only could he observe among the celibates of Oxford many a victim of the fell disease, but its power and effect had already manifested itself in his own family, and Burton must have been familiar, even in childhood, with the hapless fate of his mother's brother, the gallant and comely Anthony Faunt. Now, this valiant soldier was chosen, at the rumoured invasion of the Spaniards in 1588, Lieutenant-General of all the forces of Leicestershire; but, being crossed in his resolution by the Earl Huntington, who appointed his own brother to that service, he ' fell into so great a passion of melancholy, that within a short time after he died.' Burton was attacked by the same plague which untimely carried off Anthony Faunt, and with less excuse. ' I writ of

contents please thee, and be for thy use, suppose the Man in the Moon, or whom thou wilt, to be the author, I would not willingly be known.' And then by a characteristic inconsequence, he signs the 'Conclusion of the Author,' which appears only in the First Edition, 'from my Studie in Christ Church, Oxon. December 5th 1620. Robert Burton.' The famous title-page engraved by C. Le Blon first appeared in the Third Edition. ' How comes it,' asked Mr. Bullen in 1893, 'that the *Editio Princeps* of the *Anatomy* is not in Christ Church library ?' There is one excellent reason : the copy, which Burton presented to the most flourishing college in Europe, is now in the British Museum. The inscription on the back of the title-page is unmistakable : *Ex dono Roberti Burton aedis hujusce alumni.* But how it escaped from Oxford to London is unexplained.

melancholy,' says he, ' by being busy to avoid melancholy ' ; and so he shaped his work by turning over such physicians as the libraries of Oxford could afford. He owns that divinity is a worthier subject, but he would rather preach sermons than print them, and none knew better than he that to engage in the polemics of theology was to cut off an Hydra's head. ' One had much better provoke a great Prince than a begging Friar, a Jesuit, or Seminary Priest,' says he, in a phrase which he borrowed from Pope Alexander, and which Rabelais also echoed. Nor did he care when the doctors murmured *ne sutor ultra crepidam* : if physicians take orders, why shouldn't he write of physic ? ' I am by profession a divine,' said he, ' by inclination a physician. I had Jupiter in my Sixth House.' Even the wise are sometimes blind to their own merits, and, if Burton thought that his book would be read for the physic that was in it, he was cruelly deceived.

For Burton selected his subject not merely because it agreed with his temper, but because it was of universal application. It enabled him to say to his reader, ' thou thyself art the subject of my discourse.' In his opinion all men are mad. ' All fools are mad,' quoth he, ' though some are madder than others. And who is not a fool ? Who is free from melancholy ? ' Look where you will, you will find more need of Hellebore than of Tobacco. Joy or sadness makes no difference, since laughter like tears is but an expression of folly. In vain we pretend that wealth

and power are the outward signs of wisdom. Princes
and rich men are as crazy as philosophers. Even the
most learned are at fault : they will attempt to square
the circle, and neglect that which is of far greater
value, the proper conduct of their lives. If Democritus
were to revisit the earth, what would he see, but
' *Cumane* asses, maskers, mummers, painted puppets,
outsides, phantastick shadows, gulls, monsters, giddy-
heads, butterflies.' All changes, save folly, which
alone is constant both in men and states. There is
not a single profession which escapes the universal
plague. Religion is but a mad mockery in a world
where there are ' so many Christians, yet so few
imitators of Christ, so much science, so little conscience.' Rabelais gives the same sentiment another
turn, and there is no doubt whence they both borrowed
the phrase. And to what shall we liken the Jesuits,
who, pretending poverty, have infinite treasure and
revenues ? To what but to ' watermen, that row one
way, and look another ? '
    Then this preacher of sound sense turns from re-
ligion to war, and proves that madness has driven the
bravest soldiers to indiscriminate slaughter. Cæsar
killed a million ; Mahomet, the Turk, three hundred
thousand ; and to what end ? Thus he deplores the
proper men, able in body and mind, annually sacrificed
to Pluto ; thus he holds Ostend up to horror, ' the
Devil's Academy, a poor town, but a great grave.'
Yet he would not follow the fantastical Anabaptists,
and condemn war of all kinds, knowing in his wisdom

that, as some wars are necessary, so valour is the best ornament of a wise man. The law, again, is more mad than carnage, and the market-place than either. For there ' our *summum bonum* is commodity ; and the goddess we adore *Dea Moneta*, Queen Money, to whom we daily offer sacrifice, which steers our hearts, hands, affections all.' And there is madness in states as in men ; there is madness even in vegetals. Mad, mad, mad ! All are mad. ' Begin where you will, go backward or forward, choose out of the whole pack, wink and choose, you shall find them all alike, *never a barrel better herring.*'

So it was for this that Burton determined to discourse of melancholy : it is the universal malady. With melancholy for his excuse, he might describe all the passions and foibles of mankind ; he might indulge to their utmost the waywardness and eccentricity of his style. For be it remembered that Burton's theme is as little to his main purpose as Rabelais' fable. Each is a mere excuse for humour and rhetorical embroidery. His attempts to cure the disease, which he detected in every manifestation of human folly, are neither serious nor seriously meant. He was less intent to find a remedy for others than to indulge his own genius, and merely rejoiced that he had chosen a subject which should express his erudite fancy. To compare Burton's work with his predecessor Timothy Bright's *Treatise of Melancholy* [1] is to note the essential

---

[1] Timothy Bright's *Treatise of Melancholy, Containing the Causes Thereof, and Reasons of the strange effects it worketh in*

difference between the two methods. Burton, to be sure, was perfectly familiar with Timothy Bright's work, which he quotes with deference; and it is possible that but for the learned Doctor's example he might have given his own masterpiece another colour. Indeed, though it is idle to force a comparison, Bright anticipates many of Burton's characteristic reflections. He, too, contrasts the Sardonian laughter of Democritus with Heraclitus' tears; he, too, sings a pæan to the Air, and praises with what skill he may a ' pleasant garden and hortyard with a lively spring'; he, too, insists that a house should be ' cheerful and lightsome, trim and neat,' lest it seem to the eye of melancholy rather a prison or dungeon than a place of assured repose. But these resemblances arise from the subject, and it is by their differences that they must be judged. Nor would the veriest pedant deny Burton's infinite superiority. While Bright composed an erudite tract in a dry, if dignified, style, Burton, under the shadowy pretence of dealing with melancholy, discussed at large of the one subject that is of eternal interest, Mankind.

But, precisely because his book was human rather than scientific, it amused him to adopt a scientific

our minds and bodies: with the Physicke Cure, and spirituall consolation for such as have thereto adjoyned afflicted Conscience, was dedicated to the Right Worshipful Mr. Peter Osborne in 1586. Its author is chiefly remembered to-day as an inventor of a system of shorthand, but his *Treatise* would be worth reading, even if Burton had not shed upon it the light of his own immortality.

terminology. The title—*Anatomy*—was fashionable in his day, and was lightly turned to all uses, but the pompous division into Partitions, Sections, Members, and Subsections was a mystifying whim of his own. And, if none of his readers ever scrutinised too closely his entertaining apparatus, it is part and parcel of his plan, and wholly characteristic of his scholarly humour. No doubt he arranged his subdivisions with a conscious mirth, and we may share his own Democritean smile as we note them. *The Anatomy*, however, is scientific in aspect alone, and Burton, firm in the belief that the disease is universal, surveys all the vices and virtues of mankind. Wherever he finds excess— either of vice or virtue—there he detects the seeds of melancholy. Gluttony and abstinence, poverty and riches, Venus ' omitted ' or ' intemperate,' all produce the same melancholic result. Indeed, if so eloquent a rhetorician as Burton can be said to have a gospel, it may be summed up in the single word—moderation. But his aim is always epideictic rather that didactic. He would always rather display his own skill than teach his readers a lesson, and he willingly interrupts his main theme with the portrait of a vice or a Theophrastian character.

Above all, when he gives a full rein to his borrowed eloquence, you know not whether it is a dirge or a pæan that he sings. With an inextinguishable gusto he tells you that ' gluttony kills more than the sword,' declaring that, despite the misery which follows a surfeit, we still ' rage and luxuriate in this kind.' In other words, 'Lucullus' ghost walks still, and every man desires to sup in Apollo.' Then in rapid sentences he paints the joys and pleasures of the table, quoting Rabelais, that French Lucian, to the effect that wine is better for the body than physic, because there are more old drunkards than old physicians. ' 'Tis now come to that pass,' he exclaims, ' that he is no gentleman, a very milk-sop, a clown, of no bringing-up, that will not drink, fit for no company ; he is your only gallant, that plays it off finest, no disparagement now to stagger in the streets, reel, rave, etc.' What cares he that his prose is too scant of breath for grammar or logic ! On he goes down the swift current of eloquence and quotation, and then pulls his Muse up suddenly at a contrast. If some offend by gluttony, others offend in over-much fasting, ' pining adays and waking anights ' ; or they draw the mischief of melancholy on their heads ' by too ceremonious and strict diet, being over-precise, Cockney-like and curious in their observation of meats, times.' Who, then, since there is no happiness in this world, shall escape the common ban ? If you avoid gluttony and drunkenness, if a starving delicacy of appetite do not overtake you, then idleness, the badge of gentry, or solitude, its cousin-german, may involve you in ruin, sorrow may gnaw your heart, fear may freeze your blood, shame drive you to madness and a rope, or ambition, that dry thirst of honour, that pleasant poison, will send you to seek in anguish what you had better be without. ' They climb and climb still, with much labour, but never make an end, never at the top.'

More foolish yet is the covetous man, possessed by his money rather than its possessor, bound prentice to his goods. ' He is of a wearish, dry, pale constitution,' says Burton in a passage which recalls Theophrastus, ' and cannot sleep for worldly cares and business.' Though he be always adding to his heap of useless gold, he dare not spend a penny, lest he should die in want. And miserable as is the harpy, still more unhappy is the poor man. For Burton never accepted the conventional view that poverty is a blessing in disguise. He knew that in his gullish times wealth swayed all. 'Tis money that gives life and soul ; the poor man is ' under hatches, dejected, rejected, and forsaken, poor in purse, poor in spirit.' Worse still, poverty makes men ridiculous, and ridicule pierces the stoutest courage, the gayest indifference. Nor are these miseries the only fruitful sources of melancholy. He who escapes the snares of poverty or wealth is still a prey to the treachery of friends, the dread of death, the decay of strength, and a thousand haunting superstitions. Of what profit is it then to strive and cry ? Were it not ' much fitter for us to be quiet, sit still, and take our ease ' ?

It is when he comes to consider Love-Melancholy that Burton proves his highest qualities of humour and eloquence. Nowhere outside Rabelais will you find so fine a gallimaufry of fantastic words and conceited phrases. Here, at last, Burton lets his imagination run its fullest riot ; a careless frenzy takes him ; and the old scholar shows plainly enough that he has learned from books and life all the secrets of the art, which he declares he never practised himself. Though he heaps up his quotations with as lavish an erudition as before, he finds a style that is wholly and inevitably his own, and he treats with an open candour those things concerning which English writers have generally been silent. At the outset he proffers the conventional apology, though he declares that he needs no excuse. He asserts that the most of men would rather read Apuleius than Plato, and he cites the example of Heliodorus, who, bidden to choose between his book and his bishopric, let the bishopric go. Thereafter he quotes Catullus, Martial and Ovid gaily to his purpose, and he omits none of the stock arguments, which have been adduced since the beginning of time in favour of frank and open speech. *Omnia munda mundis,* says he, having already declared of his famous Partition, ' 'tis not scurrile this, but chaste, honest, most part serious, and even of religion itself.' So saying, he protests too much, and it is to better purpose that he echoes his master Rabelais : ' 'tis a Comical subject ; in sober sadness I crave pardon of what is amiss, and desire thee to suspend thy judgement, wink at small faults, or to be silent at least ; but if thou likest, speak well of it, and wish me good success.' Thus, in making a sound defence of the literature that is called ' curious,' he composes a proper prelude to his amazing dissertation.

In his eyes Love is universal, like melancholy, but, unlike melancholy, it is or should be nothing but good and fair.   Moreover, it is a passion which influences animate and inanimate alike.   As a stone falls, so the fire flies upwards, so the rivers flow to the sea.   The loadstone attracts iron, while the loves and hates of plants are known to the poet and philosopher alike. The Vine, which loves the elm, hates the bay, and the olive and bay are intertwined by a natural affection. In brief, as Shelley wrote long afterwards—

> See the mountains kiss high heaven,
>   And the waves clasp one another ;
> No sister-flower would be forgiven
>   If it disdained its brother.

And Burton is not content to put his faith in the common principle of Love which dominates the world. With the simple credulity, characteristic of his age, he believes in all the fables related by Jovianus Pontanus, Saxo Grammaticus and the rest.   In perfect gravity he tells the story of two palm-trees, of which the male grew at Brundisium, the female at Otranto, and which were barren, until they came to see each other's increasing height, though separated by many stadiums.   In brief, so sure is he of the doting of dumb things, that he puts a poet's credence in the amorous spindle, fired by a Lady's looks, and in the cold bath, which suddenly became hot, when Cælia entered it.   And then he pictures with a swift fancy the manifold allurements of Love,—the face, which is Beauty's Tower, the eyes, which are Love's Fowlers, the comeliness of apparel, the seduction of wealth, the power of opportunity, to Burton, as to Montaigne, irresistible. The tricks and prankings, moreover, which lovers use are innumerable—a sweet voice and music, the singing of such songs as ' O Cupid, Prince of Gods and Men,' kisses, nods, jests, and winks, and above all the incitement of dancing, that honest disport. If all these fail, there is the last refuge of tears, but tears, in the old philosopher's view, are of small service. ' As much pity is to be taken of a woman weeping,' says he with customary cynicism, ' as of a goose going barefoot.' And, even when tears prove unavailing, there remain philters and amulets, spells and charms. To such as find a certain hair in a wolf's tail of no effect, he recommends, on the soundest authority, a swallow's heart, or the dust of a dove's heart. Thus, for all his knowledge of books and men, he bows the knee in patient slavery to the picturesque superstitions of his age, and proves that intelligence need not be at variance with a constant faith.

It is the symptoms of love and jealousy which best display his ingenuity of thought and word. To these symptoms he owns there is no end. " 'Tis a bottomless pit,' says he, and he confesses by way of apology that in the matters of love he is a mere novice, a simple contemplator. No apology is needed, for, novice or not, he has made the subject his own, and his supremacy is never likely to be challenged. The reflection that lovers are not merely brutish and doting, but blind also, inspires that purple passage which is his greatest achievement in the art of invective. 'Every lover admires his mistress,' says he, 'though she be very deformed of herself,' and thereupon he heaps epithet upon epithet, until in describing the ugliness of woman he has exhausted the vocabulary of vituperation. Then in an instant all is changed to graciousness, deformity becomes beauty, in phrase at least, and he gathers into a few pages the fair imagery which the poets, both classic and mediæval, have invented to do their mistresses honour. This, then, is the Partition, which is most vividly characteristic of our Democritus. The eloquence has no tinge of melancholy ; rather it is as many-coloured as the wing of a bright-plumaged bird, as swift as the current of a winter stream. His wit shifts and turns with his rapid thought ; a gust of humour blows through every page ; and you recognise that it was not in vain that he stood at the bridge-foot in Oxford. The causes and cures of jealousy succeed one another in breathless haste ; he has as many reasons why you should or should not marry as Panurge himself ; and having arrived sudden at the end of his argument, he increases the mystification by telling you that there is one other sovereign remedy against jealousy which he is not willing to publish. Yet, 'if you be very desirous to know it, when I meet you next, I will peradventure tell you what it is in your ear,' and each one must interpret this irresistible, unspoken antidote after his own guise.

And the book which gave its author an enduring immortality, how was it composed ? All of the spoils of other men. Never was there so desperate a pirate as Burton. He flew the black flag upon every high-sea of literature, and let the ships which he encountered scuttle to forgetfulness, when they had yielded him their proper plunder. In other words, he depended with an easy confidence upon his library, and when once he had decided that melancholy should excite his fancy, he ransacked all the books of the world for episode or illustration. ' I have laboriously collected this *cento* out of divers writers,' says he with open-hearted frankness ; and he justly compares himself to an apothecary, who makes new mixtures every day, pouring out of one vessel into another. The result belongs as much to him as the mixture belongs to the apothecary. For, paradoxical as it may seem, his outlook is all his own, though books are the medium of his vision. And it is not merely his facts that he owes to others ; he affects to be in debt for his feelings also. If he laughs, it is with Lucian ; if he is satirical, it is with Menippus ; his tears flow at the bidding of Heraclitus. He was, however, no plagiarist. He could not say with Molière, *je prends mon bien où je le trouve,* because he had no excellence that he did not find ; but his robberies were all made *sine injuria*. ' I have wronged no authors,' said he, ' but given every man his own.' Yet in this very dependence there is a kind of origin-ality. None before him, not even Athenæus, had

ever presented so fine an example of the encyclo-
pædic mind. Montaigne, in spite of his devotion
to the classics, shines through every page of his book.
Burton reveals himself by his preferences and his
curious gift of style. None the less, though he
uses the words of others, he can express his own
opinions in the plainest terms, and it is not his fault
if we do not know what views he held upon all the
questions which engrossed his contemporaries.

Omne meum nihil meum—that is his own and the
truest description of his book. And if there is no
news here but what he stole of others, he had an
unrivalled genius for happening upon the pocket best
worth picking. His authorities are chosen with the
most erudite catholicity. The classics, the middle
ages, the fathers, the profane Latin writers, the
masters of his own day in prose and verse,—he gives
an excellent account of them all. No man that ever
lived could match him in the art of apposite quotation, and his readiness seems the more remarkable,
when you remember that he did not score heavily the
volumes in his library, and that he must have carried
the literature of the whole world in his head, if he
had not recourse to commonplace books. The width
of his reading is proved by the fact that some of his
citations still elude the vigilance of scholars, though
his own margins afford not a little aid. And, as he
collected his authorities from a thousand sources, so
he flung them down higgledy-piggledy upon the page,
content only if they echoed to his purpose. Often-

times he is reckless enough to quote from memory, and he will follow up his Latin, not by a translation, but by a hasty paraphrase. Greek authors he cites in the Latin of their interpreters, because the originals are not ready to hand, and it amuses him to clip and cut the poetry of all tongues into the homeliest doggerel. The classics, of course, leap ever to the tip of his pen. Plato and ' our great Mr. Aristotle ' are constant guides unto his footsteps, and there is no master of Greece or Rome with whom he is not intimately familiar. Moreover, he knows the decadence as well as the Golden Age, and he is unwilling to press any argument without the support of Austin and Tertullian. With a wise frequency he embellishes his page with many conceits from the *Metamorphoses* of Apuleius, and he proves his just appreciation of Petronius by calling the *Satyricon* a ' fragment of pure impurities.' And then he summons to his aid Lucian and Aristophanes, Erasmus and Aretine, who, less known then than now, gave to his pages a fresh sparkle of wit. Above all he rescued from oblivion the names at least of inaccessible authors, who were long ago buried beneath the weight of their own Latinity, and who, but for Burton's borrowings, would have passed silently into the night of forgetfulness—Cardan and Bodine, Joachimus Camerarius and Peter Alcioneus, Villanovanus and Leo Suavius, Avicenna and Jason Pratensis. Whatever debt he owed these authors he repaid tenfold, since under his auspices they escape for a moment from their dusty folios, and live a brief while in his vivid para-phrase.

And while he sought the most of his illustrations in the dark obscurity of Latin, he did not overlook the gracious poets of his native land. The works of Chaucer, you may be sure, lay ever at his elbow, for he quotes him with a cheerful heart, and he pays ' our English Homer '—for thus he styles him—the noble tribute of always printing his lines in black letter. No mark of respect could be more fitting or more fittingly bestowed, and it is characteristic of Burton's wide sympathies that, while the masters of the past are living guides to him, he sees his own English authors in a just and equal perspective. Perhaps he did not pay due honour to Shakespeare, whom, in citing *Venus and Adonis*, he describes as ' an elegant poet of ours '; but to Spenser, ' our English Maro,' he gives his true character, and if you hardly recognise Drayton as an ' English Ovid,' you cannot doubt the wisdom of Burton's admiration. Daniel's *Complaint of Rosalind* is manifestly among his favourites, a near rival to Marlowe's *Hero and Leander*, while for the rest he quotes Ariosto in Harington's translation, and proves his acquaintance with both Jonson and Wither. Among the prose-writers of his time he shows the highest honour to ' our Camden,' to whom his own Christ Church once gave shelter, and after him he commends, as well he might, Richard Hakluyt, the panegyrist of English courage and adventure, which the old stay-at-home loved so

well. And then he applauds Reginald Scot, for a
scepticism, which he did not wholly share; and
more than once cites that strange treatise concerning the *Passions of the Mind,* which we owe to
Thomas Wright, the Jesuit. But the two dominant
influences of Burton's book, discerned far oftener
than named, are Montaigne and Rabelais. Had not
Democritus Junior studied these two masters, his
Anatomy would have assumed another shape and
impress. To be sure he casts his net wider, and
catches many more strange fish, than Montaigne;
but his book is a *cento* in a closer sense even than the
famous *Essais.* And he borrows so many tricks of
style and diction from Messer Alcofribas, that it is
with perfect justice that he has been called the
English Rabelais. He had the same love of bold,
fantastic words as the ' French Lucian '; he delighted
with the same gay heart to play upon his vocabulary
as upon a musical instrument, to increase his effect
of pleasure or vituperation by adding epithet to
epithet; and he knew, as well as his master, the
humour that twinkles in the sly arrangement of
living words. And his sympathy with Rabelais and
Montaigne is far deeper than a mere trick of style or
cadence might suggest. On the one hand, he shared
Montaigne's wise scepticism; and still relying on the
ancients as his guides, he examined the conclusions of
his contemporaries with the caution which the old
essayist would have approved. On the other, he
was a convinced Pantagruelist, a philosopher, who

took all things in good part, and who tempered even his fiercest satire with a kindly shrug.

The plan upon which his book was composed perforce affected his style, which is inevitably disjointed, ecstatic, and full of surprise. Its rhythm breaks as merrily as a shallow brook bubbling among the stones. Now his sentences are unfinished, now they come to an abrupt conclusion in an inextricable tangle of Latin and English. Dignity and repose are not for him, and he obtains his most brilliant effects by the curious choice, or rather the intricate jumbling of words. His thoughts, and even his sentences may be borrowed from the Latin, but his diction is all his own. Where others gain glory by a skilful phrase, he wins the garland by his vocabulary. In the mere lust of words, he rivals Sir Thomas Urquhart. As I have said, he loves a catalogue as dearly as Rabelais himself, and he has so fine a mastery over the language, that he can tumble you out a dozen synonyms at will. If he wishes to describe a woman to whom Nature has been unkind, ' a filthy knave,' says he, ' a deformed quean, a crooked carkass, a maukin, a witch, a rotten post, an hedge-stake.' Nor does he show a pedantic preference for words of Saxon or Latin origin. He is determined to use the full resources of the language, and he does not scruple to mix the dialect of the street with the pompous, high-sounding terms of the study. Thus, like a modern decadent, he speaks of 'stupend and exquisite textures,' 'circumforanean rogues,' ' facete comparisons,' and ' turgent

titles.' Thus in set terms he condemns 'such as
personate, rail, scoff, calumniate, perstringe by name,
or in presence offend.' And then he will flout the
vast mob of ' whifflers, outsides, noses of wax, wittols,
afternoon men, counterfeit cranks, hog-rubbers, prick-
louse tailors.' In brief, his supreme talent is a talent
of invective. No writer has ever collected within a
single book so many varied and ingenious terms of
abuse. He has a torrent of contumely ready for
every wrongdoer, and though the wrongdoers be
many, the torrent never fails.

He can change his tone in an instant, and bring
himself back from the digressions, which he loves so
well, with a single exclamation, such as ' But I rove,'
or ' Halloo, my Fancy,' Elegance itself is not beyond
his reach, and if he will, he can gather the pearls of
gracious speech upon the thread of fancy. ' Whiteness in the Lily,' writes he, discoursing of beauty,
' red in the Rose, purple in the Violet, and lustre in
all things without life, the clear light of the Moon,
the bright beams of the Sun, splendour of Gold,
sparkling Diamond, the excellent feature of the Horse,
the Majesty of the Lion, the colour of Birds, Peacocks'
tails, the silvery scales of Fish, we behold with singular
delight and admiration.' And it is upon Charity
that he has composed his most eloquent rhapsody,
leaving for a while his habit of quotation, and point-
ing his noble satire with a haunting refrain : ' He
cares not, ride on,' which Sterne was presently to
assume for his own. Thus, the energy of this *aquæ*

potor never flags, nor did he need the encouragement
of wine, which ' so much improved our modern
wits.' Nevertheless, despite its tireless energy, it is
the book of an old man, for Burton perchance was
never young; and whatever be its faults of ' bar-
barism, Dorrick dialect, tautologies and apish imita-
tions,' *The Anatomy* is the mirror of an erudite and
lively mind, fed by books as by experience, and still
original, in spite of many borrowings.

Again, for all his dependence upon his library,
Robert Burton was a prophet of the open air, and in
his longest digression he considered all that was *sub
dio*. Here, he is far indeed from melancholy, and
yet nearest to his own soul. For this old scholar
would, if he could, have visited the uttermost parts
of the world. The problems of geography tempted
him as actively as the mysteries of Love. He would
have sought out Manoa or Eldorado, he would have
tested Marco Polo's ' lies,' and would have found
them true. He would have answered the question
whether Hecla was the mouth of Hell, and whether
Christ died for the Antipodes. He would have discovered the character of Nations and Climates, and
explained the diversities of hot and cold. Nothing
should have escaped his curious eye, neither the goose-
bearing tree of the Orcades, nor that strange Cirk-
nickzerksey lake in Carniola. Then he would have
been the spectator of mighty events. And, alas!
he never travelled but in imagination; he never
knew the great doings of great men, save by hearsay.

It was not for him to be present at mighty battles, such as Agincourt, or to witness the interviews of famous monarchs, such as Henry VIII. and Francis I. He must be content to read of the 'feasts, triumphs, interviews, nuptials, tilts, tournaments, combats, and monomachies,' which he was never destined to see. Yet even the perusal of these solemnities was 'pleasant and acceptable,' and, if it were not permitted him to appear upon the vaster stage of life, he might still enjoy *deambulatio per amoena loca*, he might still make a petty progress, a merry journey now and then, with some good companions, to visit friends, see Cities, Castles, Towns. He might still walk amongst gardens and orchards; he might still ' take a boat in a pleasant evening, and with musick row upon the waters.' Above all, he would inhabit a pleasant house, fronting the south, and in a good air. And if perchance melancholy overtook him, he would retreat to his library, that Physick of the Soul. There he would study algebra or ' divine Opticks '; there he would ponder upon the eternal problems, how man should walk on the water or fly in the air, how nativities should be cast or circles squared. And, after all, why should he repine that an untoward fate forbade him to wander abroad ? 'Tis the mind, not the place, that gives tranquillity, and enlarge our experience as we will, we are still slaves. What is Life but a Prison ?

While Burton harboured the soundest views concerning the conduct of life, he gave a cheerful credence, as I have said, to the manifold superstitions of the past. Like many another erudite, he seems to have preserved a kindly faith in the printed page. He was of those for whom the Pagan Gods not only had lived, but survived. He was ready to take warning by Jupiter, or to shape his virtue by the example of Hercules. With a touching simplicity he believed all the fables of Pliny and the poets, and he thought his case well proved when it had gained their support. Moreover, he doubted as little of spirits as of werewolves, and he gravely discusses whether there be more Angels than Devils in the air. Nor was he wholly sceptical concerning the power of witchcraft, and, though he thought that spells, charms, and barbarous words were merely used by the Devil to delude mankind, he was convinced that Magicians could cure and cause most diseases in such as they love or hate. Again, being an astrologer, he professed a calm confidence in the Stars, but he set upon their action a definite limitation. 'If thou shalt ask me what I think,' said he, 'I must answer, *nam et doctis hisce erroribus versatus sum*, they do incline but not compel ; no necessity at all, *agunt non cogunt*, and so gently incline, that a wise man may resist them ; *sapiens dominabitur astris* : they rule us, but God rules them.' And then, to cap his superstition, he asks, with guileless sincerity, 'Why doth a carcase bleed when the murderer is brought before it some weeks after the murder hath been done ? '

The same man who accepted the many popular
illusions of his time set forth the wisest opinions upon
science and theology. None saw more clearly, than
he who had studied all things, the limits imperiously
put upon human knowledge; none confessed with
better humility that, if too large a return were asked
of science, she must soon be bankrupt. And when he
heard Philosophasters contending about the Sun and
Moon, ' it is to be feared,' said he, ' that the Sun and
Moon will hide themselves . . . to make an end of
all those curious controversies, and scatter them
abroad.' Still more bitterly he hated the arrogance
and fanaticism of those, who believed that they
engrossed the truth. For him the Spanish Inquisition was the fourth fury, and he esteemed priests and
monks no more highly than did Rabelais. Accordingly, he drew a bitter picture of the Papists, who
keep the people in ignorance, and conceal the Scripture
beneath an impenetrable cloak of Latin. ' Whom
do they begin with,' demands he, ' but collapsed
Ladies, some few tradesmen, superstitious old folks,
illiterate persons, weak women, discontent, rude, silly
companions, or sooner circumvent.' Equally foolish
in his eye are schismatics and schoolmen, who take
God's office out of his hands, who ' will bind and loose
in Heaven, release, pardon, forgive, and be quartermaster with him.' ' Be quartermaster with him ' !
Where shall you match that excellent phrase, save in
that other, wherein he reproaches the heretics who
take upon themselves to be familiar with God, and to

be of his Privy Council ? With similar insight and irony he throws scorn upon the vanity of missionaries, thus anticipating the fuller wisdom of to-day. He denounces the many Christians who leave their native countries to seek martyrdom in the Indies as the victims of a slavish superstition, and he can find little pity for them when they fall beneath the rude knife of savages. But, for all his contempt of heretics, schismatics, land-leaping Jesuits, and false prophets, Burton was always loyal to his own order, and devout according to his own creed. Though he could find no, terms too harsh for the priests, who domineered over Princes, and especially for the High Priest of Rome, ' the dam of that monstrous and superstitious brood, the bull-bellowing Pope,' he declared that Justice and Religion were the two chief props of a well-governed commonwealth, and he acknowledged with Sabellicus that ' a man without Religion was like a horse without a bridle.' In truth, he was a zealous foe both to fanaticism and to heresy, and his chapter upon Religious Melancholy, in which he trusted to his own invention more freely than was his wont, is a sound defence of untrammelled reason and liberal thought. And deeply as he loved laughter, gaily as he indulged his genius of irony, he did not say farewell to his readers without a valiant exhortation. ' Only take this for a corollary and conclusion,' he wrote on his last page, ' as thou tenderest thy own welfare in religious, and all other melancholy, thy good health of body and mind, observe this short Precept, give not way to solitariness and idleness. *Be not solitary, be not idle.*

'SPERATE MISERI, CAVETE FELICES.'

And Burton was no less wisely guided in politics than in religion. Though satire was his aim, he once turned aside from his purpose to sketch a Utopia of his own, and in sketching this he proved himself a prophet of real foresight. The country of his imagination should be perfectly designed and equitably governed. Each of its twelve provinces should have a metropolis, where should be sold all things necessary to the use of man, and no market-towns, markets or fairs should be permitted to beggar the cities. Churches, theatres and hospitals should be built by the state, not by gouty benefactors, who after a life of fraud, rapine, and extortion give something to pious uses, and scruple not to rob a thousand to relieve one. From the shame of these benefactors we still suffer to-day, and Burton's denunciation of *Dea Moneta,* Queen Money, has not lost one word of its force and truth. His paternal government, moreover, would neglect no detail of administration. There should be not a barren acre in all its territories ; and, that prosperity should be generally diffused, noblemen and gentlemen should be tied to residence in their own towns. But because all things were well ordered at home, travellers should not be discouraged, and he would have certain ships sent out every year to make discoveries. In the law-courts all causes should be pleaded *suppresso nomine*, and, though peace at any price should never be advocated, Scholars should come before Soldiers in the public esteem.   He who performed any noble exploit at home or abroad should be honoured and preferred.   'He that deserves best shall have best.' If people over abounded they should be eased by colonies, for Burton was a pioneer, in thought at least, of our colonial system, and he had so just a perception of our military needs, that he would have a navy always ready and soldiers *in procinctu*.   For those modern organisations, which we call trusts, Burton had no sympathy.   'I will have no private monopolies,' said he, 'to enrich one and beggar a multitude.'   And having come thus far he shouts *Manum de tabula*! But not before he has detected some of the evils which plagued (and plague) our state, and suggested for the worst of them a wholesome remedy.

For Burton, though he lived and died a scholar, had a keen instinct for affairs ; and, being a patriot, he has sung a lofty pæan to his native land, 'a blessed, a rich country, and one of the fortunate Isles.'   But affection did not blind his vision ; and, if he detected some thistles among the roses, it was that they should be rooted out with all speed.   So he deplored the idleness and love of drink, which were the ruin of Englishmen, the over-crowding of our cities, the lack of navigable rivers, the bad transport from town to town—'we are,' said he, 'like pigs in a sty' ; and he concludes that we need some general visitor, who shall reform what is amiss. Had his faculty of reflection been transmuted to action, who knows but he might have proved a great statesman ? In truth the master-quality of his mind was prudence. Though he chose melancholy for the subject of his work, he was always busy to avoid it ; and, though he vowed that all men were mad, by his achievement he proved himself sound in mind and body. And an historian of literature has described his book as a neurotic compendium. Neurotic ! Was ever an epithet thus misplaced ? So little neurotic was this brave old filibuster of words, this tireless satirist of human folly, that he preserved in the reign of James i. the daring of the Elizabethan age, and felt in the seclusion of his study in Christ Church something of that spirit of enterprise that animated Drake and Hawkins.

The success of Burton's masterpiece was immediate and still endures. Not only were six editions published in thirty years, not only did Cripps, the bookseller, get an estate by it, but, as Burton robbed libraries after his princely fashion, so others pilfered from him. ' 'Tis a book so full of variety of reading,' wrote Wood of *The Anatomy*, ' that gentlemen who have lost their time and put to a push for invention, may furnish themselves with matter for common or scholastical discourse and writing.' And its influence was soon seen in the literature of the time. When Thomas Heywood writes, in *Love's Mistress* : ' Say she be a foul beast in your eyes, yet she is my syren ; and showing foul to others, and fair to me, I shall live the happier, and she the honester,' he doubtless has in his mind the famous tirade in the Partition of Love-Melancholy. Moreover, the splendid passage in the same dramatist's *English Traveller*, wherein a set of revellers, ' in the height of their carousing,' conceive ' the room wherein they quaffed to be a pinnace,' and, fearing shipwreck, fling overboard ' stools, tables, trestles, trenchers, bedsteads, cup, pots, plate, and glasses,' and swim for their life upon the floor, is imitated from a well-known passage in Burton (Part I. Sect. ii. Mem. iv. Sub. vii.), who himself translated it from Caelius Rhodiginus.[1] Nor is Heywood the only poet who put his hand in Burton's cupboard. If the Passionate Lord's song in Fletcher's *Nice Valour*, ' Nothing's so dainty sweet as lovely Melancholy,' gave a hint for the *Abstract of Melancholy*, wherewith Burton prefaced his book, Milton himself did not disdain to borrow both from Burton and Fletcher, when he composed *Il Penseroso*.[2] But it was Sterne who stole from Burton

---

[1] The same story had already been told by Athenaeus, and it did not arrive at the end of its wanderings in the page of Heywood. ' This pleasant piece of exaggeration,' says Charles Lamb, (' which for its life and humour might have been told, or acted, by Petruchio himself) gave rise to the title of Cowley's Latin Play, *Naufragium Joculare*, and furnished the idea of the best scene in it.' But its introduction into modern literature is Burton's handiwork.

[2] Warton not only points out Milton's debt to Burton's verses, but also surmises that he owes not a little to a certain passage of prose in the chapter entitled *Exercise Rectified* ; and it is natural that Milton, writing of melancholy, should refer to

with the most reckless daring. He put no limit upon
his depredation. To embellish his own narrative,
he lifted phrases, turns of style, and episodes. He
even stooped now and again to a literal transcription
of such passages as suited his purpose, and Dr. Ferriar
does not exaggerate when he declares that ' the singu-
larities of Mr. Shandy's character were drawn from
the perusal of Burton.' From one point of view,
indeed, *Tristram Shandy* is put together from the
pages of *The Anatomy*. And when Sterne played the
Apothecary, he did not reveal whence he procured his
drugs; he could not say with Burton that he mixed
them always *sine injuria*.

While Sterne pursued Burton with a secret and
furtive adoration, Johnson professed a reverence for
our English Democritus that was open and unashamed.
And even the great Doctor himself once picked
Burton's pocket without acknowledgment. While all
the world is tired of hearing that Burton's was the
only book that ever took Johnson out of bed two hours
earlier than he wished to rise, all the world forgets
that the Doctor's celebrated definition of oats—' a
grain which in England is generally given to horses,
but in Scotland supports the people '—is but an echo
from *The Anatomy*. Now Burton tells us that ' Joh.
Major, in the first book of his History of Scotland,

Burton's treatise, then at the top of its fame. Another of
Burton's debtors is Margaret, Duchess of Newcastle, whose
Dialogue between Melancholy and Mirth recalls, even verbally,
Burton's *Abstract*.

contends much for the wholesomeness of oaten bread.' On this point the authorities disagree, and ' Wecker (out of Galen) calls it horsemeat, and fitter for juments than men to feed upon.' Thus, the Lexicographer has borne the reproaches of Scotland for five generations, though his sin was not a sin of wicked invention, but merely a piece of genial plagiary. And after Johnson, Byron and Thackeray with loyal eloquence have acclaimed the genius of the old Anatomist, and no word of their panegyric is undeserved. For has he not presented to English Literature the wisdom of all the ages, and proved by his single masterpiece that skilful arrangement and a sturdy style may endue with originality the sweepings of a library and the confused pilferings of other men's brains ?

JACQUES CASANOVA

JACQUES CASANOVA, the most reckless adventurer who ever rescued a damsel in distress or broke a faro-bank, was born of roving parents in 1725. His father was an actor whom his mother, the daughter of an honest shoemaker, had married against the will of her parents. She not only married Gaëtan Casanova, but she also embraced his profession ; and, though her son amiably insisted that she possessed no talent whatever, she remained an actress until the end. Jacques had such a bringing-up as Bohemia affords, but his quick wits were in his favour, and at sixteen he was received Doctor of Law by the University of Padua. His own bent was to study medicine, and it would have been wiser, says he in a brilliant flash of self-knowledge, had he been permitted to follow his bent, since in medicine charlatanism is more useful than in law. His mother was determined to make him an advocate, and it was only his own resolution which saved him from a distasteful career. The truth is, he hated all work that was not a pleasure, and after a brief interval devoted to the Church, he chose the only profession which suited his peculiar talents—the profession of an adven-

turer. Henceforth he served no harder master than
his own inclination, and if 'he emptied his friends'
purses,' as he said, 'to satisfy his caprices,' the
money cumbered his pocket but a moment, and
straightway passed on to enrich another.

To follow his wanderings is to exhaust the map of
Europe. He was but eighteen when he found his
way to Constantinople, on what errand he knew not
himself. His instinct to keep the best of company
was already awake, and he carried with him a letter
to M. de Bonneval, an indiscreet Frenchman, who had
turned Mussulman, and who wore the turban as he
wore a uniform. 'Had the Jews offered me the
command of fifty thousand men,' De Bonneval told
Casanova, 'I would have laid siege to Jerusalem.'
Under such auspices Casanova had a foretaste of the
grandeur which was presently to be his. He played
and he won; he indulged his fancy for elegant
banquets and fine raiment. Wherever he went he was
courted by the fair, and applauded by the witty.
But disgrace, which dogged his footsteps to the end,
soon overtook him, and he was thrust into prison on
a charge (so he says) of thrashing a servant. However, he was soon at liberty, and shaking the dust of
Constantinople from his feet, he made his way back
to Venice. Here, too, bad luck awaited him. He
lost at the tables, and with his money vanished health,
courage, and repartee. His self-confidence was not
yet perfect. He knew not how to ruffle it with an
empty pocket, and, professional gamester though he

was, he had not yet learned the art of correcting fortune. He was, therefore, compelled for a while to earn a crown a day fiddling at a theatre, and it is not surprising that he regarded this episode as a blot upon his career.

Casanova was born under a fortunate star. He was not destined to spend his life scraping music in an orchestra, and before long came an opportunity which he was quick to seize. He had played at a wedding, and going homeward overtook a red-robed senator, who offered him a place in his gondola. Suddenly the senator was seized with apoplexy; Casanova hastened to find a doctor, and having taken M. de Bragadin (such was the senator's name) back to his palace, he complacently installed himself there. ' If I leave the poor man,' he said sententiously, ' he ' will die ; so long as I remain he will live.' He could not have pursued a wiser policy. M. de Bragadin was an amateur of the occult sciences, and he at once took Casanova for an adept. The rascal did not contradict him, for he was never reluctant to claim the knowledge thrust upon him by others. He modestly invented an old hermit who had taught him to make certain calculations, which M. de Bragadin instantly recognised as the *clavicula* of Solomon, called *cabbala* by the vulgar. Thus Casanova became the hierophant of M. de Bragadin and his friends. He told them what they wished to believe, and they construed his answers as best suited their purpose. Henceforth they did nothing without consulting their adept, and

he in return was adopted by M. de Bragadin as a son.
'You need have no thought for the future,' said the
worthy man ; 'you have nothing to do but to amuse
yourself, and whatever may happen be sure that I
shall always be your father and your friend.'

Casanova wished nothing better. To be rich and
protected was the career which of all others he would
have chosen for himself. He threw a loose rein to his
inclination. He gambled, he talked, he wrote verses,
he made love to all the beautiful women who crossed
his path, and he was supremely happy. 'I began to
give myself airs,' said he, 'to lay down the law, and
to quote authors whom I had never read.' If ever
he was involved in a difficulty, Serenus (the cabalistic
name of M. de Bragadin) was ready to extricate him,
after a brief consultation of their oracle, which they
had agreed to call Paralis. Paralis, indeed, was omni-
potent, and served Casanova loyally until the day
came when he hung his arms upon the wall, and retired
beaten from the contest. Meanwhile he rode gaily
down the highway of fortune. Henriette succeeded
Christine, Esther rivalled Thérèse, Casanova's heart
beat susceptibly, yet never broke. And like all men
of enterprise he desired to see the world. Venice,
despite her attractions, was too small for his ambition,
and as he had won money all the winter he determined
(in 1750) to set out for Paris.

What delight was his ! To be young, rich, and for
the first time in Paris ! Though he wrote his *Memoirs*
an angry old man in the seclusion of Dux, he could not

keep from his pages the joyous enthusiasm of youth. He visited the Palais Royal as a pilgrim visits a shrine, and his ardour was unchecked by the bad chocolate and worse coffee which they gave him to drink. He marvelled open-eyed at the crowd waiting to have its snuff-boxes filled at the Civet Cat, where they have been filling snuff-boxes ever since; he instantly caught the habit of the place, took his part in the comedy played around him, and in two days the famous men of Paris were his friends. Crébillon taught him French, though he could not cure his pupil of Italian idioms; he saw the King and Madame de Pompadour; he listened to the modest eloquence of D'Alembert. To this first visit to France he looked back with enduring pleasure, and when he described it, he knew that he had seen the city he loved best for the last time. 'The popular effervescence there,' said he in the tone of a true courtier, 'has disgusted me, and I am too old to hope to see it calm down.' So he returned to Venice after three years of wandering, conscious that his time had not been wasted. 'I had gained experience,' said he, 'of men and manners. I was acquainted with the laws of honour and politeness. I felt I was superior to my surroundings.' And in this assurance he took up his old life with an added moderation and reserve.

For all his good resolutions, he was soon as careless as ever, and in M. de Bernis he found a most suitable comrade for his revels. No place seemed sacred in his joyous eyes; at a wave of his hand even

the convent parlour became a ball-room, and he drank
the cup of pleasure unalloyed, until suddenly he
attracted the attention of the State Inquisitors. To
what he owed this awkward courtesy is uncertain, for
his own account is untrustworthy. It is characteristic of the man that, brutally frank in all else, he is
careful to conceal the causes of his many imprison-
ments, and to explain tortuously his frequent expulsions from foreign capitals. However, he declares
that Manuzzi, a spy of the Inquisition, visiting him
on a false pretence, detected on his bookshelves certain
books and manuscripts which dealt with magic. Now,
though he indignantly protests that he was never a
dupe himself, Casanova always found it both pleasant
and profitable to dabble with the occult sciences, and
this time, if we may believe him, he paid for his taste.
A few days after Manuzzi's visit, the Great Inquisitor
arrested Casanova before sunrise, seized his suspected
library, which contained such works as the *Zecor-
ben*, the *Clavicula Salamonis*, and an essay on the
Planetary Hours, and sent him after a hasty examination to the notorious state prison of Venice—the
Leads. His cell was neither elegant nor commodious.
The poor window which it boasted was blocked by a
huge beam placed athwart, and its ceiling was so low
that Casanova could not stand upright within it.
Worse still, it was infested with rats and fleas. Such
was the dungeon in which the hero was forced to lay
down his paduasoy mantle, his beautiful new coat, his
hat trimmed with a long white feather and Spanish

point lace, like a strayed reveller in a hovel. The surroundings harmonised so little with Casanova's taste, that he felt his mind totter. When his right hand touched his left, cold and numb from the hardness of the boards on which he lay, he thought he was touching the hand of a dead stranger. In his own words, ' what was true appeared false, and what was false appeared true.' But like a brave man he called philosophy to his aid, and resolved never to surrender the hope of freedom while life was in him. Nor were the books with which an indulgent gaoler provided him designed to cool his heated imagination. *The Mystical City*, by Maria d'Agrada, tortured his sleep with extravagant dreams, which, like the man of letters that he was, he longed to put upon paper. Despite visions, solitude, and vermin, he preserved his courage, and instantly began to make a plan of escape. His only chance was to pierce the floor of his cell, and where were the instruments fit for so difficult an enterprise ? Here again luck and philosophy aided him. ' I have always held,' said he, ' that what a man wants to do, that he will do, in spite of all difficulties, but he must begin early, for after a certain age fortune forsakes one, and cannot be whistled back.'

Casanova was but thirty, and he did not whistle in vain. One day, walking up and down a large cell next his own in which he was allowed to take exercise, he espied among other rubble an iron bar and a piece of black marble. Instinct told him their value, though when he first concealed them among his shirts he did not know the precise use to which he would put them. It was not long, however, before he had made a long octagonal dagger by rubbing the bolt upon the marble, and with this implement he set out to bore a hole in the floor. After sawing through two stout boards, he came upon a layer of what the Venetians call *terazzo marmorin*, and was in despair, until he remembered that Hannibal had made a passage through the Alps with vinegar. Straightway he poured the vinegar from his salad through the hole, and with excellent effect. The omens, too, were propitious : escape seemed within his reach ; and then the blow fell upon him. As an especial favour, he was moved to pleasanter quarters, and not only was all his work made vain, but his plot was revealed to his gaoler.

Yet he was undaunted. He reduced his gaoler to silence by threats of exposure, and speedily devised another plan. Through the gaoler's mediation he had exchanged books with a fellow-prisoner, a monk named Balbi, and the two lent or borrowed books, and presently began a correspondence. Casanova, with his keen sense of character, soon summed up the miserable Balbi, and in spite of the monk's stupidity determined to make use of him. He was the more easily persuaded to this course, because escape could only be made from Balbi's cell, and he conveyed his precious dagger to the monk, concealed in the binding of the *Vulgate*. It was Balbi's business not only to pierce the floor which divided him from Casanova, but also to make a passage from his own cell out upon the roof. The monk set to work in fear, and Casanova, as he translated an ode of Horace, listened in jubilation to the tapping overhead. Now the hero, consulting the *Orlando Furioso* as to the time of his escape, had pitched upon the line *Fra il fin d'ottobre e il capo di novembre*, and it was near midnight on 31st October when he and Balbi made their way through the holes pierced by the monk on to the roof. The Inquisitors were in the country, and the gaolers had seized the chance of a carouse, so that the fugitives had a fair start, and Casanova surveyed the city from a gable in the roof with a proud satisfaction. Two hundred feet in front were the cupolas of St. Mark's, and as he looked out upon the church, the bell struck twelve. The tag from Ariosto came to his mind, and then he was sure that success was his. But there was many a difficulty still unsolved. To enter the garret window was easy enough, and one of them could be let down by the cord which Casanova had made of his bed-clothes. But what of the other ? They dared neither lose their cord nor leave so obvious a clue. Balbi, of course, insisted upon going first, and Casanova was left to wander alone over the roof. And there upon a sort of terrace he found that which never eludes an escaping prisoner,—a ladder, which, with infinite toil, he pushed through the garret window, and so descended. He found himself in a vast gallery, and then, incapable of further effort, he fell into a deep slumber, to the great fear and disgust of Balbi. When he awoke it was five o'clock, and outside Venice was beginning to stir. Exploring the gallery he found it led to the Ducal Chancery, whence they emerged, by smashing the panels, on to the staircase of the palace. Between them and freedom was but a vast door, too strong to batter, which would yield only to the porter's key. There was nothing left but to put a bold face upon it, and setting his fine hat trimmed with gold Spanish lace on his head, Casanova gazed nonchalantly out of the window. He attracted instant attention : the porter, fearing he had locked in a senator by mistake, hastened to undo the door, and as the door turned upon its hinges, Casanova and Balbi fled across the square on to the quay, and before the signal of alarm could be given, they had leapt into a gondola.

Free at last, Casanova stood upon the pinnacle of good fortune. He was proud of his escape, and justly proud, until the day of his death. Moreover, he had won fame as well as freedom. Henceforth, wherever he went, he was pointed out as the notorious Casanova who had escaped from the Leads. Kings and popes asked him, in all humility, to relate the story of his flight, and with a characteristic arrogance he was wont to put them off with an excuse. But he was never tired of telling the tale to his friends, and he told it, says the Prince de Ligne, with inimitable spirit and energy. So, gay and famous, he wandered up and down the world, always suspected of this crime or that, until he might boast that he had been expelled

from every capital in Europe. Gambling was the real
business of his life, now as always, and none ever
showed finer courage at the green table. When he
was in good fortune he kept the bank; and if luck
frowned on him, he did not disdain to punt with the
most reckless. He played to win, and therefore was
not too scrupulous in the handling of the cards.
Thackeray borrowed his philosophy for Barry Lyndon,
and it may be summed up in the words: ' Never
cheat, but get the better of fortune.' This happy end
may be ' attained by some happy stroke of fortune,
some touch of dexterity, independent of luck '; and
Casanova considered that ' a prudent player can make
use of either or both these means without incurring
blame or being taxed with cheating.' Nor was it only
by getting the better of fortune that Casanova filled
his pocket. He did not disdain the immemorial practice of the decoy, and with Antonio della Croce's wife
to attract the unwary, that Milanese scoundrel and
Casanova once fleeced an English Jew and a wealthy
Swede of many thousands. And in the eighteenth
century gambling did more than fill the pocket; it
took its professors into the best company. Thus it
was through the cards that Casanova knew Fox, to
whom he once lent fifty louis, which the statesman
paid him back years afterwards in London. Through
the cards, also, he encountered the Duke de Roseburi,
that diffident youth who bowed oftener than he spoke,
and whom Casanova saw smile only once. Though
generally lucky, he knew, like other gamblers, what it

was to be fleeced, since fortune sometimes refuses to be corrected ; and once, when he broke the bank at *biribi*, he was paid in light coin, for passing which he came near to imprisonment. Yet for many years he had no other means of livelihood than magic and the card-table, and since he most often lived in splendour, it is evident that he knew how strokes should be made and had the courage to make them.

On one occasion he rose to heroism. It was at Salsbach, where a Frenchman, named D'Entragues, offered him his revenge at piquet. Casanova was indifferent, and complained that the Frenchman always gave up after a brief hour of play. D'Entragues, in anger, pressed his adversary, and proposed that the first who left the table should lose fifty louis. This was a bet after Casanova's heart, and he eagerly accepted it. At three o'clock they sat down, and at nine D'Entragues suggested supper. 'You are free to go,' said Casanova, 'but I shall pocket the hundred louis.' They played through the night, and when the water-drinkers appeared at six in the morning, they found the heroes still absorbed. Throughout the next day they faced each other across the table with no other food than chocolate and a cup of broth. Casanova boasts that he is still fresh, and declares that his adversary 'looks like a dug-up corpse.' In vain their friends intervene. Obdurate they sit through another night, until at nine o'clock the next day D'Entragues rocks in his chair, and falls fainting to the floor. 'He was carried to bed,' says Casanova with

pride ; ' I gave six louis to the marker, who had marked
for forty-two hours, put my gold in my pocket, and
walked down to the apothecary's. I then went to
bed and slept till three.' It is superb ; and who can
wonder that Casanova counted this conquest of
D'Entragues among his loftiest triumphs ?

When the cards failed him, he fell back upon magic,
and here he was no mean rival of Cagliostro, who more
than once crossed his path. For many years he lived
upon the amiable credulity of M. de Bragadin, and he
found Madame d'Urfé an easier and yet more profitable dupe. For Casanova she was Semiramis, and he
was her Galtinarde. An extravagant vanity persuaded
her that she was an adept, and Casanova befooled her
with flattery, until she obeyed him in all things, and
paid whatever price he chose to ask for his counsel.
For many years he consoled and plundered this poor
lady. She bought him out of prison, she gave him
jewels, she squandered money on him, while he in
return conducted a correspondence between her and
the moon, and as a final act of chicanery, superin-
tended the great metamorphosis, whereby she was to
be born again in the shape of a man. This masquerade
of mysticism is eminently characteristic of the age
which respected Cagliostro, and one knows not
which is the more surprising, the simplicity of Madame
d'Urfé, or the cold shamelessness of Casanova, who
set down the facts with no more than a word of
apology. Yet of all his achievements he liked his
domination of Semiramis the least ; and, though he

was glad enough to swindle his ' poor old friend ' while she lived, her death by an overdose of the panacea was a shock to more than his pocket.   But in dealing with the occult sciences Casanova followed the taste of the time, and his contemporaries no doubt deemed it his worst sin that he pretended to a deeper knowledge than he possessed.

And of this pretence Casanova was always guilty. The rapidity of his wit enabled him to pick the brains of others without their discovering the theft.   When he came to Paris, in all the pride of his escape, he cast about him for an honest livelihood.   M. de Bernis, always his friend, urged him to ' invent something which would bring money into the royal coffers,' and gave him a letter to M. de Boulogne, the Comptroller General.   Now Casanova knew naught of finance, but he told M. de Boulogne unabashed that he had ' a scheme in his head which would enrich the king by the interest on a hundred millions.'   Of course he had nothing of the sort in his head ; and when M. de Boulogne innocently remarked, ' I know of what you are thinking,' he feigned surprise, and wisely held his tongue.   The royal financiers were less astute, and one of them, handing him a book, said, ' There is your project, M. Casanova.'   There it was in truth,—a lottery, and M. Casanova hastened to make it his own.   Moreover, if he could not invent, he could amend, and a few suggestions so vastly improved the plan, that the patient officials readily attributed it to the man who knew least about it.

The lottery proved successful, and Casanova was clearly marked out for preferment. He was sent upon a secret mission to Dunkirk, and presently was despatched to Holland to discount the royal paper. In these enterprises his tireless energy and quick intelligence served him well, and though it is to his credit that he was always a bad spy, he had a shrewd head for business, and might have died a rich man but for his spendthrift habit. And even in Holland the beauty of Esther Hope charmed him more than her father's money-bags, for, after all, love was the ruling passion of his life.

No man was ever a more liberal lover. The image of M. M., exquisite though it was, could not wholly efface the subdued beauty of C. C.; he had room in his heart for Pauline and Mlle. X. V. C., for Hélène and Hedvige; few indeed were the ladies over whom he did not shed a tear of sensibility at parting. He loved them all, but he was the enemy of marriage, and he was forced, too often by a hard-hearted magistrate, to ride away. Whether they loved him is another question; but one at least, the peerless Henriette, remembered him to the end, and tended him with devotion when he lay ill and broken in Spain. He himself was complacent in good and evil fortune. 'My vanity was excessive in those days,' he wrote, looking back to his brilliant youth with pride. 'I considered all the women of Europe one vast seraglio destined for my pleasure.' And despite his predilection, he was no mere trifler, no indolent breaker of women's hearts.

Other interests claimed him and other ambitions. Like all the distinguished men of his time, he cultivated wit, and dabbled in scholarship. He vaunted his power of repartee with some justice, and his best sallies are at once quick and dignified. Moreover, in prison and out of it, he had always been a student; he had read books and written them. In his old age, indeed, he became something of a pedant, and bored the Prince de Ligne and his other friends by incessantly quoting Homer and Horace, both of whom he had translated. But his genuine interest in humane letters is everywhere evident in his *Memoirs*, and he talked with poets and philosophers upon equal terms. To converse with great men was, in truth, his constant pride, and in his pages we get glimpses of Rousseau and Voltaire, of Helvétius and Winckelmann. He held but a poor opinion of Rousseau, and he declined to call his own book 'Confessions,' because that title had been usurped by an *extravagant*. He confesses himself a Voltairean, and boldly exchanged pleasantries with the philosopher of Ferney. Voltaire, of course, got the better of him, for which Casanova cherished an enduring spite against him. Yet he had the grace to be sorry for it afterwards, and confessed that had it not been for Voltaire's satirical habit, he would have considered him sublime. Nor is it surprising that this link between the old world and the new should have declaimed bitterly against Goethe and Wieland, whom in his old age he met at Weimar. What pleasure, indeed, could a hoary-headed classic

take in their poetry or in their pompous gospel of
romance ?   He neither understood their language, nor
patiently endured their influence.   So he left Weimar
in a rage, and solaced himself by remembering the
sallies of Voltaire and the amiability of Haller.

As he knew the great men, so he knew the great
capitals of Europe.   Always a wanderer, he regarded
all cities as his home, save his native Venice, which
he might not enter.   At Berlin he was granted an
interview with the great Frederic, who offered him a
post which his vanity could not accept.   At Vienna
he was snubbed by Joseph II., upon whom he took
an intrepid revenge.   ' I do not like people who buy
titles,' said the Emperor.   ' And what about those
who sell them, Sire ? ' replied Casanova.   The other
Emperor, Catherine the Great, did not stir his imagination, and he left Russia unappreciative, the more
so since he disliked the Russian system of gambling,
which was to play and not pay.   In Poland he enjoyed
a social triumph, until his duel with Branecki made him
too notorious, and he was forced once more to fly in
disgrace.   And nowhere was he so happy as in England.
He liked the ' proud islanders,' the beauty of their
country, the solidity of their food, and the excellence
of their roads.   His judgment is as far apart as the
poles from the judgment of the French tourists, who
visited England in the eighteenth century, and gave
vent to their spleen in angry pamphlets.   Wherever
he went he was well received, in St. James's as in the
City ; he discovered in Madame Cornelys, the Circe

of Soho Square, an old friend, and he attended her receptions with the best of the aristocracy. He was fascinated by Lord Pembroke's delight in a fighting-cock, and by the rules of the Prize Ring, and doubtless he would have lived very happily in London, had he not been indiscreet enough to present a forged bill of exchange. The bill was none of his forging, so he is careful to tell you, but it was a hanging matter, and Casanova was forced to take refuge across the Channel.

Thus he continued his life of adventure, until he was nearly sixty years of age, and then by great good fortune he met Count Waldstein in Paris. Waldstein, charmed with his conversation, affected an interest in magic, and invited him to his house. 'Come to Bohemia with me,' said he, ' I am leaving to-morrow ' ; and for the next fifteen years, until his death, Casanova was librarian at Dux. Here his life was not happy. He was bullied (and even flogged) by an unsympathetic house-steward, and his vanity was always open to unintended affronts. When the affront seemed unbearable, he asked for an introduction to a crowned head or to a Berlin Jew, borrowed some money, and went off. But he always returned, followed by bills drawn upon his patron, and relieved the misery of an inactive life by writing comedies, or telling the thrice-told tale of his flight from Venice. That his woes were imagined rather than real is evident from the sympathetic description of the Prince de Ligne. ' It must not be supposed,' says the Prince, ' that he was content to live quietly in

the haven of refuge that the kindness of Waldstein
had provided for him. It was not in his nature.
Not a day passed without a storm ; something was
sure to be wrong with his coffee, his milk, his dish
of macaroni, which he insisted on having served to
him daily. There were constant quarrels in the house.
The cook had spoiled his polenta, the coachman had
given him a bad driver to bring him over to see me,
the dogs had barked all night, there had been more
guests than usual, and he had been obliged to eat at
a side table. A hunting-horn tortured his ear with
discordant sounds ; the priest had been trying to
convert him ; Count Waldstein had not said good-
morning to him first ; the soup, out of malice, had
been served to him either too hot or too cold ; a
servant had kept him waiting for his wine ; he had
not been introduced to some distinguished person,
who had come to see the lance which pierced the side
of the great Waldstein ; the Count had lent somebody
a book without telling him ; a groom had not touched
his hat to him ; he had spoken in German and had
not been understood ; he had got angry and people
had laughed at him.'

Such were the small grievances which distressed the
great man, who still remembered the exploits which
had astonished half Europe. The truth is, his vast
energy chafed against inaction, and his talent was not
satisfied by the production of little plays for the amusement of his patrons. He was, moreover, hopelessly
out of fashion. He was like Bassompierre when he

came out of the Bastille.   As he grew old a generation arose which understood neither his manners nor his costume.   To them his grave stateliness appeared as ridiculous as his cloth-of-gold coat and paste buckles. To him the young were all Jacobins who forgot the respect due to rank and age.   The intolerable dullness of his life was enlivened by the composition of his *Memoirs*, which, read in manuscript by his friends, brought him fame even in his lifetime.   So he declined upon a premature old age, preserving until the end a love for Venice and a pride in his own career.   ' I have lived a philosopher and I die a Christian,' were his last words, and they are eminently characteristic of the most abandoned pagan of his generation.

Nemo sapit qui sibi non sapit ;   such was the motto which Casanova chose for his *Memoirs*, and he believed in his self-knowledge as confidently as in his candour. When he met the Marquis d'Argens at Aix, that famous gossip warned him not to write his autobiography.   ' In my intense desire to write the truth,' said the Marquis, ' I have made myself ridiculous.' The warning fell on deaf ears, and for seven years Casanova did his best to tell what he conceived to be the truth.   He spared neither himself nor his friends. He castigated such vices as he detected in himself without mercy, and if these vices were few, it was because his moral code was easy and his own.   From one end of his book to the other there is an air of frankness which is irresistible.   He set veracity above reputation, and despite his arrogance he does not hesitate to recount the snubs and insults put upon him. When Kaunitz with superb disdain tells him to ' go and sin no more but not in Vienna,' he writes it down without shame or comment. When Voltaire repulsed his attempt at impertinence, he acknowledged his defeat, though he never forgot the affront. Few men, especially those who have known the glitter of high society, will cheerfully record that the policeman's hand is always on their shoulder. And Casanova remembers every *lettre de cachet*, every hasty order to cross a frontier, that ever he received. As has been said, his only reticence touches the cause of his frequent expulsions. His candour, then, we may accept without reserve. His self-knowledge is not quite so certain. No doubt he made a valiant attempt to understand his career and its motives ; no doubt he was scrupulously veracious according to his lights. But he was not a realist, writing with a wakeful eye always on the object. He did not confide such secrets to his note-book as most men dare not whisper to themselves. He was, on the contrary, of a romantic turn, and he saw with perfect justice that his life contained the material of a dozen novels. Moreover, he wrote his book long after he had mingled in the fray ; and, seen through the mist, which in his eyes always overhung Dux, the adventures of his youth perhaps appeared too brightly coloured. For, above all, his book is the book of a veteran, looking back with pride upon the past, and seeing the old enchantments through the entrancing glass of time. Again and

again he regrets his vanished prowess in small things
or in great. Once, he confesses, he was passionately
fond of ship-biscuit,—surely not a vicious taste ; but
in those days, ' I had thirty sound teeth,' he writes,
' than which it would be difficult to find any whiter or
finer. I have but two left now.' That is a cry from
the heart. Again, when he is describing the charms
of M. M. and his own ascendency over that beautiful
nun : ' Dear reader,' says he, ' be patient with me, who
am to-day only the shadow of the gay, the fascinating,
the dashing Casanova that was. I love to dwell on
memories of myself.' Thus, when we estimate his
self-knowledge, we must take this love of old memories
into account. In brief, if he did not describe himself
always as he was, he loyally pictured his youth as it
appeared to his age, and we can ask no more than this
of any ancient chronicler.

Concerning the plan and purpose of his book he
wrote with perfect candour. Dividing the world into
two parties, ' the one, and by far the greater, composed
of ignorant and superficial men, and the other of deep
thinkers,' he addresses himself to the deep thinkers
alone, and is confident that they will appreciate his
veracity. Nor has he any doubt as to the moral value
of his work. ' If ever I am read,' says he, ' I shall not
pervert any one's mind ; to do so, at least, is far from
being my object ; but my experience, my vices, my
virtues, my principles, may be of use to some who
know, like the bee, how to extract honey from all sorts
of flowers.' This judgment of the book is not unfair.

No one, not already perverse, could be perverted by its gay and humorous romance, and for those who will read it in a spirit of justice, it presents such a picture of the time as it is difficult to find elsewhere.

Casanova has drawn his own character both incidentally and of set purpose; and it is by no means easy to understand. Opposing qualities jostle one another in his temperament, and he cannot be dismissed as a mere blackguard. Adventurer and pedant, cynic and sentimentalist, he mixed his virtues and his vices with a careless liberality. The card-sharper is not a rare actor upon the stage of life, but when was there a card-sharper other than Casanova who bored his companions with quotations from the classics? Again, though Casanova is shameless in the confession of what are commonly known as vices, he was a true sentimentalist, to whom things were always more than they seemed, and who was ever ready to shed a sympathetic tear over the misfortunes of others. To solve the puzzle is to answer the riddle of the eighteenth century. And short of that vast enterprise, the man's own portrait offers a partial solution. The hungry eye, the hawk-like nose, the savagely determined chin indicate the selfish necessity of acquisition and enjoyment. On the other hand, the high receding forehead bears witness at once to intellect and fatuity. To discuss his morals were an idle task, since morals shift with time and place, and since Casanova by confessing what he deemed his worst fault has clearly revealed his own code. When he was at

Barcelona he was indiscreet enough to tell a ruffian, named Fraiture, all that he knew concerning the antecedents of Manucci, a Venetian who had befriended him. He declared that Manucci had no right to the name he bore, that, in fact, he was masquerading under a false title. His motive was not infamous, since, as he confesses, he betrayed his friend without malice and for the mere love of babbling ; but Fraiture, after the manner of his kind, blackmailed Manucci, and it is not surprising that Casanova was too ashamed to ask forgiveness. Such, in his eyes, was the worst crime he ever committed. All his infidelities to women, all the deceits which he had practised upon the innocent, all the corrections which he had administered to fortune, are forgotten in this one supreme act of treachery. He bore Manucci no ill-will : the wrong he did him was merely the effect of carelessness ; yet he bowed his head in dishonour, and thus bowing his head interpreted for all men his code of morals.

For the rest, he was a man of vast energy and tireless enterprise, to whom nothing came amiss, and though he bore patiently the affronts incident to his career, he was ready enough to draw the sword in defence of his honour. For such as offended him he had the famous lunge that never failed, and he thought that he won the spurs of knighthood by running a Polish general through the belly. But he was not one to kick against the pricks ; he revered the majesty of the law ; he praised the English because an English malefactor accepted arrest at the hands of a single soldier; and he obeyed without a murmur the mandate of superior force. Withal, he showed until the end his lack of breeding. Morals apart, he was never a gentleman, though he declared that he had learned to behave as one. Yet despite a certain coarseness of nature, he was as devoted to humane letters as the best of his contemporaries. After a full pocket he best loved intelligence. ' I hate fools so bitterly,' he said, ' that I feel myself degraded in a fool's company.' The Prince de Ligne declared that it was only his comedies which were not comic, only his philosophical works in which there was no philosophy; and in truth philosophy tempered the whole comedy of his life. He was vain, yet his vanity was accessible to humour, and he claimed the title of Seingalt as his own because he was the author of it. He knew nothing of the finer shades, the subtler flavours of life. ' I like highly spiced dishes,' he said, ' macaroni made by a Neapolitan cook, the *olla podrida* of Spain, fine, white salt cod from Newfoundland, high game, and strong cheese.' His morals and his temperament resembled his palate, and there are still those who think his *Memoirs* as highly spiced as the dishes which he loved.

Detractors have unjustly denied the authenticity of his book. And it is proclaimed genuine on every page. Its very inaccuracies are an undesigned argument in its favour, since the forger makes it his first care to verify his dates. Again, the evidence of the Prince de Ligne is clear and irrefragable. He read the *Memoirs* in the hero's own lifetime, and most wisely appreciated them.

The letter which Casanova addressed to the Prince de Courland, and which he printed in his book, was preserved in the archives of the Bastille, an eloquent proof of the Venetian's veracity ; and a hundred other arguments may be adduced in his favour.   Indeed, only those who believe that Bacon wrote Shakespeare's plays, and everything else printed in his lifetime, will doubt the authenticity of Casanova's *Memoirs*, which are the quick presentment of a reckless adventurer, and which brilliantly illustrate their author's cynical and ingenious theory that the chain of events is always independent of conduct.